MW01166285

Young Thomas More and the Arts of Liberty

What does it mean to be a free citizen in times of war and tyranny? What kind of education is needed to be a "first" or leading citizen in a strife-filled country? And what does it mean to be free when freedom is forcibly opposed? These concerns pervade Thomas More's earliest writings, writings mostly unknown, including his 280 poems, declamation on tyrannicide, coronation ode for Henry VIII, and life of Pico della Mirandola, all written before *Richard III* and *Utopia*. This book analyzes these writings, guided especially by the following questions: Faced with generations of civil war, what did young More see as the causes of that strife? What did he see as possible solutions? Why did More spend fourteen years after law school learning Greek and immersing himself in classical studies? Why do his early works use vocabulary devised by Cicero at the end of the Roman Republic?

Gerard B. Wegemer is professor of literature at the University of Dallas, and since 2000 he has been the founding director of the Center for Thomas More Studies. Among his publications are *A Thomas More Source Book*, *Thomas More on Statesmanship*, and *Thomas More: A Portrait of Courage*. He has served as an editor for *Moreana*, the international journal on Thomas More and his times. He is editing a paperback series of Thomas More's major works and has written articles and reviews on Thomas More, Shakespeare, and Renaissance humanism in such journals as *Renascence, Philosophy and Rhetoric, Review of Politics, Ben Jonson Journal*, and *Moreana*. Wegemer has master's degrees in political philosophy and in literature from Boston College and Georgetown University, respectively, and earned his doctorate in English literature from the University of Notre Dame.

Young Thomas More and the Arts of Liberty

GERARD B. WEGEMER

University of Dallas

CAMBRIDGE
UNIVERSITY PRESS

CAMBRIDGE UNIVERSITY PRESS
Cambridge, New York, Melbourne, Madrid, Cape Town,
Singapore, São Paulo, Delhi, Tokyo, Mexico City

Cambridge University Press
32 Avenue of the Americas, New York, NY 10013-2473, USA

www.cambridge.org
Information on this title: www.cambridge.org/9780521196536

First published 2011

Printed in the United States of America

A catalog record for this publication is available from the British Library.

Library of Congress Cataloging in Publication data

Wegemer, Gerard, 1950–
Young Thomas More and the arts of liberty / Gerard B. Wegemer.
    p. cm.
Includes bibliographical references and index.
ISBN 978-0-521-19653-6 (hardback)
    1. More, Thomas, Sir, Saint, 1478–1535 – Criticism and interpretation. 2. More,
Thomas, Sir, Saint, 1478–1535 – Political and social views. 3. Liberty in literature.
4. Great Britain – Politics and government – 1485–1509. 5. Great Britain – Politics and
government – 1509–1547. I. Title.
PR2322.W44   2011
828'.209 – dc22   2010039390

ISBN 978-0-521-19653-6 Hardback

Contents

Illustrations

Acknowledgments

Gratitude for assistance from numerous friends over the past decade is a joy to express. Without the vision and support of Steven A. Bennett, Joseph Coleman, Myles Harrington, Charles LiMandri, Thomas Spence, Glen Thurow, and codirector Stephen W. Smith, the Center for Thomas More Studies would never have been founded, and therefore the many fruitful conferences and research projects that made this book possible would not have occurred. No scholar could have asked for better conversationalists than these colleagues, as well as Clarence H. Miller, Elizabeth McCutcheon, Seymour House, John Boyle, Travis Curtright, Michael Foley, Louis Karlin, Joseph Koterski, Jeff Lehman, Tamara Kuykendall, David Oakley, and the faculty and students at the University of Dallas, especially John Alvis and Scott Crider, and Josh Avery and Matthew Mehan. Special thanks go to Mary Pawlowski for her help with Greek texts and with compiling the indices of terms at www.thomasmorestudies.org/IndicesofLatinTerms; to Paul Weinhold for the index; to Lewis Bateman, senior editor of Cambridge University Press; and to Brian MacDonald, production editor, for their patience and good advice through the long process of this book.

Thanks to the following institutions for permission to use their materials: the President and Fellows of Harvard College for permission to quote from the Loeb Classical Library, Yale University Press for permission to quote from *The Complete Works of St. Thomas More*, HarperCollins Publishers for permission to quote from ©2008 David Starkey's *Henry, Virtuous Prince*, the journal *Moreana* for an earlier version of Chapter 10 that appeared in volume 173 (June 2008), and those institutions identified in the List of Illustrations.

Abbreviations

Corr.	*Correspondence of Sir Thomas More*
CSPS	*Calendar of State Papers, Spanish*
CUP Utopia	Cambridge University Press edition of *Utopia*
CW	*The Yale Edition of the Complete Works of St. Thomas More*
CWE	*The Collected Works of Erasmus*
EE	*Erasmi Epistolae*
OLD	*Oxford Latin Dictionary*
SL	*St. Thomas More: Selected Letters*
TMSB	*A Thomas More Source Book*

Young Thomas More

Why Do Peace and Prosperity Require Arts of Humanitas?

[Wisdom is] the skilled artisan of life . . . , her voice is for peace, and she summons all mankind to concord.

Seneca, *Epistulae* 90.26–27

[Liberal] arts were devised for the purpose of fashioning [*fingerentur*][1] the minds of the young according to *humanitas* and virtue.[2]

Cicero, *De Oratore* 3.58

Humanitas, or the idea of man, [is that] according to which man is fashioned [*effingitur*] . . . as Plato says.[3]

Seneca, *Epistulae* 65.7

"Work out your own ideas and sift your thoughts so as to see what conception and idea of a good person they contain"; otherwise you can end up as a "Caesar [who] overturned all the laws, human and divine, to achieve for himself a *principate* fashioned [*finxerat*] according to his own erroneous opinion."[4]

Cicero, *De Officiis* 3.81, 1.26

---

[1] See www.thomasmorestudies.org/IndicesofLatinTerms for the uses of this verb in More's *Epigrams, Richard III,* and *Utopia.* This verb also appears in the one passage that can be read in the near life-size *Sir Thomas More and His Family* (see Illustration 7 in Chapter 10). *Fingere* is a term commonly used in sculpture, meaning "to make a likeness of or to represent (from clay, wax, molten metal, etc.)" (*OLD*). For examples where Cicero associates this term with Plato or Socrates or in the senses of Platonic representation, see *Tusculanae Disputationes* 2.27, 3.31; *De Oratore* 1.224; *De Officiis* 3.69, 1.26; *Pro Sexto Roscio Amerino* 47.

[2] "Artibus quae repertae sunt ut puerorum mentes ad humanitatem fingerentur atque virtutem. . . ."

[3] "Ipsa autem humanitas, ad quam homo effingitur, permanet, et hominibus laborantibus illa nihil patitur . . . ut Plato dicit. . . ."

[4] Cicero, *De Officiis* 3.81: "Explica atque excute intellegentiam tuam, ut videas, quae sit in ea [species] forma et notio viri boni"; 1.26: "Caesaris . . . omnia iura divina et humana pervertit propter eum, quem sibi ipse opinionis errore finxerat, principatum."

In 1515, as part of their plan for international peace, Thomas More and Erasmus both called for a renaissance – a "rebirth" – of the "so-called liberal studies."[5] That "so-called" referred to Seneca's famous statement: "Hence you see why 'liberal studies' are *so called*: because they are studies worthy of the free. But there is only one really liberal study, that which gives a person his liberty. It is the study of wisdom, and that is lofty, brave, and great-souled."[6] In calling for this renaissance, they were agreeing with their classical predecessors that education in the "liberal arts,"[7] or what Cicero often called the *studia humanitatis*, is the best path "to lead the state in peace,"[8] because "the fostering of a virtuous and educated citizenry provides the key" to peace and liberty.[9] But what did they mean, and were they and their fellow humanists not woefully misguided as critics such as Machiavelli would later claim?[10]

In 1515 More wrote book 2 of *Utopia* with its provocative promises of liberty, peace, and *humanitas*;[11] in the same year, Erasmus "dreamt of an age truly golden," only to discover "the severity of that worse than iron age we live in."[12] The iron age of war rather than the golden age of peace was also portrayed in *The History of King Richard III*, which More had been writing since 1513 but never published in his lifetime.

---

[5] *CW* 15, 18/13 (volume, page/line): "bonas renasci litteras"; *EE* 337/328: "renascantur bonae litterae." References are regularly to the Latin text because translations are often adjusted. When quoting sixteenth-century English, spelling and punctuation are modernized.

[6] *Epistulae* 88.1–2 (emphasis added). This collection of Seneca's letters was of such importance to More that it is one of only three books definitely identified in the portrait *Sir Thomas More and His Family*.

[7] Like Cicero, More uses several expressions for liberal education. See Cicero's *De Inventione* 1.35 ("artium liberalium"), *De Oratore* 3.127 ("has artes quibus liberales doctrinae atque ingenuae continerentur"), *Tusculanae Disputationes* 2.27 ("a Graecia . . . eruditionem liberalem et doctrinam putamus"), and *Pro Archia* 3 ("studia humanitatis"). See More's uses of "humanis literis" (*Corr.* 255/37, 42–43; 121/14ff.; *CW* 3.2, Epigram 143/103, 107–8; *CW* 15, 138/7, 11), "lyberall artes" (*CW* 6, 132/8), "liberales artes" (*CW* 15, 134/12, 138/24, 220/13), "liberalibus disciplinis" (*Corr.* 255/37–38), "ingenuis artibus" (*CW* 3.2, Epigram 19/117), and "bonis artibus" (*CW* 3.2, Epigrams 143/176–77, 264/43; *CW* 4, 158/8; *CW* 15, 26/10; *Corr.* 122/74). For Erasmus's summary of More's views on the value of liberal studies, see *EE* 1233 or *TMSB* 221–26.

[8] Mitchell 1984 38, but see his fuller argument with references beginning on p. 35.

[9] Skinner x.

[10] In their introduction to *The Prince*, Quentin Skinner and Russell Price point out striking instances in which Machiavelli directly counters Cicero's and Seneca's views on effective rule and good government (xvi–xxii esp.).

[11] See Chapter 9 for an assessment of the provocative uses of these terms.

[12] *CWE* 3, Letter 333 (15 May 1515), lines 9, 51.

Did the shattering of this golden dream prove to More and Erasmus that the fashionings of *humanitas* lacked the power they hoped?

In 1515 the playful "Triumph of Humanitas" (Illustration 1) decorated Erasmus's newly published edition of Seneca's collected works, the edition that Erasmus had worked on during his stay in England from 1509 through 1514, using manuscripts from English libraries. The figure Humanitas in the top of the frame is pushed by the Latin authors Cicero (Tully) and Virgil and pulled by the Greek authors Demosthenes and Homer – all four of whom wrote on war in ways that deeply affected their cultures. Lady Humanitas is peacefully reading, even while riding in her triumphal chariot pushed and pulled by these laurel-crowned poets and bareheaded statesmen, all under a triumphal canopy held by plump, happy cherubs. On the left side of the engraving is the figure of a child, and lest there be any doubt after one sees the sickle in his hand or the wings at his feet, a sign in Greek identifies this figure as "Time." On the right, another label in Greek identifies "Nemesis," who is holding her traditional measure and spool of fate. Erasmus, in his *Adages* (II.vi.38), describes Nemesis as "a goddess, the scourge of insolence and arrogance, whose province is to forbid excessive hopes and punish them," possessing "a general power of supervising the fates, surveying above all human affairs as queen and arbiter of all things."[13] In this frontispiece, however, the triumphal march that takes place above Time and Nemesis seems to present Humanitas as the greater queen and arbiter. This reading is confirmed by the comparative-genitive constructions, which lead us to read the text in this frame as "Humanitas greater than Time, greater than Nemesis."[14]

But how could *humanitas* ever have such power? Cicero was murdered, and Seneca's death was ordered by the Roman *princeps* he loyally served.[15] Cicero's head and hands were nailed to the rostra in the Roman forum where he had served as lawyer, senator, and consul of the Roman Republic.[16] He lived to see the Roman Republic become an empire, ruled by one despotically powerful *princeps* instead of many *principes*

---

[13] CWE 33, 310–11.
[14] My gratitude goes to Joseph Koterski and Jeffrey Lehman for this revealing grammatical point.
[15] In the portrait *Sir Thomas More and His Family*, one of the three books identified is *The Consolation of Philosophy* by Boethius, another philosopher-statesman unjustly imprisoned and executed by his prince. See Illustration 7.
[16] Rawson 296; Plutarch 2.441.

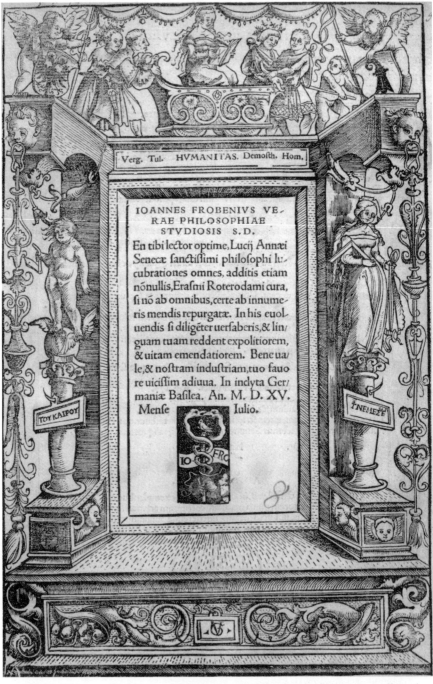

ILLUSTRATION 1. "Triumph of Humanitas." Title page of Seneca's collected works of 1515, the collection Erasmus edited from English manuscripts while staying with Thomas More in London.

civitatis.[17] As we will see in the following chapters, these *principes* – that is, these leading or "first" citizens – were an integral part of the *humanitas* Cicero sought to advance, exemplified by Cicero's rendition of Rome's greatest *principes* as educated in *studia humanitatis* and trained in the arts of governing.

After the fall of the republic, Seneca continued the appeal to the leading citizens' *humanitas* but not to the laws and *libertas* of self-governing Romans. Instead, Seneca had to appeal to the *clementia* of a despotically powerful emperor.[18] As Chaim Wirszubski has shown, *libertas* requires rule by law;[19] as we will see, Thomas More agreed.

The importance of Seneca during the medieval and early modern periods is witnessed by the title page of the 1515 edition of his collected works (Illustration 1), where Erasmus introduces him as "most holy" and "philosophical." In the prefatory letter[20] to this large volume,[21] Erasmus reports that "Seneca was so highly valued by St. Jerome that alone among Gentiles [Seneca] was recorded in the *Catalogue of Illustrious Authors*";[22] Jerome "thought him the one writer who, while not a Christian, deserved to be read by Christians" and "by all who aspire to a virtuous life."[23] Years later, however, Erasmus would give even greater praise to Cicero: "Never have I more wholly approved of Quintilian's remark that a man may know he has made progress when he begins to take great pleasure in Cicero.[24] When I was a boy Cicero attracted me less than Seneca." Erasmus then goes on to urge "the young to spend many long hours in reading him and even in learning him by heart."[25]

---

[17] For the changing use of this term from the late Republic to Augustan's conception of *princeps*, see Ogilvie 392.

[18] See Seneca's masterful appeal to Emperor Nero for *humanitas* in *De Clementia,* and especially Seneca's praise of Augustus Caesar as "mitis princeps" (9.1), echoing Cicero's similar praise of Julius Caesar at *Epistulae ad Familiares* 6.6.5.

[19] For the central importance of *leges-libertas*, see Wirszubski 1954 and 1968.

[20] "To Thomas Ruthall," CWE 3, Letter 325, 7 March 1515. In this letter, Erasmus expresses his gratitude for use of the manuscripts of Seneca provided by King's College at Cambridge and by Archbishop Warham of Canterbury.

[21] This volume is 665 large folio pages and contains Seneca's twelve moral essays, 124 moral letters, ten books of natural questions, ten books of declamations, six books of suasoriae and controversiae, St. Jerome's praise of Seneca, and the pseudocorrespondence between Seneca and St. Paul. It concludes with a seven-page listing of "Senecae Proverbia," a twenty-one-page "Index Locorum," and another snake-and-dove device (more elaborate and elegant than the one on the frontispiece) with the Hebrew, Greek, and Latin quotations that appear in the *Utopia* version of this device.

[22] See St. Jerome, *On Illustrious Men* 26–27.

[23] CWE 3, Letter 325/81–83, 109–10.

[24] Quintilian, *Institutio Oratoria* 10.1.112.

[25] CWE 10, Letter 100.

Thomas More agreed that Cicero and Seneca should be included among the greatest of classical thinkers. In defending the study of Greek at Oxford University, More wrote: "For in philosophy, apart from the works left by Cicero and Seneca, the schools of the Latins have nothing to offer that is not either Greek or translated from Greek."[26] What specific contributions did Cicero and Seneca make to philosophy that were distinct from the Greek?

Cicero's view of *humanitas,* that is, his philosophy of human nature and society, formed the basis for his conceptions of civic and international law and of the philosopher-rhetorician's duty as "first citizen" to be equipped with those arts needed to promote and protect justice, liberty, and peace.[27] This duty was based on the view that there is "no difference in kind between man and man" and that the "whole universe [is] one commonwealth"[28] because all human beings have reason – the view eventually written into Justinian's *Digests*[29] and into subsequent codes of law that Thomas More knew and defended.

Although Seneca could not appeal to such a universal code of civil law, he did consistently appeal to the principles of human nature and to the natural consequences of just and unjust behavior – most dramatically in his powerful tragedies.[30] Seneca affirmed, however, Cicero's arguments for *ius gentium,* the law of all peoples,[31] and an ideal society based on friendship, justice, liberty, and peace.

For Seneca, *humanitas* is "the idea of man" (*Epistulae* 65.7) and therefore "the first thing which philosophy undertakes to give" to society (5.4). *Humanitas* forbids arrogance and greed and teaches kindness to all (88.30, 33, 35); it toils against the madness of war, crime, and cruelty (95.31–32), teaching that "man [is] an object of reverence in the eyes of man" (95.33), whether slave or master (*Epistulae* 47.10; *De Vita Beata* 24.3); it leads those in society to view themselves as "the parts of one

---

[26] *CW* 15, 143.

[27] *Ius gentium* is a fundamental theme in *De Oratore, De Re Publica,* and *De Legibus* and throughout his speeches. As an introduction to the complexity of Cicero's thought, see Nicgorski 1993 and Frank.

[28] *De Legibus* 1.30, 23.

[29] See especially 1.1 on "Justice and Law," 1.5 on "Human Status," and the treatment of *ius gentium* throughout.

[30] Seneca's *Oedipus* appears in the portrait *Sir Thomas More and His Family,* and selections from the important choral ode of the fourth act can be read in this near life-size painting. See also the quotations from Seneca's tragedies in the sixteenth-century play *Sir Thomas More* as noted in *TMSB* 134ff.

[31] For example, *De Otio* 6.4 and its reference to "leges . . . toti humano generi."

great body" bound by love (*amore*) and "prone to friendship" (*Epistulae* 95.52). This view of *humanitas* Seneca saw expressed in the following lines that he wished to be in the heart and on the lips of all (9.53): "I am a man; and nothing in man's lot / Do I deem foreign to me." These are the famous lines of Terence that Cicero quoted and that More knew by heart, quoting them from memory while in prison.[32]

Seneca repeats this praise of *humanitas* in *De Ira*, insisting upon it as a "duty" and ending with a call to "cherish *humanitas*" (2.28.2, 3.43.5). There he again develops the analogy of the body politic but extends it to the "greater city," the *maior urbs*, of the world:

To injure one's country is a crime; consequently, also, to injure a fellow-citizen – for he is a part of the country, and if we reverence the whole, the parts are sacred – consequently to injure any man is a crime, for he is your fellow-citizen in the greater commonwealth. (2.31.7)

As he develops this analogy, he points out again that the parts of the human community need to be united by bonds of love:

What if the hands should desire to harm the feet, or the eyes the hands? As all the members of the body are in harmony one with another because it is to the advantage of the whole that the individual members be unharmed, so mankind should spare the individual man, because all are born for a life of fellowship, and society can be kept unharmed only by the mutual protection and love [*amore*] of its parts. (2.31.7–8)

Although Seneca is the first to say explicitly that the body politic should be bound by love, he is simply advancing the concepts already developed by Aristotle and Cicero.[33]

One of Seneca's longest explanations of *humanitas* occurs in *Epistulae* 88, "On Liberal Studies":[34]

Humanitas forbids you to be over-bearing towards your associates, and it forbids you to be grasping. In words and in deeds and in feelings it shows itself gentle and courteous to all. It counts no evil as solely another's. And the reason why it loves its own good is chiefly because it will some day be the good of another. (88.30)

---

[32] Terence, *Heautontimoroumenos* 77. See Cicero's use of this quotation in *De Officiis* 1.30 and in *De Legibus* 1.33. For More's knowing this quotation by heart, see CW 14, 349/2–3 with its commentary.

[33] See Chapter 3.

[34] In Erasmus's edition of these 124 letters, only this letter has its own entry in the table of contents, and it is a letter that More echoes in his own educational writings.

Seneca insists in this letter that liberal arts can only *"prepare the soul for virtue."*[35] Because virtue is the "art to become good" (90.44), it "does not enter a soul unless that soul has been trained and taught, and by unremitting practice brought to perfection" (90.46) through free choice.[36] Seneca insists that our "primary art is virtue itself" (92.10) and that virtue is "nothing else than a soul in a certain condition" (113.2). What condition? The "perfected condition" of wisdom, which is "the greatest of all the arts" (104.19). In the last letter, Seneca explains that the highest human good is the free use of one's godlike power of reason to forge "a pure and corrected soul" (124.23).[37] Such a soul, as we will see, is most capable of leading the "sound deliberation" that prudent first citizens foster to achieve peace, prosperity, and liberty.

Thomas More will paraphrase this same Senecan language in his own letters on education. For example, in his 1518 Letter to Oxford, More argues that liberal education "prepares the soul for virtue" and helps in acquiring "prudence in human affairs," which "can nowhere be drawn so abundantly as from the poets, orators, and historians."[38] This view of education accords with Cicero's that the liberal "arts were devised for the purpose of fashioning [*fingerentur*] the minds of the young according to *humanitas* and virtue."[39] Thomas More consistently affirmed a view of freely acquired virtue and well-trained reason based on "the inner knowledge of what is right" or "right conscience" (*recti conscientia*) that gives rise to "solid joy"[40] – a view that would bring More in radical conflict with Luther.

But why would poets, orators, and historians be superior sources of "prudence in human affairs"? Eleven years later, More would repeat and

---

[35] Seneca, *Epistulae* 88.20 ("quia animum ad accipiendam virtutem praeparant"); emphasis added. St. Basil the Great makes a similar argument, drawing upon Plato, in section 2 of his *How to Profit from Pagan Literature* (385), where he gives special place to oratory, poetry, and history – as More will do – in this preparatory process of free and deliberate choice.

[36] See Chapter 2 for the treatment of this essential element of human flourishing.

[37] Seneca's *Epistulae* is another of the three books specifically identified in the portrait *Sir Thomas More and His Family*.

[38] CW 15, 139; note especially line 11: "animam ad virtutem praeparat" and compare with Seneca's *Epis.* 88.20. More makes an extended argument about wisdom in his Letter to Gonell, *TMSB* 197–200 or *SL* 103–7 and *Corr.* 120–23. As seen in note 35, St. Basil the Great gives the same list of three.

[39] See the quotations opening this chapter. Although Crassus articulates this view in *De Oratore* 3.81, Cicero in his prefaces to these dialogues affirms the view of education that Crassus defends.

[40] *TMSB* 198, 199.

expand this statement by adding "laws" to these superior sources and also by indicating the special contributions of these four areas of study:

[R]eason is by study, labour, and exercise of logic, philosophy, and other liberal arts corroborate [strengthened] and quickened, and the judgement both in them and also in *orators, laws,* and *[hi]stories*[41] much rip[en]ed. And albeit *poets* [have] been with many men taken but for painted words, yet do they *much help the judgement* and make a man among other things *well furnished of one special thing without which all learning is half lame . . . a good mother wit.*[42]

Proper study of oratory, law, history, and poetry, More explains, will "much ripen" and "help the judgment" by making one "among other things well furnished of one special thing without which all learning is half lame." Lucian, as Chapter 4 will indicate, is a master at revealing in most entertaining and effective ways what that "one special thing" is: prudence, clear-sighted practical wisdom; or, put in Chaucerian language, "a good mother wit."

Why these particular arts or areas of study? Oratory is an art that requires a thorough knowledge of human nature and a thorough, detailed knowledge of a people and its culture. The same is true of law, poetry, and history. All require an expertise in *humanitas* if they are to move and affect their audience.[43]

This expertise in *humanitas* gave rise to Seneca's and Cicero's view that all should be treated equal before the law and be subject, before that law, to equal rights.[44] Cicero forcefully argued that human flourishing required "liberty in law," and he used his rhetorical powers to attempt to persuade his fellow citizens that "we are servants of the law that we might be free."[45] Seneca, however, given the imperial despotism and ambitions for world domination of his time, had to use persuasion of another kind, but he artfully and powerfully reminded all of their common humanity and of the importance of peace.[46] Seneca's most famous essays – "On

---

[41] See the editor's note at *CW* 6, 132/10–22.
[42] *CW* 6, 131–32, emphasis added.
[43] Cicero develops this point throughout *De Oratore*.
[44] See, for example, Cicero, *De Officiis* 2.42 and *De Legibus* 3.44.
[45] *De Lege Agraria* 2.102; *Pro Cluentio* 146.
[46] That peace in the state is analogous to health in the body is a commonplace for Christian authors. See Augustine's *City of God* 19.12–13, 17, 24 or Aquinas's commentary on the *Nicomachean Ethics* 1112b14 where Aquinas expands Aristotle's remark about the end of the statesman as "enact[ing] good laws and enforc[ing] them." Aquinas adds that "a statesman or a ruler of the state does not deliberate whether he ought to achieve peace which is compared to the state of health to the human body (health consists in the harmony of wills)" (no. 474).

Benevolence," "On Mercy," "On Providence," "On Happiness" – are rhetorical masterpieces devised to move his audiences, contemporary and future, to a life ordered to peace, justice, wisdom, and care for all fellow human beings.

But how important were these matters of international peace and justice to More himself?

At the age of fifty-five – within months of his resignation as lord chancellor of England, a year and a half before his arrest, and three years before his death – Thomas More wrote the epitaph for his tomb, had it engraved in stone, and sent a written copy to Erasmus for publication.[47] When Erasmus delayed publication, More wrote again, urging immediate publication.[48] What was so important that More wanted chiseled in stone and then publicized to his contemporaries and to posterity?

The most obvious priority is set forth in the only line indented and set apart from the rest of the main text: a call for lasting world peace. (See Illustration 2.) This call is prefaced by a reference to the only specific political achievement More describes on this tombstone,[49] the August 1529 international peace treaty (*foedera*) of Cambrai.[50] Significantly for what we will see about factions and civil war, More then goes on to point out that he also maintained peace and avoided ill will (*inuidia*) in his relations with the three classes of English society[51] "all through" the "series of high offices or honors" that he received. Even in his prison letters, More would insist that he had never played the "part taker" or partisan in factional feuds.[52]

Peace was of such importance to Thomas More that he did not join the king's service until mid-1518,[53] once the king and Wolsey had agreed

---

[47] *EE* 2831[June 1533] or *SL* 178–83 or *TMSB* 305–10.

[48] More's first letter has not survived, but that Erasmus fulfilled More's second request of *EE* 2831 is clear from *EE* 2865/27 (31 August 1533).

[49] In addition to the actual tombstone, which is in Chelsea Old Church, see the printed versions of this epitaph in More's *Omnia Opera* of 1565, 1566, and 1689 as well as *EE* 2831/90. The 1557 English edition of More's *Workes* sets off this sentence in its own paragraph (on p. 1420) but does not indent and italicize it as do all three Latin editions of More's *Omnia Opera*.

[50] Consider the significance of the term *foedera* by comparing Epigram 32/4, *Utopia*, *CW* 4, 196/14, 16, 20, 31, 198/22, 24, 27, and *Richard III*, *CW* 15, 336/21 with its allusion to Sallust, *Jugurtha* 11.1.

[51] Monarch, nobles, the people ("princeps, nobiles, populus," *EE* 2831/92–93).

[52] For example, see *SL* 227 and 232.

[53] For the dating of this event, see Guy 2000 50ff. For More's repeated concern for "a general peace for which Christendom has so long been miserably yearning," see More's

ILLUSTRATION 2. The 1532 Tombstone of Sir Thomas More, with epitaph by More. In the summer of 1532, within weeks of his 16 May retirement from Henry VIII's service, Thomas More put in place this tombstone with the epitaph he wrote for himself chiseled in stone. More sent the text of the epitaph to Erasmus twice with instructions to publish it.

to international peace. This "Universal Peace" proved to be disingenuous because the king and Wolsey would violate it in just a few years when it would serve their political ambitions. Nonetheless, in 1518 their actions and a new international climate gave reasonable hope that peace could be achieved and could last.[54]

The sign of More's commitment to peace and opposition to wars of imperialism can be judged best by his opening speech as lord chancellor before the Parliament and king eleven years later.[55] Why was the best sign a speech made in 1529? Because this new position as lord chancellor gave More the strongest, and arguably the first, position in which he could influence the country's policy on war and peace. On that first public occasion, he boldly declared that "Wolsey's" wars were a mistake resulting in damage to the English economy and distraction from the important work of justice and reform at home.[56] Of course, everyone knew that these wars were initiated and fully supported by Henry VIII. No sooner had the seventeen-year-old Henry become king than he started plans to invade France – in imitation of his hero Henry V. With the invasion of 1513, Henry insisted on leading it himself despite the considerable risks to England's own security.[57]

In that first public speech as lord chancellor, More then announced the purpose of the new parliament: the reformation of the laws of England.[58] This purpose stood in striking contrast to the usual one that was all too familiar to the English people: payment for war. Throughout his address to the king in Parliament, More referred to Henry VIII as the good shepherd,[59] who recognizes the importance of "permanent peace" for England and the importance of "ensuring the peace of Christendom" while trying "by every means to increase and prosper the trade of the

---

letters to Francis Cranevelt [22 February 1526] and [8 November 1528] in *Moreana* 103:63 and 117:47 as well as More's Letter to Wolsey 21 September [1521] in *Corr.* 263/41–44.

[54] See Robert P. Adams's classic study, *The Better Part of Valor*.

[55] On 3 November 1929.

[56] Tudor historian Edward Hall and Spanish ambassador Eustace Chapuys give the only extended accounts of this speech, and they are in general agreement with the official Parliament Roll's summary (Hall 2.164–65; Great Britain, *CSPS* no. 211, 8 November 1529; *Letters and Papers of Henry VIII* 4, no. 6043, 3 November 1529).

[57] See Chapter 7; on Henry's leadership as a danger to England, see Scarisbrick 35, 37–38. On Henry VIII's crafted imitation of Henry V, see Chapter 6 and Herman 1995 220.

[58] See the sources in note 56 and their many references to the need for "reform" and "reformation."

[59] See the analysis of More epigrams on the good *princeps* as a shepherd in Chapter 6.

country."[60] Why is the good shepherd the dominant metaphor in this speech? Hall summarizes More's explanation:

[I]f a prince be compared to his riches, he is a rich man; if a prince is compared to his honour, he is an honourable man; but compare him to the multitude of his people and the number of his flock, then he is a ruler, a governor of might and puissance, *so that his people maketh him a prince*, as of the multitude of sheep cometh the name of a shepherd.[61]

Significantly, More states discreetly in this public forum what he indicated in his early literature: that the "people . . . maketh" their own prince, that is, that the people's support is the condition for an individual's becoming – and remaining – the *princeps*.[62] As More indicates here and again at the end of his life,[63] political authority belongs to the people, who can then delegate part of that authority to a known, qualified, virtuous, and trusted leader who has stood out as "first" in proven service in their protection and care. Or, as Quentin Skinner recently summarized this classic view, sovereignty is the "property of the people" [*res publica*], not "the possession of the state."[64]

But in using the metaphor of the shepherd, More the poet was doing something different from, but related to, what More the politician was doing: like Homer,[65] he was introducing an image befitting the full reality of rule, as Raphael would claim to do in *Utopia*. More the poet wanted Henry VIII and his war-loving lords to think about being courageous shepherds rather than war-hungry leaders like Henry V.

A second important motive for More's publicizing his own epitaph in 1532[66] was related to the first, and it dealt with More's concern for

---

[60] Great Britain, *CSPS* no. 211.

[61] Hall 2.164. When More then goes on to criticize Wolsey as the "rotten and faulty" "great wether" who "so craftily, so scabbedly, ye and so untruly juggled with the king" (ibid.), More draws attention to how this spiritual pastor, this cardinal whom the king "naturally supposed to be honest and virtuous," had neglected care of his spiritual flock, leaving the matter such that the "ecclesiastics needed most reform" (Great Britain, *CSPS* no. 211).

[62] In these lines, More artfully criticizes those princes set on riches and honor.

[63] See Roper 85 or *TMSB* 56–57; *CW* 13, 21; *CW* 14, 373–75, 263–65; and especially Harpsfield, appendix III, 274–75.

[64] Skinner xi.

[65] For example, see Homer's frequent use of the shepherd metaphor at *Iliad* 2.105, 2.244, 2.255, 2.772, 4.413, 11.187, 15.262, 20.110, 22.278; *Odyssey* 4.24, 4.532, 14.497, 15.151, 17.109, 24.368, 24.456.

[66] He publicized this as widely and permanently as was then possible, not only sending it in writing to Erasmus for publication but etching it in stone as well.

"integrity."[67] As he wrote to Erasmus in the letter accompanying the text of this epitaph: "I considered it my duty to protect the integrity of my reputation."[68] More then went on to explain his epitaph as "a public declaration of the actual facts" that openly invited rebuttal – just as a seasoned and shrewd London lawyer or practitioner of the "arts of peace" would know to do.[69] The letter also set forth a brief summary of what had occurred since his resignation: in thirteen months, he wrote, "no one has advanced a complaint against my integrity."[70] Quite the contrary, "it is embarrassing for me to relate," More went on, that the king has pronounced "frequently in private, and twice in public that he had unwillingly yielded to my request for resignation." More also reported that Henry VIII, in demonstration of his goodwill, had ordered both the Duke of Norfolk and the next lord chancellor to express the king's gratitude to More "at a solemn session of the Lords and Commons" and on "the formal occasion of [the lord chancellor's] opening address" to Parliament. What More did by publishing his own epitaph was literally to chisel in stone proof of his lifelong reputation for integrity.[71] More acknowledged that some would accuse him of boasting, but he argued that his duty to protect his reputation for integrity overrode that concern.

This concern for integrity draws attention to another part of the title page of Erasmus's 1515 edition of Seneca: the two snakes and the dove toward the middle of the page (Illustration 1). This was a favorite drawing that Johann Froben came to use as his printer's mark in many of his humanist publications,[72] including his 1518 editions of More's *Utopia*.

---

[67] On the epitaph of his tombstone, More includes integrity among the qualities he admired in his father: "homo ciuilis, suauis, innocens, mitis, misericors, aequus et integer" (*EE* 2831/96). These qualities are quite close to those required by Cicero's and Seneca's *humanitas*. A sampling of More's other uses of "integrity" are *CW* 1, 64/14 (claimed to be the first use in English as indicated at *CW* 1, L, note 1, but the *Medieval Dictionary* points out one earlier use: in the 1425 translation of Paul's Letter to Titus 2.7 – I thank H. A. Kelly for this earlier reference); *CW* 4, 102/11; *CW* 15, 358/23, 392/2; *EE* 2831/42, 46. Erasmus uses the term to describe More at *EE* 999/209, 221 or *TMSB* 10. For More's earliest recorded concern that word and deed should harmonize and not be in "dispute," see *TMSB* 177, *SL* 5, or *Corr.* 3/47, but also *CW* 3.1, 29/20–22, 172.

[68] *EE* 2831/41–42: "arbitrabar oportere me integritatem nominis mei defendere."

[69] See *CW* 4, 56/24.

[70] *EE* 2831/46–47: "nec adhuc quisquam prodiit qui de mea integritate quereretur"

[71] One indication of this early concern is that More wrote of various characters' "reputation for integrity"; see, for example, in *Richard III*, the power of "integritatis opinionem" (*CW* 15, 358/23; also 393/2).

[72] See Muller, catalog entries 124 and 124a: "Druckermarke von Johannes Froben."

In 1515 it appeared in a rather rough form,[73] but by 1518 a much-refined image by Hans Holbein appeared in *Utopia,* as seen in Illustration 3.

This illustration shows the two serpents as crowned, thus depicting a central tenet of Seneca's, Cicero's, Erasmus's, and More's *humanitas,* a tenet Luther would strongly attack: that for human beings, a well-trained reason must be king.[74] This illustration also shows the serpents so artfully fashioned around the staff of Asclepius (god of healing) that each forms the traditional symbol of health. Instead of the traditional one snake, two work together to protect one vulnerable dove. Around the illustration are Greek, Latin, and Hebraic poetic expressions of one judgment shared by these different cultures about the nature of human flourishing and of human happiness. The Latin is from Martial's ode on what constitutes a happy life: "shrewd simplicity and love of doing right" (10.47). The Greek at top and bottom is from Matthew: "[S]o be prudent as serpents, innocent as doves" (10:16). And the Hebrew at the right is from Psalm 125: "Do good, O Lord, to those who are good and to those who are upright in their hearts." From his earliest to his last work, Thomas More drew attention to the importance of this poetic summary of *humanitas*: good persons of integrity are "prudent as serpents and innocent as doves."[75]

---

[73] See the bottom of the framed space in the middle of Illustration 1.

[74] For this commonplace in Plato and Cicero, see note 35 of Chapter 3; in Aristotle, notes 34 to 36 of Chapter 2.

[75] A decade before the *Utopia*, in the letter prefaced to his translations of Lucian, More pointed out that "the thoughtless credulity of the simple-minded (rather than the wise) [*simplicium potius, quam prudentium*]" results in "foolish confidence and superstitious dread" – thus "undermin[ing] trust" in what is actually true (CW 3.1, 11ff.).

In *Richard III*, the narrator comments that ruler Henry VI was more innocent than prudent (CW 2, [Latin]6/12–13 or CW 15, 320/21). The narrator also draws attention repeatedly to a sickness in the land marked by the lack of trustworthiness: "For the state of things and the dispositions of men were then such that a man could not well tell whom he might trust or whom he might fear" (CW 2, 43/26–8; Logan 50; CW 15, 398/18–20).

In the *Utopia*, Peter Giles is praised as a person of *magna fides, simplicitas,* and *prudens* (CW 4, 48/9–10). Morus says of himself that he "would rather be good than prudent," and in the second letter to Giles, Morus points out the importance of *fides* and *prudens* in reading *Utopia* properly (CW 4, 248–53).

A few years after *Utopia*, More warns the ignorant monk who slanders Erasmus that Christ "meant [his followers] to be not only simple but prudent as well" (CW 15, 260/5–6). And in his Letter to Bugenhagen (CW 7, 44/29), More again draws explicit attention to the need "to be cunning as a serpent."

Later in life, More creates a salt-of-the-earth English persona who exhorts her fellow Londoners to "be not only simple as doves, but also prudent and wise as serpents" (CW 8, 890/3–5). She warns that "if we be slothful" and not diligent, we "will be willingly beguiled" and be made "mad fools" (890/5–6). In his last work, More also notes that

ILLUSTRATION 3. Serpent-and-dove book device of Froben. Froben used this device of two serpents and a dove for his humanist publications. It refers to Christ's statement, "Be wise as serpents, innocent as doves" (Matthew 10:16). This illustration is from the 1518 edition of *Utopia*.

Such integrity – such consistency in thought, word, and action – was a necessary quality of the classical *humanitas* More admired. Socrates, Plato, Aristotle, Cicero, and Seneca would refer to this quality as "true justice" in the individual. The classic formulation, known and quoted by medieval thinkers, is Socrates' statement in the *Republic* that "the extreme of injustice is to seem to be just when one is not" (361a).[76] In the *Gorgias,* Socrates puts it this way: "Before all things, a man should study not to seem but to be good" (527b). Xenophon reports the same idea in the *Memorabilia,* where Socrates advises that "if you want to be thought good at anything, you must try to be so; that is the quickest, the surest, and the best way" (2.6.39).[77] Cicero too stressed the need for a "self-consistent life."[78] But such a life requires, as More would put it, a "sure conscience" informed by "sure deliberation."[79]

Cicero and Sallust present Cato as the classic figure of *integritas* but in a way that shows why More would be reluctant to use that word often[80]

"those of us who follow Christ's command [are to] become wise as serpents (*CW* 14, 617/1); Christ "wished His followers to be brave and prudent," not "senseless and foolish" (*CW* 14, 59/3).

[76] For example, St. Basil the Great refers to Socrates' quote in *How to Profit from Pagan Literature,* sec. 6. Basil's document was so important to the renaissance of Florence that "it was the first Greek text translated by Leonardo Bruni," who used it "as a defense of humanism" (Basil 371–72). Bruni dedicated his translation to the city's fourteenth-century lord chancellor Coluccio Salutati.

[77] Cicero refers to these passages in *De Officiis* 2.43.

[78] *De Officiis* 1.72, 3.5 and see Chapter 3.

[79] For "sure deliberation" (*certum consilium*), see More's Epigram 198/13, especially in light of Aristotle's discussion of deliberation and "deliberate choice" at *Nicomachean Ethics* 1112a19–1113a14 and Aquinas's use of *consilium* as the term for deliberation in his commentary. For the importance of a "sure" conscience, see *SL* 242, 242, 221, *TMSB* 332, or *Corr.* 528/550, 552; see also the ironic use at *CW* 2, [English] 18/17 and the power of conscience at *CW* 2, [English] 68/31–34 and 87/11–12, 16–21 as so dramatically portrayed in Shakespeare's *Richard III.* In his first work published in English, More adds to the text he translates: "Of virtue more joy the conscience hath within / Than outward the body of all his filthy sin" (*CW* 1, 108/7–8; compare with 378). This idea is expressed again at the end of his life when he writes in prison that "the clearness of my conscience hath made my heart hop for joy" (*SL* 235). For the obligation of training the conscience "surely by learning and good counsel," see *SL* 242, 229. More stated that "for the instruction of my conscience . . . , I have not slightly looked, but by many years studied and advisedly considered" the matters at hand (*Corr.* 516 or *TMSB* 320). For the danger of "framing one's conscience" according to one's own desire, see More's comments at *Corr.* 521, 527, *CW* 13, 112, or *TMSB* 325, 331, 214. For achieving "surety," consider also *CW* 1, 40/250 and More's early argument against Lady Fortune, as will be seen in Chapter 4. That More is deliberately provocative in the use of "certum consilium," see note 5 of Chapter 7.

[80] Cicero, *Pro Murena* 3: "Catoni, gravissimo atque integerrimo viro"; Sallust, *Catiline* 54.2: "integritate vitae Cato" as well as 10.5 with its condemnation of hypocrisy whereby

and why Cicero claimed that Cato could improve by having greater education in *humanitas*.[81] Cato illustrates the dangers associated with one who is rigidly concerned about an appearance of integrity; his unbending and doctrinaire Stoicism presented a grave danger to the republic.[82] While More leaves no doubt that he is committed to consistency of word and deed,[83] he also leaves no doubt that he is well aware of the many ethical complexities and the demands of "true virtue." True virtue, consistency between word and deed,[84] is a necessary condition of Cicero's *princeps*, who must be well educated in the full range of *studia humanitatis*.[85]

Aristotle expressed this same thought in different ways, noting that "the end appears to each man in a form answering to his character"[86] and, for this reason, "it is impossible to be practically wise without being good."[87] Popularly put, "As a person is, so does he judge."[88] Experience shows that persons enslaved by uncontrolled anger or burning ambition

one's public face does not reflect one's true character. In English, More may use the word only once in this sense (*CW* 1, 64/4). The Latin uses at *CW* 15, 358/23 and 392/2, *CW* 4, 102/11 show the ambiguities and dangers involved. When More describes his father as "integer," that adjective is the last of a list of seven qualities: "civilis, suavis, innocens, mitis, misericors, aequus et integer" (*EE* 2831/96).

[81] *Pro Murena* 65.

[82] After strongly disagreeing with Cato's overly rigid behavior and judgments, Cicero praises "my master, the schools of Plato and Aristotle, men who do not hold violent or extreme views" (*Pro Murena* 63). Cicero goes on to address Cato: "If some happy chance, Cato, had carried a man of your character off to these masters, you ... would be a little more disposed to kindness" (64). However, much more than kindness was at stake in Cicero's long battle with the extremes of Roman Stoicism and Epicureanism. See Nicgorski 1984 and 2002. The best study of Sallust's exploration of these issues is Batstone.

Reflection on these reasons provide a context for Morus's criticism of Hythlodaeus's "uncivil" approach at *CW* 4, 98; in response to Morus, Hythlodaeus invokes a rigid dichotomy between corruption and integrity (102/10–11).

[83] From one of his earliest letters, More states his concern for the consistency of *vita* with *verba* (*TMSB* 177, *Corr.* 7/47).

[84] Cicero often uses the word *constantia* for this quality; see *De Officiis* 1.69, 72, 119.

[85] On the necessity of an unwavering *fides* and love for truth and justice, see *De Officiis* 1.15, 61–65, 153. See also Cicero's frequent insistence that the true statesman must have the full range of learning, as in *De Oratore* 3.122 especially, but also 1.20, 1.53–54, 1.71–73, 2.5–6, 3.20–21, 3.54; *Pro Archia* 15–16; *De Legibus* 1.59–62; *De Republica* 1.28–28, 2.24–25.

[86] *Nicomachean Ethics* 1114a33. Rhetoric is essential because, Aristotle observes, all are "so much influenced by feelings of friendship or hatred or self-interest that they lose any clear vision of the truth and have their judgment obscured by considerations of personal pleasure or pain" (*Rhetoric* 1354b.). More makes a similar point at *CW* 6, 262.

[87] *Nicomachean Ethics* 1144a36–37.

[88] A free rendering of *Nicomachean Ethics* 1114a33. See also *Rhetoric* 1388b32–1391a19.

or blinding greed cannot judge clearly; they lack the integrity of self-government that human beings need for consistent sharp-sightedness, *humanitas*, and, consequently, prudent action. Hence, we can understand why More would write with his typical wit, "I would rather be good than practically wise."[89]

These views about character, perception, and self-government are expressed in two classic images: the ship's captain at sea and the shepherd protecting his flock, images that More used throughout his life.[90] As these examples indicate, it is one thing to think or even to boast of facing dangers; it is another to do so in fact, especially in the face of death. The captain or the shepherd might perceive clearly what must be done in times of danger, but each must also have a character so disciplined over time that the leader can act courageously in obedience to that perception, at the cost of one's own life if necessary.

Sir Thomas used such examples not only in his earliest publications[91] but also before the king in the 1529 Parliament and right up to the months preceding his own death. In his last book, he warned that the weight and difficulties of duties could "drown and oppress" the mind with sorrow unless such sorrow is "ruled and governed by reason." If reason does not rule, then reason freely "gives over her hold and government,"[92] like "a cowardly ship's captain who is so disheartened by the furious din of a storm that he deserts the helm, hides away cowering in some cranny, and abandons the ship to the waves."[93] More goes on to indicate in no uncertain terms that such a captain could never be called good or just. As More used this image, he showed that the captain's character, his *ethos*,[94] is at least as important as his intellect or his skill. He showed that a certain kind of character is needed to free the intellect to utilize the very skills it has acquired.

---

[89] Thomas More's prefatory letter to *Utopia*: "malim bonus esse quam prudens," CW 4, 40/29.

[90] For example, see the *Republic* 341c and 488d, 345c and 440d, and the references to Homer in note 65.

[91] CW 4, 98/27–28; guarding sheep: CW 3.2, no. 115; sarcastic play on protecting sheep: CW 15, 358/25, the lamb entrusted to the wolf (*agnus certe consulto in lupi fidem creditus*).

[92] CW 14, 263, but I follow here Mary Basset's translation given at CW 14, 1113. The verb used is "infrenet," alluding to Plato's famous image of the charioteer governing his two powerful horses at *Phaedrus* 246, 254.

[93] CW 14, 265.

[94] This Greek word for character is the root of our word "ethics."

Despite his own fear, the effective captain must have the character and clarity of perception to do as Morus says in *Utopia*, "You must not abandon the ship in a storm because you cannot control the wind."[95] As More implies here and explains in his later writings, not only must the captain know when to lower his sails and carefully supervise his crew, especially during storms, but also the captain must have the tested skills and virtues needed to do so.[96] That is precisely why special care must be taken beforehand to acquire all the arts of the captain's trade: good captains need sufficient knowledge of the ship, the sea, the winds, and their own crews; they need sufficient skill in the many arts required for piloting, for *gubernans* (the root of our word "govern"). Just as important, however, they need proven strength of character to fulfill their duty in the face of grave dangers.

Why did More join Erasmus in calling for "the renascence of good letters"? How could a "rebirth" of old books be of any help in the face of new and pressing contemporary problems? Those "good letters" – that is, those classical, biblical, and patristic texts in Latin and especially Greek[97] – he considered to be not only the basis for but also the best-fashioned exercises to achieve the prudence that is a prerequisite for all the other arts needed by "the leading citizens" or *principes*. More and his fellow humanists were convinced of this truth because liberal education gives access to the time-tested truths and also to the intellectual training of the highest, most effective, and most profitable kind.[98] One such intellectual exercise is More's famous *Utopia*, which raises the fundamental issues about *humanitas*, and hence about the soul and the nature of happiness, justice, virtue, wisdom, and government. True, Raphael's report leaves the reader uncertain whether Utopia is really a tyranny or a free republic and whether the common Utopians are enslaved and broken subjects, or wise and virtuous citizens. But for More, "good letters" or the "liberal arts" are not just entertaining pastimes; they are the very

[95] CW 4, 98/27–28.
[96] Some of the uses of this piloting metaphor can be found at CW 1, 45/7–8 and SL 233; CW 4, 98/27–28 and negatively at 52/18; CW 5, 270/28–29; CW 12, 6/13, 29/6, 57/30–31; CW 14, 265/1–3; CW 15, 476/12, and the text from Seneca's *Oedipus* shown in portrait *Sir Thomas More and His Family* (Illustration 5). The image is used in abbreviated form at CW 3.2, Epigram 19/184.
[97] CW 15, 139ff.; SL 100ff.
[98] In reflection upon the title and theme of St. Basil the Great's *How to Profit from Pagan Literature*, one can appreciate why Bruni's translation from Greek to Latin was dedicated to the chancellor of Florence, Coluccio Salutato (Basil 371).

means to achieve the strength of mind and character needed for free self-government rather than enslavement to passion, false ideas, or other persons. They are the means to become free and effective citizens.

In this context, one can appreciate why Thomas More disagreed fundamentally with Martin Luther's denial of free choice of the will,[99] belief in a class of "pure elect,"[100] and claim that human nature was so corrupt that the reason and will were powerless either to find truth or to live justice.[101] These doctrines were, in More's judgment and in the judgment of Christian *principes* then in Europe, false and seditious opinions sure to lead to war and social chaos.[102] The greatest evidence for this view – from their perspectives – was the Peasants' Revolt of 1525, which ended with the slaughter of sixty thousand to eighty thousand peasants in one summer.[103] Luther's ideology – claiming that he and some few were the "pure elect" unable to lose salvation by sin and saved by their faith alone – went against the entire humanist project advanced by More, Erasmus, and their fellow advocates of international unity, peace, and reform based on the development of law, virtue, public deliberation, and education.

When in conversation with one of Luther's followers who claimed that personal inspiration from reading the Bible was sufficient education, More made this reply:

Now in the study of scripture, in devising the sentence, in considering what you read, in pondering the purpose of diverse commentaries, in comparing together diverse texts that seem contrary and are not, although I deny not but that grace and God's special help is the great thing therein, yet he uses for an instrument man's reason thereto. God helps us to eat also but yet not without our mouth. Now as the hand is the more nimble by the use of some feats, and the legs and feet more swift and sure by custom of going and running, and the whole body the more wieldy and lusty by some kind of exercise, so is it no doubt but that reason is by study, labour, and exercise of logic, philosophy, and other liberal arts corroborate [strengthened] and quickened.[104]

---

[99] CW 6, 373; CW 8, 498; CW 5, 269, 271, 207; CW 7, 49.

[100] CW 6, 368–69; CW 8, 57; CW 5, 691–93, 279, 281.

[101] See More's extended discussion throughout CW 6, especially 122–32, 152–53, and his comments about Luther's confusion of license with liberty in CW 5, 270–78, 414/19–29, 688/17–18.

[102] CW 6, 369–72; CW 7, 149; CW 8, 28–33; CW 9, 162, 167.

[103] More's estimates ranged from 60,000 (CW 7, 149) to 70,000 (CW 6, 369 and CW 7, 102) to 80,000 (CW 8, 56).

[104] CW 6, 131–32, but modernized.

Later in life, More put this view even more strongly, stating that *no* virtue is possible without well-trained judgment – that "strength of heart and courage in a reasonable creature can *never* be without prudence."[105]

Plato, Aristotle, Cicero, Seneca, Erasmus, and More's fellow humanists agreed on this view of reason, of a *humanitas* of free and self-governing citizens. Luther did not, and in contrast, More emphasized throughout his life the importance of a well-fashioned reason, a well-fashioned character, and a substantial body of well-fashioned laws, resulting from many generations of prudent citizens and rulers guiding human affairs. Therefore, More followed Plato, Aristotle, Cicero, and Seneca in affirming wisdom and virtue to be the proper ends of education and of life because they alone could equip the individual and the nation to fashion the integrity of thought and action needed to be just, happy, and free. This is a quality we would call "integrity" today, and it is significant that Thomas More is one of the first to use that English word.[106] And like Socrates and Cicero, he died in a deliberate attempt to live it.

Along with these mentors, More agreed that such an education is the most useful education precisely because it best equips human beings to pilot their ships through uncharted waters and through those mighty storms that always come. And in this prudent piloting, More emphasized the absolute necessity of the legislator's expertise in the art of law making.

More saw law as itself an ongoing work of prudence, yet despite his respect for it, More had modest expectations because even the best laws cannot protect every innocent person. This view More learned from history and from his own experience: that often laws are, in words More quoted from Plutarch, "just like spiders' webs; they would hold the weak and the delicate who might be caught in their meshes, but would be torn in pieces by the rich and powerful."[107] More was acutely aware from his earliest days that even the best laws could be manipulated unless learned, prudent, and courageous *principes* exercised constant vigilance and prudent care.

That such prudence is best fashioned with the help of good letters or *studia humanitatis* or the "liberal arts" was a conviction that arose from an understanding of art.

[105] CW 12, 130, emphasis added.
[106] See note 67.
[107] CW 12, 225, quoting Plutarch, *Solon* 5.2–3.

2

Fashioning Peace and Prosperity

What Are the Necessary Arts?

[M]ost *principes* apply themselves to the arts of war . . . instead of the good arts of peace.

Thomas More, *Utopia* 56/22–24

The *princeps'* art of rule . . . is easily seen in our faces and is made conspicuous in the prosperity of the people.

Thomas More, Epigram 19/82–85

[A]rt produces nothing without reason. . . . When you see a statue or a painting, you recognize the exercise of art; when you observe from a distance the course of a ship, you do not hesitate to assume that its motion is guided by reason and by art.

Cicero, *De Natura Deorum* 2.87

Art is necessary to perfect nature – this classical principle More learned during his long and formative study of Plato, Aristotle, Cicero, and Seneca. He also learned this by his experience in a prosperous and self-governing London, home of many master artists. When young More, therefore, wrote that the "*princeps'* art of rule . . . is easily seen in [joyous] faces and is made conspicuous in the prosperity of the people," he was drawing from firsthand London experience as well as from classical and medieval history and political theory.

Plato's Socrates showed how each art is a specific type of making that requires habits and skills based on extensive practice, careful reasoning, and long deliberation about best practices, or what one might call the laws that arise from the "nature" of what is made.[1] To achieve excellence

---

[1] See *Phaedrus* 277b–c.

in that making, the best carpenters or musicians or warriors acquire intricate habits, a detailed knowledge, and active deliberation fostered since childhood, first through play,[2] imitating the craft of their parents, then through free competitions that encourage excellence in that practice and knowledge. Play and then free and thoughtful and willing engagement are essential because, as Socrates puts it, "no forced study abides in the soul" and no one can force a human being to put in the labor of the many years required to master the skills and knowledge needed for true excellence.[3] Human beings must freely decide to exert the effort and to endure the pain that excellence in a specific art requires; in addition, they must have the necessary aptitudes and opportunities.

Few, however, have both. Some, for example, are not gifted in music or gymnastics or dance; others who have these capacities are not willing to practice and study to achieve the highest levels of excellence.[4] In addition, external factors such as wealth can corrupt the potential artisan by taking away the incentive to work as hard as artistic excellence requires.[5]

Excellence in an art comes at a high cost for the artisan, as seen in the many hours of arduous study and practice required to become a great musician or athlete or ruler. Good doctors do not seek pleasure or their own good when working to heal another, and at times they endanger their own lives in practicing that art. The same is true for the expert captain faced with "the dangers of the sea";[6] he must master his fear of storms to be able to "pay careful attention to year, seasons, heaven, stars, winds, and everything that's proper to the art, if he is really going to be skilled at ruling a ship."[7] In a similar way, the art of politics is ordered to knowing and bringing about the good of those ruled, even

---

[2] *Laws* 643b, 764c ff., 812–813a; *Republic* 466e–468a, 537a.

[3] *Republic* 536e.

[4] *Republic* 349e; *Laws* 812d–813a, 764c–765d.

[5] *Republic* 421d.

[6] *Republic* 332e–333a, 341c–d.

[7] *Republic* 488d is the longest of at least fifteen passages developing this metaphor. See Thomas More's metaphorical use of the pilot's skill at CW 4, 98/27–28 and the opening metaphor of book 2 of *Utopia*: navigating the secret rocks and channels in Utopia's harbor, CW 4, 110/21–34. More writes of the need for a "substanciall conying pylot" who can navigate not only harbors with "secret rokkes vnder the water on both the sides" but also through Scylla and Charybdis (CW 12, 120/11–18 and 148/2–8). As mentioned earlier, he writes of the "cowardly ship's captain" who through fear deserts the helm in time of storm (CW 14, 265/1–3); he compares law to the rudder of the country (CW 5, 270/28–29) and uses frequently the image of sailing on stormy seas (SL 233, 255).

at the expense of the ruler. To act as a good shepherd, for example, the guardian of the flock must be willing to endure pain and possible death.[8] And in each case, the master artisan must reason a great deal about all factors involved in that art.

Like Plato, Aristotle develops the Socratic analogies between well-known arts and the less-known political art: just as each art has an activity or function proper to it as seen in its perfection, such as the well-made shoe or well-made chair,[9] so the art of politics has an activity proper to human beings, an activity that orders groups of people to their particular excellence, which for Plato and Aristotle is synonymous with "virtue."[10] As Aristotle puts it, "every virtue or excellence both brings into good condition the thing of which it is the excellence and makes the work of that thing be done well." Two classic examples he gives are these: "[T]he excellence of the eye makes both the eye and its work good; . . . the excellence of the horse makes a horse both good in itself and good at running and at carrying its rider and at awaiting the attack of the enemy. Therefore, if this is true in every case, the virtue of man also will be the state of character which makes a man good and which makes him do his own work well."[11]

Aristotle explains that art "exists to aid nature and to fill up its deficiencies." Just as flourishing harvests depend on the art of the farmer, so flourishing lives of human beings require "many arts for preservation, both at birth and in the matter of nutrition later."[12] Because this nutrition is both physical and educational, Aristotle notes that "all art and education wish to supply the element that is lacking in nature."[13] Ultimately,

---

[8] This common truth about art Socrates used to counter Thrasymachus's claim that the artful ruler seeks his own good rather than the good of the ones ruled in book 1 of the *Republic*. See Thrasymachus and Socrates' exchange on the shepherd at 343a–345e, and consider Thomas More's Epigram 115. In his *Apology*, Socrates defends himself before the city, saying: "I have neglected all my own affairs . . . , approaching each one of you as a father or an elder brother to persuade you to care for virtue." He explains that he has endured poverty in exercising his distinctive art, rather than seeking his own advantage by charging fees (31b–c). See also Chapter 1 for More's comparison of Henry VIII to a shepherd.

[9] *Nicomachean Ethics* 1097b21 ff.

[10] *Nicomachean Ethics* 1097b23, 1101a18, 1102a1–2, 1153b17.

[11] *Nicomachean Ethics* 1106a15–17, 1106a18–24.

[12] *Protrepticus* xi; *Parts of Animals* 639b15–19; *Physics* 2.2 and 13; *Nicomachean Ethics* 1140a10 ff.; *Metaphysics* 981a, 1034a8 ff. Compare these with Cicero's *De Natura Deorum* 2.57–28 and Seneca's *Epistulae* 65.3 and 17.

[13] *Politics* 1337a2.

the art of arts or the science of sciences is wisdom, that is, "knowledge about principles and causes that are certain."[14] In the human sciences, the master or architectonic art of that wisdom is political philosophy.[15]

In the field of politics, Aristotle's master artisans have as their aim the happiness of their people, which in turn requires obedience to good laws.[16] Such laws are in a special way "the 'product' of the political art,"[17] because they are those dictates of reason[18] which look to the good of the whole without reference to personal or special interests.[19]

Because these laws look to the true good of citizens, the legislator must "have studied virtue above all things," and he must know "the facts about the soul" because "legislators make the citizens good by forming habits in them."[20] To develop these habits of "excellence," to develop the "best state" of the human soul,[21] Aristotle explains that "it is from the same causes and by the same means that every virtue is both produced and destroyed, and similarly every art."[22] Just as builders or harpists become good artisans by repeatedly doing their arts well, so souls develop excellences or virtues by repeatedly doing human actions well. The reverse is true regarding poor artistry and vice. In this way art and virtue are analogous:[23] both require habits guided by knowledge and deliberation about the best and most appropriate means to the best and most appropriate end.[24]

Therefore, any artisan, Aristotle explains, whether a physician or a builder or a political ruler, "starts by forming for himself a definite picture . . . of his end – the physician of health, the builder of a house"[25] – or, in the case of the political ruler, a definite picture of happiness for his people, that is, "the best way of life" for human beings, or what Cicero

[14] *Metaphysics* 982a1.
[15] *Nicomachean Ethics* 1094a14.
[16] *Nicomachean Ethics* 1102a9–10.
[17] *Nicomachean Ethics* 1181a24.
[18] *Nicomachean Ethics* 1134a36 and Aquinas's commentary no. 1009.
[19] See Aristotle's discussion of political justice and rule by law rather than rule by individuals at *Nicomachean Ethics* 1134a24 ff.
[20] *Nicomachean Ethics* 1102a17, 1103b3–4.
[21] *Nicomachean Ethics* 1106a16, 1139a15.
[22] *Nicomachean Ethics* 1103b7–8.
[23] See, for example, Cicero, *De Finibus* 4.4.
[24] *Nicomachean Ethics* 1103a16.
[25] Aristotle, *Parts of Animals* 639b15–19. See also *Metaphysics* 981a: "[A]rt arises when, from many notions gained by experience, one universal judgment about a class of objects is produced." Consider again the importance of "sure deliberation" in such judgments. See also *Nicomachean Ethics* 1140a 9–14.

called *humanitas*. Because all art "indeed consists in the conception of the result to be produced before its realization in the material,"[26] the art of politics also requires "a definite picture" of the best way of life. *Utopia* stands in this tradition, but not as one unskilled in the art of reading Platonic or Ciceronian dialogues might conclude.

That "definite picture" or "idea" or "universal judgment" of the fully flourishing human life – of Cicero's and Seneca's *humanitas* – is the central and most important issue of ethics and of political philosophy. The greatest disagreement among philosophers in the classical era[27] was between the "pleasure philosophers" and the "virtue philosophers" represented by such thinkers as Epicurus and Socrates in the Greek tradition and by Lucretius and Cicero in the Roman tradition.[28]

Pleasure is commonly confused with happiness because the very concept of happiness implies an element of pleasure. Therefore, as Aristotle points out with his usual clarity, "most men...identify the good, or happiness, with pleasure."[29] So important in fact is this perception that Aristotle concludes that "the whole concern of both virtue and political science is with pleasures and pains."[30] Why? Because every human "action is accompanied with pleasures and pains" and because virtue is both "increased and...destroyed" by pleasure and pain.[31] Because of the extraordinary power of pleasure and pain, Aristotle joined Plato in calling for good education from childhood so that youth could come "to delight in and to be pained by the things that we ought."[32]

The "ought" leads to another element that Aristotle emphasized in the achievement of virtue and happiness: free choice. As seen in the previous chapter, Seneca explained that our "primary art is virtue itself" – in part because of the role that must be played by the free and deliberative

---

[26] Aristotle, *Parts of Animals* 640a32–33.

[27] And, arguably, in any age.

[28] These opposing views are cleverly dramatized in More's *Utopia* by the novel philosophy of the Utopians, which claims that human beings can be perfected by seeking maximum personal pleasure while simultaneously achieving genuine virtue and political justice and peace. Epicurus or Socrates, Lucretius or Cicero and Seneca would find such a formulation not only novel but untenable because such a claim goes against all previous classical accounts of the human condition, including their own. As Chapter 9 indicates, More cleverly engages each of these schools of thought, deepening the level of his readers' dialectical engagement.

[29] *Nicomachean Ethics* 1095b15–16.

[30] *Nicomachean Ethics* 1105a11–12.

[31] *Nicomachean Ethics* 1104b14–15, 1105a14–15.

[32] *Nicomachean Ethics* 1104b12–13, referring to such passages in the *Laws* 653a ff. and *Republic* 401e ff.

exercise of reason. Therefore, because human beings are by nature free, the *princeps* must have a mastery of those arts needed to govern the free – especially those arts identified by Plato, Aristotle, and Cicero: the arts of education, law, and rhetoric. All involve choice.

Aristotle, in fact defines virtue in terms of choice, emphasizing that "virtue is a state of character concerned with choice, and choice is deliberate desire."[33] This choice is based on "what we best know to be good"[34] as "a result of deliberation,"[35] a deliberation that has taken good counsel into consideration because counsel is part of prudence and therefore precedes choice.[36] Such "voluntary" actions will, by Thomas More's time, be called free actions of the will or just "free will"[37] – a subject that erupts with Luther as *the* crucial issue of More's and Erasmus's humanism and its program of free government based on liberal education.

Education, law, and rhetoric are so necessary for free government that faction and war cannot be avoided without them, and in fact the government will not long remain free without them.[38] Just as expertly trained pilots are needed to navigate safely through violent storms and through unknown seas, so *principes* expertly trained in human and political realities are needed to guide their fellow citizens freely to achieve peace, justice, liberty, and prosperity.

Rhetoric, for example, is one of those master arts needed for liberty because artful speech unites a people upon accepted principles of justice in decisions that build a society in goodwill and mutual prosperity. Cicero's myth about the origin of society makes the provocatively exaggerated claim that artful speech alone had the power "to gather scattered humanity into one place" and "to give shape to laws, tribunals, and civic rights."[39] As Chapter 3 shows, Cicero portrays the greatest of Rome's

---

[33] *Nicomachean Ethics* 1106a14–15 and Aquinas's commentary no. 308. See also Cicero's *De Legibus* 1.19 and 2.11 where he defines law in terms of choice.

[34] *Nicomachean Ethics* 1112a7–8.

[35] *Nicomachean Ethics* 1113a5, 1112a15–17, 1135b10–12, 1139a22–26.

[36] See Aristotle's perceptive analysis of counsel and deliberation at *Nicomachean Ethics* 1112a13–1113a14 and Aquinas's commentary, especially no. 457.

[37] See Sparshott 387n58 and his commentary for *Nicomachean Ethics* 1109b30 ff., where he points out that Aristotle's term for what is often called "voluntary" is *hekousion*, and he supports the argument that the best translation is "intended." Aquinas uses the term *will* throughout his commentary on these sections; see his *Summa Theologica* I.83.1 ff. for his defense of free will and his interpretation of Aristotle's analysis of choice.

[38] See the extended discussions of this point in Cicero's *De Oratore*.

[39] *De Oratore* 1.33, but at 1.35–40 Scaevola immediately refutes this exaggerated claim. Even as a youth, Cicero's claims for rhetoric were more moderate than in this mythic account (*De Inventione* 1.1–3).

leaders (especially Scipio, Laelius, and Crassus) as all well educated in rhetoric as part of their *studia humanitatis*. As Crassus says, "In every free nation, . . . this one art has always flourished above the rest and ever reigned supreme."[40]

Just as Plato and Aristotle did,[41] Cicero emphasized that all human and political excellence is cultivated in ways analogous to excellence in the arts:

Well these philosophers observed that we are so constituted as to have a natural aptitude for the recognized and standard virtues in general, I mean justice, temperance and the others of that class (all of which resemble the rest of the arts, and differ only by excelling them in the material with which they work and in their treatment of it); they observed moreover that we pursue these virtues with a more lofty enthusiasm than we do the arts; and that we possess an implanted or rather an innate appetite for knowledge, and that we are naturally disposed towards social life with our fellow men and towards fellowship and community with the human race.[42]

The art of cultivating human excellence is based on recognizing and fostering the "natural aptitude[s]" that Stoics liked to compare to seeds inherent in every human soul.[43] Precisely because all human beings have souls that are similar in this essential way, Cicero and Seneca agreed with Socrates' claim that human beings were citizens of the world,[44] not just citizens of their own country – a position that would come to distinguish Cicero's and Seneca's "idea of *humanitas*" that recognizes a human nature common to all.[45]

Human nature achieves its full flourishing when governed by those guidelines or laws arising from the very structure of its being, just as with the arts of farming, doctoring, and navigation.[46] The "most fruitful of all arts," for Cicero and Seneca, is the "true and refined philosophy" that

---

[40] *De Oratore* 1.30.

[41] Cicero gives Plato and Aristotle high praise when he says they "had developed a teaching that left nothing to be desired either in fullness or finish" (*De Finibus* 4.3).

[42] *De Finibus* 4.4.

[43] Notice that even here, in his "popularization" of the Stoic position (*De Finibus* 4.24), Cicero indicates his own preference for "innate" rather than "implanted."

[44] *Tusculanae Disputationes* 5.108; *De Legibus* 1.23, 61; *De Officiis* 3.26, 28; *De Finibus* 3.64; *De Natura Deorum* 2.133, 154; Seneca, *Otio* 4.1, 6.4.

[45] Seneca, in *Epistulae* 65.7, attributes his understanding of *humanitas* "or the idea of man" to Plato; he maintains that *humanitas* is, along with *congregationem*, the "first thing which philosophy undertakes to give" (5.4) because the alternative is *demens* or madness (5.4 and 95.31–32). See Cicero, *De Legibus* 1.33 and 42.

[46] *De Finibus* 4.16–17.

teaches the way of good living."[47] This same position Thomas More held from his earliest published work.[48]

This "true and refined philosophy," this "art of living" (*vivendi ars*), helps human beings to "guard the gifts that nature has bestowed and to obtain those that are lacking."[49] Because it is based on the careful study of the "nature" of the body and of the soul, philosophy can be "the guardian and protector of the whole person, as being the comrade and helper of nature."[50]

The emphasis on guarding and protecting is given special attention by Cicero, who claims that the Romans both understood and cared for this dimension of life more effectively than did the Greeks. The accomplished statesman-orator-general-lawyer-philosopher Crassus, arguably Cicero's greatest *princeps*,[51] makes this case in both subtle and confrontationally forceful ways in Cicero's *De Oratore*. Cicero gives, for example, a vivid report of Crassus's greatest and final speech in the Senate when he stands against the tyrannical and illegal actions of "a consul whose duty it was to be [the Senate's] fostering parent and faithful guardian [but who instead] was plundering like some unprincipled brigand" (3.3). With a "superlative energy of spirit, intellect, and force," Crassus fearlessly stood against the consul Philippus, challenging him in the name of Roman *libertas* if he insisted on continuing his injustice: "[Y]ou must cut out this tongue of mine – although even when this has been torn from my throat, my breath of itself will serve my liberty [*libertas*] for the refutation of your licence [*libido*]" (3.4).

This same Crassus – successful general in foreign wars, consul and honored leader in peace at home – is the one who insists on the position

---

[47] *Tusculanae Disputationes* 4.5–6. That Seneca follows in this same Socratic tradition can be seen in *Epistulae* 92.10, 44, 46; 88.28; 90.1–2; 104.19; 117.12, 16.

[48] *SL* 4–6, 103–7 or *TMSB* 175–77, 197–200, and More's humanist letters (*CW* 15). See also his introduction to Pico della Mirandola's "Letter to Andrew Corneus," where, contrary to Pico's own opinion, More states that one reason to study philosophy is "for the instruction of [the] mind in moral virtue" (*CW* 1, 85/10–11).

[49] *De Finibus* 3.4, 4.16, 19; *Tusculanae Disputationes* 4.15; Seneca, *Epistulae* 88.28, 33; 90.27, 95.7, 117.12; Augustine, *City of God* 9.4.

[50] *De Finibus* 4.16–18, where Cicero explains that careful study of the soul reveals "in the first place...seeds of justice [*iustitiae semina*]," which provide the "origin and growth of all the virtues." "Innate love of knowledge" is another seed that gives rise to "the contemplation of the secrets of nature."

[51] As Mitchell explains, Crassus is, "for Cicero, the great exemplar of the arts of peace, the civilian statesman par excellence." Crassus's "position as a *princeps* of the highest *auctoritas* in a dominant Senate was Cicero's own fondest ambition" (1991 47). For Cicero's own high praise of Crassus, see *De Oratore* 2.1–4, 6; 3.2–7, 74–77.

that Cicero himself affirms:[52] that the *princeps* needs a full and complete education in *studia humanitatis* – that "wide domain of science" not "split up into separate departments" (3.132). Otherwise, leaders come "to office and to positions in the government quite naked and unarmed, not equipped with any acquaintance with affairs or knowledge" (3.136). Only such a well-educated leader can "win freedom for his native land," having been "equipped ... with weapons for the task" (3.139). The dangers of a partial education are seen by two extremes: those Cynics and Stoics who "in the Socratic discourse had been captivated chiefly by the ideal of endurance and hardness"; and those Epicureans "who had taken delight rather in the Socratic discussions on the subject of pleasure" (3.62). This second extreme "that has undertaken the championship of pleasure"[53] is especially unfit, Crassus argues, "to be the author of public counsel [*consilii*] ... pre-eminent for wisdom and eloquence in the Senate, in the assembly of the people, and in public causes" (3.63).

But the first extreme, pride in personal endurance and hardness, is also an unfatherly, uncivil, and "inept" hindrance to social harmony, as Crassus points to in the beginning of *De Oratore,* where the superiority of Romans' wearing shoes and holding chaste conversation in the safety of a walled household is contrasted implicitly to the primitiveness of barefoot Socrates' conversations about illicit loves, conversations held in the midst of nature under the noonday sun, outside home or city.[54]

Cicero also compares the educational work of the true and artful *princeps* to the farmer's task of proper cultivation, of bringing all "its parts into the most thriving condition."[55] In an analogous sense, the wise philosopher-statesman's "office and duty" is "entirely centered in the work of perfecting man."[56] When artfully cultivated, human beings come to "full flower and perfection," marked by *honestas*[57] and *humanitas*.[58] In determining the "nature" of this full flowering, Cicero says that he

---

[52] In *De Oratore,* see Cicero's own comments in the prefaces to each day of his Crassus dialogues, especially 1.5 and 16, 2.5–6, and 3.15.

[53] This same phrase occurs in *Utopia,* CW 4, 160/25, in direct opposition to this passage and to *De Officiis* 2.27.

[54] Consider the parallels and contrasts of the settings of *De Oratore* and Plato's *Phaedrus,* especially at *De Oratore* 1.28–29, in light of these later comments of 3.62 and 138–39, as well as More's use of Lucian's dialogues as seen in Chapter 4. I am grateful to Scott Crider for his illuminating reflections on these contrasts.

[55] *De Finibus* 4.38.

[56] *De Finibus* 4.36.

[57] *De Finibus* 4.18 and throughout *De Officiis*.

[58] See Chapter 1.

follows Plato,[59] who was the first to insist that one cannot separate what is useful (*utile*) for human beings from what is *honestas* or right (*ius*).[60]

Cicero describes as the "paragon" of Stoic humanity those possessing "integrity [*honestas*], serious-mindedness, self-control, magnanimity, and justice,"[61] but he states explicitly that this understanding of human excellence is the result of artful education in the *studia humanitatis*.[62] Cicero follows Socrates in defining virtue as "nothing else than nature perfected and developed to the highest point," based on "a likeness between man and God."[63] Thomas More would make the same point in his first humanist work published in English, his *Life of Pico della Mirandola*.[64]

Seneca places himself in this same school of philosophy, and he also presents virtue as an art, "man's primary art."[65] All human beings are free to "fashion" deliberately their own *ethos*,[66] or character, by developing habits through the repetition of actions guided by a view of life considered proper to human beings. In Seneca's classic formulation, "[V]irtue does not enter the soul unless that soul has been trained and taught, and by assiduous practice brought to perfection."[67] Implied in this formulation is the freedom of one who has made a deliberative choice to train and to practice freely and assiduously: "For nature does not bestow virtue; it is an art to become good"[68] – that is, it requires long and deliberate and arduous labor.

---

[59] That Cicero favors Plato over Socrates, see Nicgorski 1992 and DiLorenzo.

[60] At *De Legibus* 1.33 and *De Officiis* 3.11. Cicero seems to make an opposite claim at *De Oratore* 3.60 and, by implication, at 1.46–47, but notice the distinction he makes between Socrates and Plato. For Cicero, Socrates but not Plato is responsible for separating philosophy from its useful political art, rhetoric. To consider the issues involved, see especially Nicgorski's articles of 1984, 1991, and 1992.

[61] *Pro Murena* 60: "Finxit enim te ipsa natura ad honestatem, gravitatem, temperantiam, magnitudinem animi, iustitiam, ad omnis denique virtutes magnum hominem et excelsum." It is significant that Cicero does not include prudence in this list and that he goes on in this passage to indicate that Cato could improve himself with more "studiis humanitatis" (61). Compare, for example, the use here of *finxit* with the "forged and fashioned" (*conflatur et efficitur*) of *De Officiis* 1.14. Contrast this understanding of self-fashioning with Stephen Greenblatt's use in *Renaissance Self-Fashioning*.

[62] *Pro Murena* 61.

[63] *De Legibus* 1.23–26; *De Officiis* 1.153; *De Natura Deorum* 2.154 and 2.16–18, 78 and 3.26.

[64] See Koterski as well as *CW* 1, 77 and 111–12, where More draws attention to the importance of human beings understood as created in the image of God.

[65] Seneca, *Epistulae* 92.10. The limitation of this metaphor is shown by reflection on *Nicomachean Ethics* 1105a27 ff. and 1106b13–14, where Aristotle explicitly denies this comparison.

[66] *Ethos* in Greek means "character"; it is the root of our word "ethics."

[67] Seneca, *Epistulae* 90.46.

[68] Seneca, *Epistulae* 44.

Although everyone has the nature to exercise the art of virtue, few have the nature to excel in the wide range of diverse arts needed by the *princeps* to pilot the ship of a free state, as Cicero makes clear in *De Officiis*. There he points out that "it is each person's duty to weigh well what are his own particular traits of character" before "choosing his role upon the stage" of life. Only in this way can people "work to the best advantage in that role to which [they] are best adapted [*aptissimi*]" and therefore "not falter in the discharge of any duty."[69] This choice presents "the most difficult problem in the world" because "it is in the years of early youth, when our judgment is most immature, that each of us decides what his calling in life shall be."[70] It is no wonder, then, that Margaret looks so pensive in the Thomas More family portrait as she points to a passage from Seneca about the art of self-fashioning and the art of governing.[71]

So difficult are the *princeps*'s arts and sciences of rule, so rare are the many gifts needed, and so much extraordinary labor is required to achieve them that one could understand why five widely divergent London playwrights would join forces in praising a Londoner who exerted the "great . . . study" and "loyal industry" to "forge" the "peace / That shines upon our commonwealth." Poet and politician Lord Surrey voices this praise in *Sir Thomas More* in a scene in which Surrey is speaking to Erasmus about Thomas More:[72]

> This little isle holds not a truer friend
> Unto the arts. . . .
> He's great in study; that's the statist's [statesman's] grace
> That gains more reverence than the outward place.
>
> . . .
>
> Now shall you view the honourablest scholar,
> The most religious politician,
> The worthiest counsellor that tends our state.
> That study is the general watch of England;
> In it the prince's safety and the peace
> That shines upon our commonwealth are forged
> By loyal industry. . . .[73]

---

[69] *De Officiis* 1.113–14, 119.
[70] *De Officiis* 1.117.
[71] See Chapter 10.
[72] In this scene, More is away because he is involved in a play of his own, as part of a joke on his unsuspecting guest Erasmus.
[73] *TMSB*, 3.1.116–17, 120–21, 128–34. In the sixteenth-century manuscript that was censored and not published until 1844, the five "hands" are commonly identified to be the handwriting of these playwrights: Anthony Munday, William Shakespeare, Henry Chettle, Thomas Dekker, and Thomas Heywood. Despite the wide political and religious differences of these playwrights, the play itself is entirely praiseworthy of their

Singled out in this description of the prudent statesman is the industrious study of the liberal arts that are able to "forge" peace and safety. Seventy years earlier, More had written that a true leader must, by practicing a "civil philosophy," "know his stage, adapt himself to the play at hand, and perform his role appropriately" – even if that role would be to remain silent, rather than play the comedian in a tragedy or the tragedian in a comedy.[74] These lines echo Cicero's description of his "first citizens," who are "like skilful actors who have played well their parts in the drama of life to the end, and not like untrained players who have broken down in the last act."[75]

> fellow Londoner, characterized in the play by good-humored wisdom exemplified in the "Marriage of Wit and Wisdom," a play in which More himself has a significant part.
>
> [74] CW 4, 98/11–14; compare with *De Officiis* 1.70–73, 114 and *De Senectute* 64. See Skinner 220n47 and 222.
> [75] *De Senectute* 64.

3

Cicero's and More's First Citizens

How Do They Avoid Faction and Civil War?

[I]n a matter affecting the state, I could not but mark the inspired words in the writings of my master Plato: "As are the first citizens [*principes*] in a commonwealth, so are the other citizens apt to be." [W]e should all have as our one aim and object what I have so repeatedly urged – the *maintenance of peace with dignity.*

> Cicero, *Epistulae ad Familiares* 1.12, 21 (emphasis added)

In every free nation, and most of all in cities which have attained the enjoyment of peace and tranquility, this one art [of speaking] has always flourished above the rest and ever reigned supreme.... [W]hat other force could have been strong enough either to gather scattered humanity into one place, or to lead it out of its brutish existence in the wilderness up to our present condition of civilization as men and as citizens, or, after the establishment of social communities, to give shape to laws, tribunals, and civic rights?

> Cicero, *De Oratore* 1.30, 33

Young Thomas More began his literary career – as would Shakespeare in his first four plays – with a probing study of England's civil wars. Faced with generations of such wars and aware of the people's growing discontent with tyrannous Henry VII, what did this brilliant, well-educated Londoner see as possible solutions to England's internal warfare? He studied carefully the writings and experiences of ancient Athens and the Roman Republic, as well as the institutions and practices of his own self-governing and relatively peaceful city of London. What solutions did he see?

The striking, indeed obtrusive, presence of vocabulary distinctive to the Roman Republic remains one of the unsolved mysteries of Thomas

More's early works. Why, for example, does More repeatedly use terms[1] such as *res publica, maiestas,*[2] *senatus,*[3] *forum, senatusconsultum, consulconsilium,*[4] and *bona fides*? Or why in provocative ways use special words referring to unique historical developments such as *patrocinium,*[5] but especially those developments that arose to protect the rights of Roman citizens such as *provocatio,*[6] *appellatio,*[7] and *auxilium*[8]? Or why use terms, if not coined by, certainly invested with new meaning by Cicero, terms such as *humanitas* and *principatus*?[9] Obviously, without saying so directly,[10] More invites a comparison between the Roman Republic and England's strife-filled government. But what was young More suggesting?

Most striking is the frequent use of *princeps* in More's *Richard III, Utopia,* and *Epigrammata* – all three of which even use the highly charged

---

[1] For the many uses of these terms, see www.thomasmorestudies.org/IndicesofLatinTerms.

[2] See Gordon's important treatment of "*Maiestas* in Thomas More's Political Thought."

[3] At *CW* 15, 320/20, More does use *Parlamentus,* but he commonly uses *senatus* to refer to both the council of England (320/20, 322/13, and implied at 450/17) and England's council of mayor and aldermen (358/15, 420/11, 424/11, 454/19, 474/5). More's sensitivity to the difference in these uses is made clear at *CW* 8, 187/9–12. In Epigram 198, see More's references to a senate at lines 1, 2, 7, 9, 28.

[4] Cicero and Augustine point out that the Roman "consul" derived his title by his office as "one who consults . . . for the public good" (*City of God* 5.12; *De Legibus* 3.8). Consuls and all Roman magistrates were to consult with the deliberative body of the senate and with *ius* and *lex* (*Verrine Orations* 2.1.107; *In Pisonem* 23; *Respublica* 1.41, 43 and 2.30, 53; *Pro Sestio* 137, 91).

[5] For Cicero's most famous use of this term, see *De Officiis* 2.27; see also 2.66, 69. For More's ironic uses of this term, see *CW* 4, 160/25 and *CW* 15, 462/4.

[6] See *CW* 4, 144/12. As Andrew Lintott points out in his 1999 study, *provocatio* was eventually "regarded as one of the principal rights of the individual Roman citizen, a theoretical guarantee against execution without trial" (33). One might ask, What recourse – and protections – did the Utopian citizens have? Lintott's "Provocatio: From the Struggle of the Orders to the Principate" shows why Cicero considered *provocatio* "one of the cornerstones of Roman criminal law" (226–27); Lintott's article and his earlier book on *Violence in Republican Rome* help to appreciate the history of this practical solution to a perennial problem of rights versus power, the *ius* versus *vis* (*Sestio* 92, *Caelio* 27) that Cicero recognized.

[7] See *CW* 4, 230/12, and Lintott 1972 233–34 and 264.

[8] In *Utopia,* every use of this term refers to foreign allies and the care given to them; no such care – that is, legal protection – is given to fellow Utopians (*CW* 4, 200/8, 208/14, 214/16, 216/4). This term is used in a similarly ironic way at *CW* 15, 470/22. See Lintott's 1972 article for suggestive comments on the importance of this "Republican practice" (263, also 230) and Wirszubski 1968 25–27.

[9] See notes 34, 35, 37, 45, 60, 94.

[10] Morus, the character and narrator in *Utopia,* advises and uses the same "indirect approach."

phrase *pius princeps*.[11] Although it has been recognized that *princeps* "inevitably recalls Rome's complex political legacy to the sixteenth-century Europe,"[12] much scholarly work has yet to be done to recover Thomas More's interpretation and use of that legacy. With the fall of the republic, for example, Augustus Caesar adopted the title of *princeps*, but with no real sense of his being first among equals. Tacitus says that Augustus "found the whole state exhausted by civic dissensions and took it under his *imperium*, using the name of *princeps*" (Tacitus, *Annales* 1.1). Utopus found Utopia in this situation of "universal dissensions" and therefore it was "easy to conquer the whole country because the different sects were too busy fitting one another";[13] Utopus, too, took *imperium* using the name of *princeps*.[14]

More himself draws attention to the *princeps* and "our *respublica*" in two letters written to Erasmus shortly after the 1516 publication of

[11] See *CW* 15, 424/8; *CW* 4, 92/3; *CW* 3.2, Epigram 111. No Renaissance humanist could read *princeps pius* in *Richard III*, in *Utopia*, or in Epigram 111 without thinking of Virgil's *Aeneid*. In Epigram 147, More describes Virgil as a "poet who is second to none," a poet who "wrote long ago that in piety [*pietate*] Aeneas was second to none." Aeneas was the leader famous for the fatherly care of his people, for strong obedience to the gods, and for founding a Rome to be ruled by law. As classical scholar R. G. Austin explains, *pius* or *pietas* "is a very Roman concept, embracing many aspects of man's relationship to the gods and to fellow men: duty, devoted service, responsibility, compassion, the full consciousness of what is due to others" (33). It is the most frequent epithet Virgil used to describe his Roman hero, Aeneas; common translations are "duty-bound," "loyal," "devoted," "pious," "noble," "who reveres the gods," or "the good." No one translation is adequate; hence, this example gives some indication why More, after experimenting as early as 1513 with English and Latin versions of *Richard III*, might have decided to use Latin in writing *Utopia* in 1515–16.

[12] David Baker 36. Why *princeps* is a "complex" term can be seen by its history. In the early Roman Republic the "*princeps (civitatis)*...was a value term applied to the man judged to be the most prominent or influential of the *principes*"; by the "late Republic the term *principes (civitatis)* described the collective body of ex-consuls," and the *princeps* referred to the oldest of these (Ogilvie 392, where he also points out that Livy consistently uses *princeps* with its "Republican usage," with "no hint of the Augustan conception").
  In *Utopia*, conqueror Utopus finds Abraxa in a similar condition, and *princeps* is the official term used in his new state of Utopia for the lifelong head of each city. We are also told that the Utopians have mastered all the arts of the Roman *imperium* (*CW* 4, 108/7–8). What do *Utopia* and *Richard III* suggest about the way to judge military conquerors such as Conqueror Utopus or Princeps Caesar Augustus or Henry VIII? Would, for instance, Thomas More agree with a Montesquieu and a Gibbons who judged such a *princeps* to be a cunning and subtle tyrant, or would he agree with those who judged Princeps Augustus as "the benevolent leader of Rome, Italy, and the reunited empire, bringer of peace, reformer, and organizer" (Raaflaub xii)?

[13] *CW* 4, 218/34; *CUP Utopia* 223.

[14] See note 12 and Chapter 9.

Utopia. In the first, More writes that all of his imagined *principes* "are distinguished for learning and virtue"[15] and that they all "rule over free people"[16] rather than over "subjects, as the term is now used by kings to refer to their people, who are really worse off than slaves."[17] He goes on to say that what distinguishes his *principes* is that they are "far removed from that ill-will [*inuidia*][18] which desires others to suffer while they are well off themselves."[19] Instead of the ill will characteristic of rivalry between factions, his *principes*'s rule of the free is characterized by virtue and learning.

In the second letter, More writes of his desire to be a *princeps*[20] whose principate[21] is distinguished by a "rule of clemency" (*clementiae imperium*)[22] not affected by fortune.[23] He then imagines himself to be a *princeps* who wears a general's "military cloak" that is conspicuously "Franciscan."[24] This letter again points to a rule "far removed from . . . ill-will" by focusing on a "rule of clemency" symbolized by the striking

---

[15] More's letter of 31 October 1516, *EE* 481, line 67: "litteris ac virtute tanti"; see the translation of *SL* 80.

[16] *EE* 481, line 73: "imperare liberis."

[17] *EE* 481, lines 71–72: "subditos ac subiectos, quomodo nunc reges populum vocant, hoc est plus quam seruos." Compare this situation with the contrasting description in Augustine's *City of God*: "Illi in principibus eius vel in eis quas subiugat nationibus dominandi libido dominatur; in hac serviunt invicem in caritate et praepositi consulendo et subditi obtemperando" (In the one [city], the lust for dominion has dominion over its princes as well as over the nations that it subdues; in the other, both those put in charge and those placed under them serve one another in love, the former by their counsel, the latter by their obedience") (14.28, Loeb edition). See also 5.12 for the nature of Roman rule and the tendency of the Roman "father [to oppress] the people as slaves." That More knew the *City of God* exceptionally well, see Stapleton 7–8 and Wegemer 1996 128–49.

[18] As Chapter 8 shows, *inuidia* plays a dominant role in *Richard III*; it is, however, conspicuously absent from *Utopia*. For the importance of this term, see www .thomasmorestudies.org/IndicesofLatinTerms.

[19] *EE* 481, lines 73–74: "ac longe absint tam boni viri ab ea inuidia vt optent male esse aliis, quum sibi sit bene."

[20] *EE* 499, line 57.

[21] *EE* 499, lines 41 and 59.

[22] *EE* 499, line 56: "clementiae regit imperium."

[23] *EE* 499, lines 49–50. See *Jugurtha* 2.3–4 and *Catiline* 2.5–6 for Sallust's accounts of why it is important to have a character that does not change with fortune. For the source and importance of such a character, see Tacitus's *Historiae* 4.5 and *Annales* 4.20.

[24] *EE* 499, lines 42–44: "conspicuus paludamento Franciscano, praeferens venerabile sceptrum e manipulo frugis." Because he imagines himself also carrying "a handful of wheat as my venerable scepter," his attire seems to be the same as any Utopian *princeps*. See *CW* 4, 194/5 ("gestatus frumenti manipulus") and *CW* 4, 132/34 for the "natural color" of their woolen attire. Dominic Baker-Smith explains the Franciscan allusions in *Utopia*; see, for example, 143ff. and 205.

combination of the military leader's *imperium* with a garb expressing the Franciscans' distinctive poverty.[25]

Cicero too emphasized the importance of an *imperium* of clemency[26] ordered to peace,[27] an *imperium* distinguished by contempt for both wealth and transitory human goods. Cicero repeatedly insisted that true *humanitas* requires one to have "contempt" for passing human things (*humanarum rerum contemptio*) if one is to achieve truth, the common good, and "greatness of soul."[28] He explained, as he had done "so often,"[29] that such "contempt" is a necessity especially for statesmen:

> Statesmen, too, no less than philosophers – perhaps even more so – should carry with them that greatness of spirit [*magnificentia*][30] and indifference to outward circumstances [*despicientia rerum humanarum*] to which I so often refer, together with calm of soul and freedom from care, if they are to be free from worries and lead a dignified and self-consistent life. (*De Officiis* 1.72)

These, then, are some of the necessary elements of Cicero's new type of *princeps* that the Roman Republic would need to survive, if it would survive. Or, as Cicero in his last major work sets forth the ideal: the "highest ambition of our magistrates and generals" should be justice and trustworthiness, *aequitas et fides,* "so our government could be called more accurately a protectorate [*patrocinium*] of the world than a dominion [*imperium*]" (*De Officiis* 2.26–27).

What was this new leadership envisioned by Cicero and how did it relate to the new *princeps* that Thomas More envisioned for England? Working toward answers to these questions is the major task of this

---

[25] As Baker-Smith points out, More presents "himself as the prince of the Utopians in a Franciscan habit" (205).

[26] Dyck explains how *clementia* "is a peculiarly Roman concept" (225). For its importance in Rome after republican rule under law was replaced by imperial rule, see Cicero's later speeches and Seneca's classic treatments of this virtue as indicated in Chapter 1.

[27] See the quotations given at the beginning of this chapter (*Epistulae ad Familiares* 1.21 and *De Oratore* 1.30).

[28] *De Officiis* 1.13; in these contexts, *res humane* is often translated as "human vicissitudes" or "worldly conditions." In the "Dream of Scipio" (Cicero, *Republic* 6.20), the command is to "keep your gaze fixed upon these heavenly things, and scorn the earthly"; the dream allows Scipio to see "what a small portion . . . belongs to you Romans" (6.21).

[29] For example, see *Tusculanae Disputationes* 1.95: "[S]et the whole meaning of right living in strength and greatness of soul, in disdain and scorn for all human vicissitudes [*omnium rerum humanarum contemptione ac despicienda*] and in the practice of all virtue." In *De Officiis,* see these many exhortations: 1.61, 72, 106; 2.37–38; 3.24, 119.

[30] Compare this use with CW 4, 244/20, Morus's famously controversial invocation of "nobilitas, magnificentia, splendor, maiestas."

book.[31] Clearly, however, both Cicero and More saw the need for a *princeps* skillful enough – that is, learned, virtuous, experienced, and detached enough – to fashion action that would not only avoid the ill will [*inuidia*] that causes deadly civil strife but also strengthen the trust (*fides*) and friendship needed to foster "sound deliberation" (*certum consilium*) in the body politic.

Etymologically, *princeps* means "taking or capturing first [place]," from *primus* and *-ceps,* a form of *capio.*[32] Implied in the concept is society's recognition of merit – the same merit that Thucydides praised in Athenian citizens such as Pericles, Brasidas, and Peisistratus, whose excellence, prowess, generosity, and ability led them to be recognized by their fellow citizens as "first."[33] In his *De Natura Deorum*, Cicero explains *principatus* as "the equivalent of the Greek *hēgemonikon*, meaning that part of anything which must and ought to have supremacy."[34] In human beings, that ruling part is the intelligence (*mentes*), as Plato taught.[35] In philosophy, for example, the *princeps* – the person holding first place – is usually considered to be "Socrates, the person who on the evidence of all men of learning and the verdict of the whole of Greece, owing not only to his wisdom and penetration and charm and subtlety but also to his eloquence and variety and fertility easily came out *first.*"[36]

In a state, that ruling part for Cicero is the group of most eminent citizens, the *principatus,* who are responsible for "steer[ing] the ship of state."[37] These leading citizens emerge as "first" by the proven quality

[31] Because Thomas More has been virtually excluded from English academic life since 1535, More scholarship is four hundred years behind any other comparable English figure. The clearest evidence is that the first critical edition of his works was published only in 1963–97 – in the United States, not in England.

[32] For a brief account of the history of this word in the time of Augustus Caesar, see Holmes 263–65. The perennial "debate about Augustus" as *princeps* is outlined in the introduction (xi–xxi) to Raaflaub and Toher.

[33] As Agathi Georgiadou explains, such a leading citizen "in Thucydides does not only mean 'the first statesman' but 'the most capable statesman'" (225; see also 230, 236). See Thucydides' praise of such rare leaders at 1.139.4, 4.81.2, and 6.54.5.

[34] *De Natura Deorum* 2.29.

[35] At *Tusculanae Disputationes* 1.20, Cicero cites Plato as his authority for presenting reason as *principatus*: "Eius doctor Plato triplicem finxit animum, cuius principatum, id est rationem in capite sicut in arce posuit."

[36] *De Oratore* 3.60 (emphasis added); Cicero, however, seems to indicate that "the great Plato" actually has that preeminence and is responsible for Socrates' reputation. For the "great Plato," "princeps" of philosophers, see *De Finibus* 5.7, *De Legibus* 3.1, 2.39, *De Oratore* 3.15, *Scauro* 4; for Plato's being responsible for a glorified Socrates, see Nicgorski 1992 216, 220 and DiLorenzo, especially 248–49.

[37] *Epistulae ad Familiares* 1.21; *Pro Sestio* 20, 45–46, 99; and *De Natura Deorum* 2.87.

of their service in bringing about the good of the *respublica* as a whole. To these "who excelled in justice and wisdom," the people entrust their *imperium* "without which, existence is impossible for a household, a city, a nation."[38] Such leaders of government arise because they are "first in wisdom and eloquence in the Senate, in the assembly of the people, and in public causes."[39] They rise "easily"[40] to first place if they have the natural talent and have worked to achieve the mastery of the arts involved. Maintaining that position of trust, however, requires proving "their loyalty [*fides*], their steadfastness [*constantia*], their greatness of soul [*magnitudo animi*]" through many political storms, and through the whole of their lives.[41]

Those who are first in the arts of liberty and in strength of character are the natural leaders to whom citizens wish and need to entrust the authority to govern, because the ship of state requires trustworthy [*fides*] pilots skilled in the many difficult arts needed to navigate unknown or stormy seas. These "first citizens" are the ones who "have better insight into the future, and who, when an emergency arises and a crisis comes, can clear away the difficulties and reach a safe decision [*consilium*] according to the exigencies of the occasion" (*De Officiis* 2.33). In Cicero's account, such talented and skilled artisans are the only ones able to persuade and teach others to form societies:

Those who stood out as first in virtue and outstanding in counsel [*consilii*], having perceived the essential teachableness of human nature, gathered together into one place those who had been scattered abroad, and brought them from the state of savagery to one of justice and humanity.[42]

Here and elsewhere, Cicero shows that it takes an expertise of the "great and wise" to bring about peace and prosperity,[43] an expertise rooted in *studia humanitatis*. This extensive education that begins with "fashioning the minds of the young according to *humanitas* and virtue"

[38] *De Legibus* 3.3–4.
[39] *De Oratore* 3.63.
[40] Compare Cicero's explanations of the *princeps* arising "easily" at first because of talent and proven service with Buckingham's boastful claim that he could "easily find some other candidate who cared for the *respublica*" (CW 15, 480/2–3).
[41] *Pro Sestio* 139; that the *princeps* must be properly trained and adequately proved, see *De Legibus* 3.29–32 and throughout *De Oratore*.
[42] *Pro Sestio* 91: "Qui igitur primi virtute et consilio praestanti exstiterunt, ii perspecto genere humanae docilitatis atque ingenii dissipatos unum in locum congregarunt eosque ex feritate illa ad iustitiam atque ad mansuetudinem transduxerunt." See also *De Inventione* 1.1–3, *De Oratore* 1.30–33, and *Tusculanae Disputationes* 1.62–63.
[43] *De Inventione* 1.2; *De Oratore* 1.30.

is for Cicero[44] – and More – the best way to fashion justice, liberty, and peace.

Humanitas is a word specially indebted to Cicero and then developed by Seneca, and they used it hundreds of times in their promotion of a way of life ordered toward "peace with dignity," justice, and civic prosperity.[45] Cicero's "educational ideal" of *humanitas*, as S. J. Wilson describes it, "combined an aversion from war and civil strife with intellectual culture and an admiration for Greek literature and science, and which valued character as well as learning."[46] As Cicero scholar Thomas Mitchell explains:

[H]umanitas meant more to Cicero than high culture or refined manners.... It further represented the social spirit that came from a maturation of man's inner sense of fellowship and gentleness...that made possible a secure and civilized way of life in a just and harmonious society. Cicero goes so far as to present *humanitas* as the difference between primitive, ill-ordered societies with brutish concerns and brutish habits of violence and aggression, and those where moral idealism had a place and where unity and order prevailed, protected by justice, laws, courts, rights, and a concern for peace.[47]

Expertise in these many civilizing arts involved in governing is comparable to the many arts required for expert piloting – hence the origin of "governing," from *gubernans* (piloting). As Cicero explains:

But just as in sailing, it shows nautical skill to run before the wind in a gale, even if you fail thereby to make your port; whereas when you can get there just as well by slanting your tacking, it is sheer folly to court disaster by keeping your original course, rather than change it and still reach your destination; on the same principle in the conduct of state affairs, while we should all have as our one aim and object what I have so repeatedly urged – the *maintenance of peace with dignity* – it does not follow that we ought always to express ourselves in the same way, though we ought always to have in view the same goal. (*Epistulae ad Familiares* 1.21, emphasis added)

Among the skills of governing, philosophy plays an essential part in achieving "peace with dignity."[48] Why philosophy? Cicero had to be

---

44 See Chapter 1 and *De Oratore* 3.58.
45 Paul MacKendrick claims that Cicero coined *humanitas* (2, 19; bibliographic sources are given at 322n64). See Seneca, *Epistulae* 65.7, for his understanding of *humanitas* "or the idea of man" as going back to Plato. Astin gives a lucid account of what he seems to take as a distinctively "Ciceronian ideal of *humanitas*" (302–6).
46 S. J. Wilson 95.
47 Mitchell 1984 38.
48 *Pro Sestio* 98; *De Officiis* 1.76 and 80; *Epistulae ad Familiares* 1.21. See Wirszubski 1954; Wood 197–99; Mitchell 1979 198–200.

extremely careful – as did Thomas More – in addressing this question within a culture more warring than peace loving. Briefly put, however, Cicero saw philosophy as the most fruitful of arts and a necessary part of the *humanitas* needed by the orator-*princeps* whose greater and more glorious task is to bring peace to their country, as compared to military leaders who bring wealth through war.[49]

Especially at the end of his life, Cicero used all his persuasive force to appeal to this new kind of leader or *princeps*: a leader so dedicated to the good of his country that he scorns mere personal pleasure and never considers good (*honestas*) what is only personally expedient. Cicero's last appeal occurs in those "truly golden books"[50] of *De Officiis*, books that both Pliny and Erasmus recommended to be "learnt by heart,"[51] a recommendation Thomas More seemed to have followed.[52]

Cicero's leading or first citizens are so detached from wealth and even glory[53] that they dismiss petty concerns[54] to further the interests of all rather than a faction or favored part.[55] Such statesmen, as we have seen, "should carry with them that greatness of spirit and indifference to outward circumstances to which I so often refer, together with calm of spirit and freedom [of spirit], if they are to . . . lead a dignified and self-consistent life."[56] The true greatness of soul needed by these "first citizens" is, for Cicero, *humanitas* – that quality whereby wisdom [*sapiens*] and justice

---

[49] *De Officiis* 1.74–78, 82; on the Romans' suspicion of Greek learning, see *De Oratore* 2.4–5.

[50] Erasmus uses this description in 1501: "libellos vere aureos" (*EE* 152); compare with the title page of *Utopia*: "libellus vere aureus" (*CW* 4, 1).

[51] Pliny, *Natural History* preface 22, cited in *CWE* 1, Letter 152/30. Twenty-two years later, Erasmus recommends in his own name that the young "spend long hours in reading [Cicero] and even in learning him by heart" (*CWE* 10, Letter 1390/100).

[52] See the numerous references in Logan and Skinner 218–22. Skinner rightly points out that Morus in *Utopia* is "echoing *De Officiis* almost word for word" (222) in major passages.

[53] Despite Cicero-the-rhetorician's repeated appeals to what was the leading Romans' dominant passion, glory, Cicero-the-philosopher recognized the dangers of actions done to please an audience. See *Tusculanae Disputationes* 3.3–4 and *De Officiis* 1.68, 2.43, and especially *Tusculanae Disputationes* 1.109: "There is, it may be, nothing in glory that we should desire it, but none the less it follows virtue like a shadow." Even if Cicero himself was overly attached to glory, Thomas More was not. Throughout his writings, from first to last, his most persistent theme is the danger of pride. Here More's letter linking his *princeps* with the Franciscan virtues of poverty and humility seems significant.

[54] Notice the emphasis placed on this ability: *De Officiis* 1.13, 61, 66, 72, 106; 2.37–8; 3.24, 119.

[55] *De Officiis* 1.86.

[56] *De Officiis* 1.72.

are inseparable from goodness [*honestas*] marked by that greatness of soul (*magna animus*) to scorn vicissitudes of life and to resist even life's most powerful attraction of glory.[57] Cicero explains that natural "first citizens" have immense power. Fellow citizens will follow them into war or into peace, and no one person or faction can easily counter their governance.[58]

Virgil is aware of this power when he gives the first glimpse of ancient Rome in the *Aeneid*. In that scene, he presents Evander "with all the first [*omnes primi*] of his people and his unwealthy senate" as they are worshiping the gods. At this moment and in this setting, Evander welcomes Aeneas with a strange greeting and command: "Friend, dare to scorn riches; fashion [*finge*] yourself / to be worthy of the deity, and come not disdainful of our poverty."[59] This self-fashioned scorn for riches and respect for poverty – done for friendship and the gods – are just the qualities needed to eliminate ill will and hence factions as seen in More's 1516 Letter to Erasmus.

Concern for the common wealth, not my wealth; concern for the whole body, not just my part of the body – such citizen concern, in Cicero's view, is the only way of eliminating the factions or "party spirit" that have throughout history caused bitter strife such as the "disastrous civil wars" Rome experienced with Marius and Sulla, or with Caesar and Pompey in Cicero's time. Cicero in fact defines those "worthy of the leading place [*principatu*]" by their dedication "to the state in its entirety in such a way as to further the interests of all"; these true first citizens follow Plato's two rules: "first, to keep the good of the people so clearly in view that regardless of their own interests they will make their every action conform to that; second, to care for the welfare of the whole body politic and not in serving the interests of some one party to betray the rest."[60]

These "factions" – to use the term favored by the American Founders[61] – have commonly been recognized as a "disease" that can be "fatal" to any society.[62] More, for example, would maintain that

[57] *De Officiis* 1.62, 63, 65, 66; *De Finibus* 2.37–47.

[58] *De Legibus* 3.30–32, 25, 34. Consider also the famous epic simile of the "dedicated public man" who is able to quell a riot by his speech, in *Aeneid* 1.151. For More's statement that Virgil is a "poet who is second to none," see note 11 and Epigram 147.

[59] "Aude, hospes, contemnere opes et te quoque dignum / Finge deo, rebusque veni non asper egenis" (*Aeneid* 8.364–65).

[60] *De Officiis* 1.86, 85.

[61] See *Federalist Papers*, nos. 6, 10 especially, but also 14, 38, 45, 61, 81. See further commentary in Chapter 9.

[62] In the *Federalist Papers,* James Madison refers to faction as a disease "which has proved fatal to other popular governments" (no. 14); he views "the history of faction" as

party strife caused by "rulers desiring each other's dominion" was the major cause of the "war and deadly dissension" in what should have been a united "corps of Christendom."[63] Even in his last letters written in prison, as we have seen, More insisted that he was never a "part taker," a partisan, of this kind.[64]

Sallust and Tacitus, authors More studied carefully for many years,[65] agreed with Cicero's analysis regarding factions as the cause of Rome's fall. Sallust wrote that "strife of parties" is what "has commonly ruined great nations";[66] in the case of Rome, these "parties and factions, with all their attendant evils" arose from "wantonness and arrogance . . . fostered by prosperity."[67] But the deepest roots of these Roman factions were, in Sallust's assessment, originally ambitions for "glory, honor, and power" that soon degenerated into greed for money and pleasures.[68] Elsewhere, Tacitus gives accounts similar to Sallust's, about the causes of factions, the damage they bring, and important role of greed,[69] of the "wanting more" that Lucian presents in *The Cynic*[70] and that *Utopia* claims to eliminate by a Franciscan simplicity of life.

To show powerfully that the state should be unified rather than fractured by competing interests, Seneca would later develop the image of the state as a body united by bonds of love (*amor*) with its head, as he elaborated upon Cicero's original metaphor of the body politic.[71] More

"among the most dark and degrading pictures which display the infirmities and depravities of the human character" (no. 38). Alexander Hamilton also refers to factions as "diseases" (no. 61); this "natural propensity . . . to party divisions," this "pestilent breath of factions" can "poison the fountains of justice" (no. 81).

63 *CW* 6, 413.
64 See, for example, *SL* 227 and 232.
65 *CW* 2, lxxxii, lxxxvii–xcviii.
66 *Jugurtha* 42.4–5.
67 *Jugurtha* 41.2–3.
68 *Catiline* 10–11.
69 See, for example, Tacitus, *Historiae* 2.38. Aristotle gives a fuller account in *Politics* book 5.
70 See Chapter 4.
71 Seneca and St. Paul (1 Cor. 12:12–27) are the first to state explicitly that the bonds of this corporate body are love. Of course, Plato, Aristotle, and Cicero all emphasized the importance of friendship within the state, and Cicero attributes his body-politic metaphor to Plato (*De Officiis* 1.85). Plato, however, writes only of the unity of the city, comparing the city to the well-ordered soul of the just (e.g., *Republic* 420B ff.). Xenophon's *Memorabilia* 2.18 has Socrates applying the story of the body's harmony among its limbs to the harmony among brothers. Although elsewhere Socrates deals with the importance of friendship within a city, nowhere does he go as far as Cicero and Seneca in comparing the state to a human body working together harmoniously as directed by the head or mind. See Cicero's most famous comparisons of the state to a body at *De Officiis* 3.22, but also 1.85 and 3.32, as well as *Pro Cluentio* 146 ("The state

would use this same image and language in his Epigram 112, writing that "the good king and his people" should be like the head of a united body bound by love (*amor*):[72]

ON THE GOOD KING AND HIS PEOPLE

A kingdom in all its parts is like a man; it is held together by natural affection. The king is the head; the people form the other parts. Every citizen the king has he considers a part of his own body (that is why he grieves at the loss of a single one). The people risk themselves to save the king and everyone thinks of him as the head of his own body.[73]

The people and ruler are to be "held together by natural affection," not torn apart by factious ill will.

In a similar way, Seneca had written that "we are parts of one great body" created by Nature for "mutual affection" (*amorem mutuum*), friendship, fairness, and justice. Because Nature "created us from the same source and to the same end," we are "related to one another" and, as we have seen, Seneca goes on to advise that the famous verse of Terence should "be in your heart and on your lips: 'I am a man; and nothing in man's lot / Do I deem foreign to me.'"[74] Again in "On Anger," Seneca used the comparison of the body held together by love: "As all the members of the body are in harmony one with another because it is to the advantage of the whole that the individual members be unharmed, so... all are born for a life of fellowship, and society can be kept unharmed only by the mutual protection and love [*custodia et amore*] of its parts."[75]

Although this image of all human beings of the world united by love might be appealing to some, what influence could it possibly have on leaders of a country set on dominion and empire?

without law would be like the human body without mind, unable to employ the parts which are to it as sinews, blood, and limbs") and *Pro Sestio* where he calls for healing a Roman state that has been afflicted and wounded (1, 5, 17, 31, 135). More would have known Aesop's "The Stomach and the Body" (Fable 66) as well as the versions of that fable as told by Livy (2.32.9–12) and Plutarch (*Life of Coriolanus* 6, used later in Shakespeare's *Tragedy of Coriolanus* 1.1), but none of these refer to bonds of love.

[72] As emphasized in Augustine's *City of God*.

[73] DE BONO REGE ET POPVLO. Totum est unus homo regnum, idque cohaeret amore. / Rex caput est, populus caetera membra facit. / Rex quot habet ciues (dolet ergo perdere quenquam) / Tot numerat parteis corporis ipse sui. / Exponit populus sese pro rege putatque / Quilibet hunc proprij corporis esse caput.

[74] *Epistulae* 95.52–53 quoting Terence's *Heautontimoroumenos* 77. Cicero and More both use this quotation in similar contexts: *De Legibus* 1.33, *De Officiis* 1.30; More quotes from memory this statement at CW 14, 349/2–3, as seen in note 32 of Chapter 1.

[75] *De Ira* 2.31.7, as seen in Chapter 1.

Warrior barons in England, for example, preserved their land wealth and power by primogeniture and not any longer by proven virtue and merit, and certainly not by *amor* and Ciceronian *humanitas* marked by love of peace. How, then, could anyone hope to open reflection on the possibilities of the type of leadership implied in Cicero's *princeps* – that is, a leader of *honestas* and of proven practical ability with the skills needed to foster justice for the whole of the country rather than privilege and wealth for one's own bloodline and friends? How could anyone hope to make appealing to such warrior barons raised on chivalric "glory" a new kind of leader dedicated to "common wealth," to peace and prosperity for the whole of the land?

How did Cicero do it when faced with warring factions led by Catiline,[76] and later by Pompey and Caesar?

One way was to exalt rhetorically, as More would do in his 1509 coronation ode,[77] the new *princeps*'s great-souled benevolence in devotion to the *respublica,* while arguing against and scorning the ways of life based on personal pleasure[78] and personal dominion.[79] Another was to appeal to those aspects of Roman culture represented by several of its greatest leaders from the past: Scipio, Laelius, and Crassus.[80] These were the leaders who embodied friendship and republican government based on *fides* and justice as well as (at least in Cicero's representation) a *principatus* of Ciceronian *humanitas.*

As we have seen in the opening chapters, these natural "first citizens" must, Cicero insists, be fully fashioned according to the *studia humanitatis*[81] with the same arduous education needed for the highest excellence in any master art – if they are to achieve peace and prosperity, true

---

[76] In *Philippic* 11.36, Cicero states: "I am so far from honoring those enemies of quiet, concord, laws, law-courts, and liberty, that I cannot help but hate them as fully as I love the state [*rem publicam*]."

[77] See Chapter 6.

[78] Nicgorski's 2002 study of "Cicero, Citizenship, and the Epicurean Temptation" sets forth a compelling case of what was as stake for Cicero, and for the American Founders – and arguably, for what Utopia presents as the end of life.

[79] For one of the last expressions of Cicero's ideal, see *De Officiis* 2.26–27.

[80] Scipio and Laelius are the first Roman leaders that Cicero "can explicitly call philosophers" (*Tusculanae Disputationes* 4.5). See also *De Finibus* 2.59, *Tusculanae Disputationes* 5.54–56, *Pro Murena* 66, and *Pro Archia* 16. For Crassus's leadership, see *De Oratore* 3.2–8, 14–15 and *Epistulae ad Atticum* 8.11.1; for his liberal education and command of philosophy, see *De Oratore* 1.20, 53–54; 2.1–11, especially 5–6; 3.21, 54ff. For the importance of these three leaders, see Fantham 2004 313–17; see also Nicgorski 2008 86ff. For the importance of history for Cicero, see Mitchell 1991 19–21.

[81] See *Tusculanae Disputationes* 4.5; *Epistulae ad Quintum fratrem* 1.1.29; *De Finibus* 5.74; *De Officiis* 1.85 with 1.63, 67, 69; *De Oratore* 1.53–54, 3.57–59.

commonwealth; if they are to preserve their own integrity in the task; and if they are to enable right (*ius*) to conquer violence (*vis*).[82] These first citizens, as master artisans of rule, not only must pay special attention to the laws that are developed through a country's history but must also view them from a truly philosophic perspective possible only to those who have had the widest and deepest range of study.

Law has special importance because without law – and without the courts and other constitutional means to enforce them – *ius* cannot conquer *vis*. Cicero "repeatedly stresses that a state is a partnership in justice, a community held together by a common agreement about the principles of right that... must be spelled out in a state's laws, whose purpose it is to ensure that citizens may live honorably and happily in safety and peace."[83] As Cicero shows, Rome's form of government guaranteed "the rights and liberties in the definition of *respublica* [property of the people]" because it was "based on law and committed to strict equality in the administration of justice" and thus worked against "arbitrary or unchecked power."[84]

In what may be his most famous lines about law, Cicero insisted that

law is the bond by which we secure our dignity, the foundation of our liberty, the fountain-head of justice. Within the law are reposed the mind and spirit, the judgement and the conviction of the state. The state without law would be like the human body without mind – unable to employ the parts which are to it as sinews, blood, and limbs. The magistrates who administer the law, the jurors who interpret it – all of us in short – obey the law that we might be free.[85]

Once again Cicero uses the metaphor of the human body to explain the workings of the body politic: just as the mind orders the free movement of the body, so the laws order the free movement of the body politic.

This view of law (i.e., law as the prudent dictates of deliberative collective reason)[86] is part of Cicero's earliest account of the origin of society; it suggests why both he and More saw knowledge of the law as part of a leader's essential education in *humanitas* or liberal education, the education of the free.[87] Without an "equitable code of law" a city is not

---

[82] *Pro Sestio* 92.
[83] Mitchell 1991 13, rich in bibliographic support.
[84] Mitchell 1991 53.
[85] *Pro Cluentio* 146.
[86] Aristotle's *Nicomachean Ethics* 1134a36 and Aquinas's commentary (no. 1009); Cicero, *De Legibus* 1.22.
[87] CW 6, 131–132; Cicero, *De Officiis* 2.65–66, *De Oratore* 1.18, 165–203.

possible,[88] and that code of law is possible only if an agreement has been forged by a persuasive and trustworthy leader.[89]

The need for such a persuasive leader explains in part why the early modern period held Cicero in such high regard. Cicero was recognized as the philosopher-*princeps*-orator uniquely skilled and successful in bringing philosophy down from the heavens. Regarding that extraordinary skill and success, Erasmus praised Cicero as surpassing Plato and Aristotle:

> Plato and Aristotle tried to introduce [philosophy] to the courts of kings, to the senate, and even to the law-courts. But Cicero seems to me to have brought her almost onto the stage, for with his help she has learned to speak in such a fashion that even a miscellaneous audience can applaud.[90]

For example, so successful was Cicero in understanding the common ground and common understanding of justice still present in fractious Rome that he could fashion a view of the principate designed to appeal to "a statesman of the highest calibre"[91] dedicated to the good of all of Rome. Significantly, although republican self-rule had ended by the time of Cicero's death,[92] *princeps* became the favored title of Augustus Caesar in 27 B.C.[93] and continued in use until the reign of Diocletian in A.D. 284. In his brilliance as a rhetorician and philosopher, Cicero captured an essential dimension of the Romans' self-understanding when he coined the term "principate" and redefined its character in his last major works[94] – a dimension so deeply rooted in Roman history that

---

[88] *De Inventione* 1.1–3; see also *Pro Cluentio* 146; *Pro Sestio* 91–92; *De Legibus* 1.17, 19, 23, 33, 2.11–12, 14; *De Oratore* 1.30–33; *Epistulae ad Familiares* 10.1.1.

[89] See, for example, *Pro Sestio* 91, but also the quotation from *De Oratore* at the beginning of this chapter.

[90] CWE 10, Letter 97, translation adjusted. See the opening paragraphs of *De Officiis* for Cicero's own explanation of the importance of mastering both rhetoric and philosophy.

[91] Ferrary 52–53.

[92] Augustine's *City of God* 2.21 recounts the arguments by Cicero that the Roman Republic "had become entirely extinct."

[93] As Tacitus explains in the first lines of *Annales*: After decades of Roman civil war, "the interests of peace required that all power should be concentrated in the hands of one man" (1.1). Although Augustus Caesar gathered all power into his own hands to quell Rome's destructive factions, he ruled, Tacitus observes, "not by instituting a monarchy or a dictatorship, but by creating the title of First Citizen" (*Non regno tamen neque dictatura, sed principis nomine constitutam rem publicam*) – all in the interests of providing "law for the Roman citizen... in the interests of general tranquility" (*ius apud civis... quo ceteris quies esset*) (1.9).

[94] Fantham explains that *principatus* is "the state of being *princeps* (a leader, or leading man), and if this usage is common [i.e., of *princeps*], the abstract noun

the term would abide and would return centuries later in Erasmus's and More's own writings.

With its tangled history, *princeps* is a term Erasmus and More use with the full power of its accumulated connotation.[95] When Erasmus writes his *Education of a Christian Prince* in 1516, he defines the *princeps* in Ciceronian terms as the "embodiment of the laws," ideally selected by the vote of a free and willing people.[96] The custom of having a *princeps* "born to the office, not elected," Erasmus comments, "was the custom of some barbarian peoples in the past (according to Aristotle)[97] and is also the practice almost everywhere in our own time."[98] Knowing Aristotle well himself, and having studied these matters for fourteen years after completing his law studies and before accepting to work for Henry VIII, what did More consider to be possible alternatives to England's long and "barbaric" history of faction and unrest?

Of course, there might not be a solution. That was the reaction of many who had read Augustine's "pessimistic" *City of God*, which claimed that no justice existed at any time in ancient Rome and that the best of those Romans were not at all virtuous.[99] Did More agree with Augustine's dark view? Already at twenty-four, young Thomas More knew *The City of God* so well that he had given a well-attended series of public lectures on it, "not . . . from the theological point of view, but from the standpoint of history and philosophy."[100]

Or solutions might require cultural, political, and economic developments that would take generations to put in place.

Or were simpler solutions possible? After all, London had devised institutions and customs that had brought reasonable peace, and great prosperity. Since 1215, it had been self-governing, electing its own leaders

[*principatus*] – which would become the constitutional designation of Rome's government under Augustus and his successors – is not" (310). See notes 37–58, 79–82 for major references to Cicero's redefinition of the "*princeps*," especially in *De Officiis*.
[95] Consider Erasmus's use of this term in his *Institutio Principis Christiani* at *Opera Omnia* 4.1, 141/158, 152/511, 159/703, 167/8, 187/679. For More's uses, see www.thomasmorestudies.org/IndicesofLatinTerms.
[96] Erasmus, *Education of a Christian Prince* 79; also 1, 4; *De Legibus* 3.2.
[97] *Politics* 1285a17, 1285b24.
[98] Erasmus, *Education of a Christian Prince* 5. Erasmus goes on to say that, in this primitive situation, "the main hope of getting a good prince hangs on his proper education, which should be managed all the more attentively, so that what has been *lost with the right* [ius] *to vote* is made up for by the care given to his upbringing" (emphasis added).
[99] See Augustine, *City of God* 19.21, 23–25.
[100] Stapleton 7–8. We have no other record of what More said in these lectures.

annually, having its own courts and banks as well as an apprentice system that gave the poor and disenfranchised a way to advance economically and to become "free men." Could London's long experience in self-government help with the problems faced by the nation at large? That Thomas More, born and raised in London,[101] asked these questions is evident from his first great literary works, especially *The History of Richard III* and *Utopia*. As the marginal notes of *Utopia* humorously point out, the Utopian cities are "just like" London[102] – yet in provocative ways they are not. And the London citizens of *Richard III* are of such interest to all real or potential kings that all contenders vie for London's election, regardless of how ludicrous it may be.[103] As we will see in the chapters ahead, More's early works, with their numerous classical and medieval allusions, contrast in many ways the policies and ways of life of those deadly and contentious "kings' games . . . played upon scaffolds"[104] in which nobles and royalty contend for power, with the customs and practices of a London that deliberately limited the conditions allowing such power.

So what solutions could the practices of London offer for England's problems of unrest? And did those practices agree or disagree with what the greatest historians and philosophers of Greece and Rome proposed? Thomas More and his fellow civic humanists undoubtedly discussed these questions.

Before writing his first major work about this topic, More had completed the full range of *studia humanitatis* advised by Cicero and by Cicero's greatest philosopher-orator-statesmen.[105] Besides having the intellect of a genius (according to Erasmus and Colet),[106] More had the industry and drive to master Greek after completing his law studies and then to devote fourteen years to intense study of those Greek, Roman, biblical, and medieval "good letters," considering every known option to

---

[101] His family had long prospered in the city: his father was a successful lawyer who rose to become a judge of the King's Bench; his paternal grandfather had been a successful London baker and guildsman; his maternal grandfather, sheriff (Ackroyd 6–8, 136).

[102] For example, see *CW* 4, 118.

[103] Consider the powerful close of More's Latin *Historia Richardi Tertii*: "Cum ludicra illa electione . . ." (*CW* 15, 484/22).

[104] *CW* 2, 81/6–7.

[105] Crassus in *De Oratore* and Laelius and Scipio in *De Amicitia* and in *De Re Publica* – all three of whom are presented as model *principes*, as "first or leading citizens" – "first," as we have seen, in the sense of standing forth because of consistently superior qualities of the deliberative and reliable leader.

[106] *EE* 999/269 or *TMSB* 12.

solving the problems of civil unrest before he decided in 1518 to enter the service of Henry VIII.

The chapters that follow focus upon More's earliest writings before 1518, the year he joins King Henry's service. Chapters 4 through 9 treat More's earliest literary works, with special attention to elements revealing More's "solutions" to England's propensity to civil war. Chapter 10 analyzes More's pictorial representation of the educational ideal that he had for his children and perhaps for himself. Chapter 11 returns to the questions posed in this chapter: What did More learn from the classical authors and from the experience of London about solving England's pressing problem of civil unrest? What types of law and institutions did More discover as ways of securing the peace and prosperity that he and Erasmus saw as the proper ends of government,[107] and that leaders of London aspired to achieve over many centuries?

---

[107] See Chapter 1.

4

More's Earliest Views of *Humanitas, Libertas,* and *Respublica,* 1500–1506

[C]hoose which ye list, / Stately fortune or humble poverty: / . . . bondage or free liberty.

> Thomas More, "Fortune Verses" (c. 1504)[1]

The life of the ordinary private citizen [*priuatus*] is best, and most prudent.

> Thomas More's translation/emendation of Lucian, *Menippus* (1506)[2]

The law is very ready to hire a tyrannicide. . . . But when it says tyrannicide, judges of the jury, it seeks a resourceful person, . . . able in stratagem [*consilio*] rather than force; one who knows how to lay plots, hide his traps, make the most of his opportunities. . . . [But] the republic had fallen into the gravest danger, first because of this man's rashness, then by his cowardice. . . . [T]he gods wanted [this city] to be free [*liberam*].

> Thomas More, *Declamation in Reply to Lucian* (1506)[3]

What is *humanitas*? What is the fullest and best way of life? This issue is addressed repeatedly in More's earliest poems and in the humorous and subtle dialogues by Lucian that More translated and which became his first published and internationally acclaimed work.[4]

Elements of Thomas More's distinctive *humanitas* – elements such as love for liberty, hatred of tyranny, and care for rhetoric and

---

[1] CW 3.1, 39/222–25.

[2] CW 3.1, 41/34–35. Alluding to Odysseus's famous statement in Plato's *Republic* 620c, More adds the word *priuatorum* to his translation and changes the placement and form of the term Lucian had used for "wisely." See note 68.

[3] CW 3.1, 109, 123, 127. Consider the significance of *consilio* in light of the importance of "sure deliberation" seen earlier.

[4] More's translations were printed nine times during his lifetime, more than any other work he wrote (CW 1, xxv).

declamation – Erasmus noted in his first description of More,[5] pointing out that More worked for years to acquire the extraordinarily difficult and rare skills needed for rhetorical excellence[6] (as also explained in Cicero's *De Oratore*).[7]

The need for skill young More makes clear in his early poem "A Merry Jest," which opens with these lines:

> Wise men alway,
> Affirm and say,
> That best is for a man:
> Diligently,
> For to apply,
> The business that he can,
> And in no wise,
> To enterprise
> Another faculty,
> For he that will,
> And can no skill,
> Is never like to the [i.e., thrive or prosper].[8]

That this twenty-six-year-old would understand the necessary link between prosperity and freely acquired skill one would expect from the oldest son of an accomplished and prosperous "self-made" Londoner. As Erasmus noted,[9] however, the extent of More's drive to educate himself – especially in poetry, philosophy, history, and oratory – was unusual.

Years earlier, however, More's talent and love for oratory had been demonstrated in the nine dramatic speeches that constitute his first known poem, "Pageant Verses." These verses also show his preoccupation with freedom and his attention to "wise and discrete" rule for the "public weal." In these "Pageant Verses," Childhood speaks first,[10] with an apparent simplicity,[11] but also with an unmistakably strong desire to

---

[5] *EE* 999/88, 246ff.; *TMSB* 6, 11–12.

[6] *EE* 999/247; *TMSB* 11, where Erasmus explains More's "long struggle to acquire a more supple style in prose [*molliorem prosam orationem*]."

[7] Morus is identified as England's "orator" at the beginning of *Utopia* (*CW* 4, 46/12). For the rarity and extreme difficulty in achieving oratorical excellence, see Cicero's comments in *De Oratore* 1.5–22 and the description of rhetoric as a master art specially needed in "every free nation" (1.32).

[8] *CW* 1, 15/3–14.

[9] *EE* 999/246ff.; *TMSB* 11.

[10] *CW* 1, 3/12ff.

[11] But as Cousins points out, the stanza goes on to "unsentimentally suggest how ambivalent that simplicity is" (1980 49). Cousins's careful analysis of this poem in a later article shows how, ironically, "what Chyldhod's reasoning most distinctly reveals in its focus on the life of pleasure is opposition to his disciplined, intellectual development" (2008 39).

act freely as he will: "I am called Childhood, in play is all my mind." The conflict in this first line between "play" – "a metonym for 'pleasure'"[12] – and "mind" is forcefully expressed as Childhood "gives vent to his pent-up emotions"[13] aroused by study's threat to his play: he wants to "burn to powder" all "these hateful books." Then, he concludes, "might I lead my life always in play: / Which life God send me to mine ending day." Of course, we smile at this childish demand for "freedom" from work and the implied conclusion that God wants man to play rather than mind his present labors. Yet such a view, the next pageant immediately shows, is characteristic not just of Childhood but of Manhood also.

In the next speech, Manhood voices the same preoccupation with the pleasures of doing freely as he wills, but he also brags that his pleasures of hunting and hawking are superior to the boy's "peevish game" because he has "become a very man in deed." Not only does Manhood vaunt through his words but, in the painting that accompanied this poem, he also triumphs over the boy himself: "[U]nder the horse's feet was painted the same boy that in the first pageant was playing."[14]

This same pattern of boastful speaker and pictorial triumph occurs in the six pageants that follow. Age, for example, expresses great pride in being "wise and discrete" in his labor of rule for the "public weal." He no longer has time for love or its "childish game and idle business," and "lying under his feet was painted the image of Venus and Cupid," who, in the previous pageant, had triumphed over Manhood. Age wants freedom from the demands of love in order to advance his political ends. That twenty-year-old More would imagine "wise and discrete" rule for the "public weal" as the proper and prototypical work of Age might be a bit surprising except that his life in self-governing London would have presented this image to him frequently. And, after all, that would be the view of London's "ordinary citizen."[15] And that young More certainly knew the power of love he shows us in Epigram 263, which recounts his first such experience at age sixteen.

In the ninth pageant,[16] the tone changes from boast to philosophic reflection as the Poet explains this sequence of "made up images" as a means to "feast the mind on the realities themselves," just as the skillful paintings "feast" the viewers' eyes on pleasant and humorous figures. The

[12] Cousin 2008 39.
[13] Willow 93.
[14] CW 1, 3/24–4/37.
[15] See the end of this chapter, along with Chapters 5, 8, 9, and 11, for the great significance of the "ordinary citizen" for More.
[16] CW 1, 6/112–16; CW 3.2, Epigram 272.

readers who so feast their minds that they come to understand the things figured forth by the words,[17] the Poet promises,

> will see that the elusive goods of this perishable world do not come so readily as they pass away. Pleasures, praises, homage, all things quickly disappear – except the love of God, which endures forever.[18]

This same view of the transitory character of earthly goods is the main theme of More's other two earliest poems, "Rueful Lamentation" and "Fortune Verses" (c. 1503).[19] Both poems again are wholly composed of speeches. In the first, Queen Elizabeth laments of her recent death,[20] and the poem begins with her warning to those attached to "worldly riches and frail prosperity":

> Ye that put your trust and confidence
> In worldly riches and frail prosperity,
> That so live here as ye should never hence,
> Remember death and look here upon me.[21]

In this opening stanza and in the twelve that follow, the closing of each refrain is "Lo, here I lie," and every stanza shows some dimension of the "brittle" character of human wealth or the fleeting quality of "mortal folk" and "worldly vanity."

More's "Fortune Verses" is composed of competing speeches by Thomas More and Lady Fortune. The poem's prologue opens with "T. More" lamenting that poets, orators, and philosophers, despite their eloquence and inventiveness, have rarely brought forth any "fruit or sentence, that is ought worth."[22] Lady Fortune then gives an eloquent and stirring praise of herself, arguing that it is far "[b]etter to be fortunate than wise" (33/66). "Joy, rest, and peace," "pleasure or profit," "comfort, aide, and sustenance" – all these are at her "device and ordinance" (33/56–59). Power, honor, happiness, and "a common weal to govern and defend" are bestowed by her favor (34/81–87). And she ends with a challenge to her audience's freedom and self-governance: "Each man hath of himself the governance. / Let every person then follow his own way" (34/89–90).

---

[17] This important issue of the relation of *res* and *verba* is well articulated by Crassus in *De Oratore* 3.19–24.

[18] CW 3.2, Epigram 272/8–11 gives this translation of CW 1, 6/113–16.

[19] For the dates of these poems, see CW 1, c.

[20] She died at the age of thirty-seven.

[21] CW 1, 9/2–5, but with modernized spelling.

[22] CW 3.1, 31/8. Hereafter, page and line references in text for "Fortune Verses" are from CW 3.1.

More responds with equal vigor, focusing on Fortune's "slippery," "deceitful," and "unstable" character and pointing out that her attendants are Weary Labor, Pale Fear, Sorrow, Disdain, and Hatred (35/124–26), and that she is surrounded by Danger, Envy, Flattery, Deceit, Mischief, and Tyranny (35/129–30). In defiance of Fortune, More proposes instead Lady Poverty, who "with merry cheer" takes her stand with wise philosophers like Socrates, the laughing Democritus, and Bias, who counted nothing his "that he might lose" (38/190–200). "Glad Poverty" and her companions are content with what sustains nature; they do "[n]o hoarding of nature's good"; and they find their pleasure in beholding "the secret draughts [i.e., plans] of nature" (38/202–39/214).

More, as Lady Fortune did, challenges the audience members to decide freely how they will live:[23] "[C]hoose which ye list, / Stately fortune or humble poverty: / That is to say, now lies it in your fist, / To take here bondage, or free liberty" (39/222–25). Lady Fortune offers but a "fools' paradise" (39/232), More warns, and he concludes by challenging his audience to defy this ever-changing, deceitful Fortune:

> Wherefore if thou in surety like to stand,
> Take Poverty's part and let proud Fortune go,
> Receive nothing that comes from her hand:
> Love manner and virtue: they be only those
> Which double [inconstant] Fortune may not take thee from.
> Then may thou boldly defy her turning chance:
> She can thee neither hinder nor advance. (40/250–56)

As for whatever treasure from Fortune one may have, More counsels,

> Trust not therein, and spend it liberally.
> Bear thee not proud, nor take not out of measure.
> Build not thine house on height up in the sky.
> None falls far, but he that climbs high,
> Remember nature sent thee hither bare,
> The gifts of Fortune count them borrowed ware. (40/258–41/263)

This last image of a naked human being with only borrowed ware stresses the humble human condition as opposed to that of Fortune, the boastfully proud, powerful, cruel, wealthy, and tyrannous empress (especially 35/123, 130).[24]

Roughly two years after this poem, More published his first book with Erasmus, a book of Lucian translations, the "first fruits of [More's]

---

[23] Traditionally, "good letters" challenge their readers in such ways.
[24] See also More's translation of Lucian's theatrical metaphor of souls departing the stage and giving up their costumes at CW 3.1, 84–85.

Greek studies." For that book, Thomas More wrote one original speech in Latin, a bold declamation setting forth the rare Ciceronian and Ulyssean qualities[25] needed by a citizen to defend the *libertas*, safety, and prosperity of a republic[26] against the deadly dangers posed by the tyrannical ruler – or the misguided citizen. Of foremost necessity is the proven ability for shrewd planning or deliberation, *consilium*.[27]

In his 1506 *Declamation in Reply to Lucian*, More assumes what Lucian presents in his *Tyrannicide* and what Cicero defends in *De Officiis*:[28] that laws in favor of tyrannicide are just. Lucian's *Declamatio pro Tyrannicida* is in the voice of one who claims to be a tyrannicide deserving his democracy's reward for killing a tyrant's son, whose death then led to the tyrant's suicide. In response, More's *Declamation* changes the voice from an advocate for a democracy to an advocate for a republic,[29] arguing that the killer actually endangered the republic by his incompetent and misguided murder. To honor such a citizen would positively endanger the republic, or so this orator argues.

Lucian's *Tyrannicide* is one of only four works of Lucian that More chose to translate; it is the only Lucian work to which More wrote an original response.[30] What do his translation and original *Declamation* reveal about More, a young lawyer with limited but painful political experience?[31] By 1506, More's only public office had been as a representative of London in the 1504 Parliament, where he incurred such hostility for openly opposing King Henry VII that More found himself in danger of death.[32]

---

[25] *CW* 3.1, 110/6.

[26] *CW* 1, 7/37, 94/1ff. For the many references to *libertas* and *respublica*, see www.thomasmorestudies.org/IndicesofLatinTerms.

[27] *CW* 3.1, 108/28, 110/5, 120/9, 124/20.

[28] At 3.82–83 Cicero defends the killing of Julius Caesar.

[29] For More's emphasis on the republic, see examples at *CW* 3.1, 98/19, 102/32, 104/15, 106/5 and 26, 120/19 and 29, 122/5, 124/4 and 30. Hereafter, line and page references in text and notes for *Declamation* are from *CW* 3.1.

[30] As the introduction to *CW* 3.1 explains, More also challenged Erasmus to do the same. Erasmus translated twenty-eight works by Lucian (xli) and took up More's challenge, writing a response three times as long as More's (xxxvii).

[31] More was called to the bar in 1501 at age twenty-four.

[32] See Stapleton 25 for More's belief that he could "most certainly have lost [his] head" because of the opposition he voiced. Roper also reports the danger More thought he faced, concluding that "had not the King soon after died, he was determined to have gone over the sea, thinking that, being in the King's indignation, he could not live in England without great danger" (Roper 8 or *TMSB* 21).

The danger of death and the power of a tyrannical ruler are foremost in the mind of the "Orator" in More's *Declamation,* responding to Lucian's *Tyrannicide.* "Orator" is appropriate because the spokesman of this work explicitly acknowledges the importance of the "art of speaking" (98/13), as Cicero had done in *De Oratore,*[33] and because this spokesman presents himself as freely and consciously taking up the difficult duty (94/12–13, 16) of defending his city's *libertas* and future prosperity, both of which are tied to proper acknowledgments of the gods and of the kind of citizen that the city honors.

The Orator shows dramatically the importance of proper citizen character by focusing on the beastly character of the tyrant who has so distorted his nature that he is cruel rather than benevolent, murderous rather than caring. But also, the Orator explains, the reckless, rash, cowardly, and presumptuously impious qualities[34] of the alleged tyrannicide must be rebuked as grave threats and not be rewarded if the city is to achieve the favor of the gods and its safety and prosperity, in accord with its laws. The behavior of this misguided citizen, despite his possible good intentions, "plunge[d] the whole city into the greatest danger by his folly."[35] In his final appeal to the jury, the Orator pleads:

> I entreat you, then, jurors, by the immortal gods, the gods who are the sources of this most cherished liberty [*charissimae libertatis*], this unlooked-for happiness, not to allow what came to us through the design and power of all the gods to be ascribed to the madness of one man; nor to allow this city ever to be so ungrateful to the gods their liberators; nor to suffer it to confess that its safety is owed to the temerity of a human being rather than to the benevolence of the gods, who we may now hope will always be propitious toward this city if we, mindful of what they have bestowed, acknowledge them (as is right) the authors of their blessings. But if – may it never come about! – we prove ungrateful, ascribing their deeds to others, and giving to men the gratitude owed to gods, we must fear in turn, by Hercules, lest the gods curtail their favor toward us and leave off the protection of our commonwealth [*respublica*] as unworthy of their guardianship. (124)

More's Orator presents *libertas* as a "most cherished" condition of the *humanitas*[36] willed by the gods (124/19) and as dependent upon a *respublica* in which citizens respect law, the gods, and human life (101/23–24)

---

[33] Such as 1.102, 2.5, but throughout.

[34] CW 3.1, 111/13–22, 115/38–39, 121/10–11, 124/9–10, and following.

[35] CW 3.1, 125.

[36] More uses this term in the introductory letter at CW 3.2, 96/13. To appreciate its ironic tone in that context, see CW 4, 78/10, 112/5, 162/32, 164/27, 200/17 and CW 15, 344/15 and 406/26.

and in which citizen leaders have labored to acquire the skills needed
to govern the ship of state – skills that he will later compare to those
of the good pilot at sea and to the good physician healing the sick
(108, 110).

The Orator opens by presenting himself as a citizen who volunteers
to serve as *patron* of his beloved republic:[37] he does so out of duty
(*officium*, 94/16, 98/16) for the public weal (94/1–2, 8, 11; 96/17, 98/19),
motivated by *pietas* (94/16), by reverence for the gods (98/19–20). As a
patron for the city, he insists that he has no ill will (*inuidia*) toward the
supposed tyrannicide; *inuidia*, he argues – as will the narrator of *Richard
III*[38] – is the most destructive of vices (97/33–34). He elaborates this
vision of *humanitas* with rhetorical flourish: "Surely to deem another's
good fortune one's own misfortune, to rage at the success of others, to
be vexed by praise of others, to be tormented by another's happiness –
is not this the greatest misery, is it not the most extreme madness?"
(97/35–39).

The skill of the Orator is impressive, and part of that skill is evi-
denced by the vividness of his accounts of the "extreme peril" the city
has escaped, but only through the benevolence of the gods, who have
willed the city's *libertas*, moved by pity for its extended "enslavement"
to tyranny (121). Also, brief as it is, his presentation about the "nature of
tyranny" heightens the declamation's power, and it reflects what will be
the single-most dominant theme in More's later epigrams and in *Richard
III*, despite the impression that *Utopia* gives to many that tyranny is not
as great a problem as these other works insist that it is.

According to the Orator, the driving ambition for power is what blinds
the tyrant and leads to a cruelty and violence that rejects the laws of god
and men and removes all respect for life (101/23–24).[39] This ambition
affects "[e]ven legitimate authorities" who govern by law and also obey
law; yet even these leaders, who are "so much milder" than a tyrant, "are
nevertheless so dominated by the ambition for power that they spare
not the lives of intimate friends rather than allow them to share in their
rule" (101/17–21). How the Utopians could have escaped this plight is
addressed in Chapter 9.

---

37 CW 3.1, 94/9, and see www.thomasmorestudies.org/IndicesofLatinTerms for other sig-
    nificant uses of the term *patron*.
38 See Chapter 8.
39 For the strength of this passion in those who rule, see Augustine's *City of God*, the book
    that was the subject of young More's public lectures in London five years earlier, in
    1501. See especially *City of God* 1.preface, 1.30, 4.6, 5.19, 14.15, 18.2.

The Orator goes on to present tyranny as a perennial danger to any society: "Certainly tyranny is always a violent and fearsome thing" (101/38). The tyrant is "no longer master of himself" (*nec sibi iam imperans*, 103/7), enslaved as he is to his own unrestrained passions. This unleashed beast commits "all known forms of crime" against his fellow citizens (101/34). Normally the citizens' "safety and *libertas*" are protected by law,[40] but "laws ... are held captive" by the tyrant and "are laws in name only" (105/23–27). As becomes increasingly clear, safety and *libertas* are simply not possible without good laws and effective means of implementing them.

The tyrant is so opposed to the republic's welfare that the "law is very ready to hire a tyrannicide" (109/27), but – the Orator eloquently explains – when the law "says tyrannicide, judges of the jury, it seeks a resourceful man, one not only strong-handed but (much more) strong-hearted; able in stratagem [*consilii*] rather than in force; one who knows how to lay plots, hide his traps, make the most of his opportunities" (109/29–32).

What follows are several pages indicating the rare combination of virtues and skills needed by the tyrannicide – virtues and skills not possessed by the man who claims his reward as the republic's supposed liberator. Lacking the Ulyssean quick wit, courage, and talent for "careful planning" and "stratagem," this alleged liberator – argues the Orator – threw "the entire city into extreme peril, since by foolishly inciting him he made the tyrant more menacing to the citizens and more wary of plots" (111/23–25). Ultimately, the Orator concludes that the self-proclaimed tyrannicide failed because of lack of skill, fear, or negligence (115/38–39, 121).

Overall, the Orator's speech appeals to an experience of fear, enslavement, violence, and continuous danger, which his jury of citizen-judges has known firsthand. With this common ground, the Orator stresses the need for civic care, resourcefulness, prudence, and especially faith and reverence for the gods and the laws – all in the interests of the republic's

---

[40] The Orator speaks repeatedly of *salus ac libertas* as desired ends of *respublica*. See 96/12, 98/26, 120/19ff., 124/22–23. For Cicero's emphasis on safety, see *De Re Publica* 3.34, quoted in Augustine, *City of God* 22.6. And for the preeminence of *libertas* for Cicero, see especially *De Officiis* 1.68, 70; 3.87; a practical implication of *libertas* is the city's duty to safeguard each citizen's "free and undisturbed control of his own particular property" (2.78). In direct opposition, Utopus argues that the elimination of private property is the precondition for justice and happiness.

libertas, safety, and prosperity; all as necessary elements of the *humanitas* endorsed by this republic.

The Orator appeals frequently to the interconnectedness of respect for the gods, observance of the laws, *libertas,* and the safety and prosperity of *respublica.* Emphasized are the dangers of negligence, cowardice, ingratitude, and lack of skill on the part of citizen-leaders. Effective leaders of a republic need not only skills in governing – just as physicians need skills in healing (108) and pilots need skills in piloting (110) – but also sufficient virtues to exercise those skills effectively. These virtues are necessary for self-governing when confronted with those strong desires for power, pleasure, glory, and doing as one wills.

As the Orator has argued, even good rulers regularly give in to their ungoverned passions. So important is this topic to young Thomas More, that achieving "mastery of oneself" (*sibi imperans,* 103/7) is the very theme that dominates the other three Lucian dialogues he chose to translate and is the most dominant theme of his earliest writings. More explains in the prefatory letter to these translations that Lucian "fulfilled the Horatian maxim and combined delight with instruction. . . . Refraining from the arrogant pronouncements of the philosophers as well as from the wanton wiles of the poets, he everywhere reprimands and censures, with very honest and at the same time very entertaining wit, our human frailties" (3). So "skillfully" and "fruitfully" (*fruge*) has Lucian written his dialogues that, "although no one pricks more deeply," no one's "calm of mind" (*aequo animo*) is upset by his barbs. Lucian's approach is "most charming"[41] and fruitful[42] – in sharp contrast to the "fruitless contentions of philosophers" (5/10). It could be said that Lucian's dialogues are designed to appeal to and develop the "keen judgment" (*acre iudicium,* 2/25, 8/3) of readers interested in achieving the prudence of the serpent and the innocence of the dove (6/11–13) – a cast of mind requiring the "simplicity, temperance, and frugality" of life that allows the calm "testing" of stories, "carefully and with judgment" (*caute & cum iudicio,* 6/18), "as though applying the rule of Critolaus,"[43] so that "we should accept or reject them if we wish to free ourselves both from foolish confidence and superstitious dread" (7/17–21). In the three dialogues that More chose to translate, readers are invited to ask: What is

---

[41] *Lepos* is an important element of Cicero's *humanitas*; see *De Oratore* 1.27, 2.270–271, 3.29 and *De Officiis* 1.90 and 98.

[42] Besides 2/11, see 4/5, 17.

[43] See Cicero's *Tusculanae Disputationes* 5.51 where, according to Critolaus's scale, the goods of the soul easily outweigh temporal or external goods.

the source of the main characters' foolish confidence? Or what superstition or untrustworthy assumption motivates each character's particular action or way of life?

The Cynic opens with a request by Lucian[44] who asks for a defense of the Cynic's "wandering, uncivilized, and gloomy" way of life,[45] a way of life far from charming. The Cynic responds by bragging that he lives the virtue of *frugalitas* – the quality, ironically,[46] "which describes the virtue of the older Romans," who admired the "productive . . . upright, energetic, prudent, self-controlled man who keeps the right measure in all that he does."[47]

The Cynic then brags about his self-sufficiency, his meeting his own needs, and his not lacking any of life's requirements. Why should he wear clothing or shoes,[48] since these are only for protection he does not need? Nowhere, of course, does the Cynic think about his responsibilities toward the needs of others, or that his ability to go barefoot might depend at least in part on the civilized conditions that provide roads and less dangerous conditions. Nor would he accept the position of a Crassus that well-shod Roman philosopher-statesmen are superior to barefoot Greek philosophers who distance themselves from civic life and who, if required, would take up their offices "naked and unarmed," being proudly and blindly "captivated chiefly by the ideal of endurance and hardness, [as did] first the Cynics and next the Stoics."[49]

Lucian objects that nature and the gods have made the earth for all to enjoy – thus harkening back to his opening objection to the Cynic's

---

[44] Lucian named this character "Lycinus"; More's version, by changing the name to Lucian's own, seems to make the judgment, common now among classical scholars, that this character is a lightly veiled allusion to Lucian himself. See, for example, the introduction (xxv) of the edition of Lucian by Fowler and Fowler, and the commentary of *CW* 3.1, 141.

[45] *CW* 3.1, 11/7: "uaga, inhumanaque ac ferali uita." *Inhumanus*, besides meaning "uncivilized" or "inhuman" can also mean "superhuman" or "divine" (*OLD*); this latter meaning is the Cynic's view of himself, as his statements at the ending of this dialogue reveal.

[46] That More deliberately chose here to heighten Lucian's irony is seen by his choice of this term *frugalitas* with connotations distinct from Lucian's *euteleia*, meaning "cheapness" or "thrift."

[47] See the editor's note at *Tusculanae Disputationes* 3.16; at 3.16–18 Cicero explains that the Roman understanding of *frugalitas* "connotes all abstinence and inoffensiveness (and this with the Greeks has no customary term) . . . ," "embraces all the other virtues as well," and "is derived from 'fruit' [*fruge*]."

[48] See the significance of this example of shoes at *De Oratore* 1.28–29 together with 3.62 and 3.136.

[49] *De Oratore* 3.136, 3.62.

"gloomy" way of life.[50] Besides, Lucian continues, the Cynic does not recognize the "products of the arts" as "gifts of the gods" (13). Quickly and dismissively, the Cynic concedes that the arts may indeed be gifts of the gods,[51] but he immediately launches into an attack on the excesses and pride of all those who do not live as he does. In the long and gloomy rant that follows, the Cynic claims to live most closely to the ways of the gods; in this boastful ranting, however, he reveals excesses and pride of his own. He is proud to live as he wills: unshaven, unshod, unwashed, with no home or unwanted friends to infringe upon a *libertas* that is his own form of *libidino*.[52] With great comic irony, the Cynic criticizes his interlocutor, Lucian:

[Y]ou would have us change and you reform our manner of life for us because we often are ill-advised in what we do, though you yourselves bestow no thought on your own actions, basing none of them on *judgment and reason, but upon the custom of appetite*. (167, emphasis added)[53]

Lucian, of course, is most famous for going against established customs in using comedy to bring judgment and reason to bear by satirizing those characters dominated by various forms of that "custom of appetite."

The Cynic continues with the very critique that Lucian himself often gives throughout his comic dialogues:

Therefore you are exactly the same as men carried along by a torrent; for they are carried along wherever the current takes them, and you wherever your appetites take you. Your situation is just like what they say happened to the man who mounted a mad horse. For it rushed off, carrying him with it; and he couldn't dismount again because the horse kept running. Then someone who met them asked him where he was off to, and he replied, "Wherever this fellow decides," indicating the horse. Now if anyone asks you where you're heading for, if you wish to tell the truth, you will simply say that it's where your appetites choose, or more specifically where pleasure chooses, or now where ambition, or now again where avarice chooses; and sometimes temper, sometimes fear, or sometimes something else of the sort seems to carry you off. (167; 23)

---

[50] At CW 3.1, 11/7, More's choice of *feralis* (meaning literally, "associated with death," "funereal"; "suggestive of the underworld") is a significant change from Lucian's *theriode* ("beastly"); the Cynic's "gloomy" outlook on life is in sharp contrast to the advice given by Teiresias in the underworld at the end of *Menippus:* laugh and attend to the present life.

[51] Consider the importance of this "passing" concession in light of Chapter 2.

[52] In ranting against everyone else who follows like a beast their "libido" (23/3), this Cynic never considers that he himself might be moved by appetite more than by "judgment and reason" ("iudex et ratio," 21/39).

[53] Translation adjusted for 21/29–23/1.

The comedy of this passage and of the entire dialogue is bound up in Lucian's revealing the Cynic's own ungoverned and unrecognized appetites: the appetites for "a quiet life doing whatever I want to do and being with whomever I want to be" (167),[54] as well as pride in his own supposedly godlike virtues – a danger of special importance as More will indicate.[55]

Powerfully, nonetheless, the Cynic does set forth the danger of "softness" (which, as we will see in the next chapter, is one of Pico's dominant faults)[56] and the danger of ungoverned appetite. As he points out, the "fountainhead" (*fontem*) of "all men's ills – civic strife, wars, conspiracies, and murders" – is "the desire for more" (166).[57]

The importance of governance by right reason, rather than by appetite or inherited custom, is emphasized in Lucian's *Lover of Lies*, another comic dialogue exposing both the excesses of supposed philosophers and the ease of smart people in deluding themselves.[58] As Tychiades points out, confronted by several thinkers like the Cynic, the antidote to philosophers' nonsense is "truth and sound reason brought to bear everywhere"[59] (196; 77 /25–26).

The problem of finding sound guidance in the midst of *res humanae* is also the focus of the third Lucian dialogue More chose to translate, *Menippus*. Here we find another cynic, but a rich one, with so much wealth and leisure that he can pay "whatever price" and take off more than a month (172) to consult yet more experts about the meaning of his life. When we first see Menippus the Cynic, he is dressed in a ridiculous Hercules costume, with lion skin and club[60] – but also carrying a lyre. His friend reacts to Menippus by exclaiming that "surely [you are] out of your mind" (170; 25/27). Menippus then reports to friend Philonides about his recent trip to the underworld, which he visited to find out "the best way of life, the life that the wisest and most powerful would

---

54 "uitam quietam . . . agam quicquid uolo, uerserque cum quibus uolo" (23/19) – compare this with Raphael Hytholodaeus's "uiuo ut uolo" at CW 4, 56/1.

55 See Chapter 5 and More's *Life of Pico, CW* 1, 94.

56 CW 1, 55, 73–74.

57 "Omnia nanque mala inter homines ex horum cupiditate nascuntur, & seditiones, & bella, & insidiae, & aedes. Haec omnia fontem habent plus habendi cupidinem" (21/3–5).

58 For an extended analysis of this dialogue, see Wegemer 1996 84–88.

59 "ueritatem rectamque omnibus in rebus rationem."

60 More makes the costume funnier by changing the felt hat to a club, which sets up a greater contrast with the lyre.

choose."[61] Of course, by wanting to know what the wisest and most powerful would choose, Menippus reveals his own confusion – and character – because what the wisest will choose would often differ from what the most powerful would choose.

Menippus certainly has been confused. The contradictory accounts of poets and lawgivers drove him, he reports, to ask philosophers about a "simple and certain path in life,"[62] but despite enduring all their abstractions, Menippus found that "they expressed the most contradictory of opinions" (172). More disturbing and "far more unreasonable," Menippus discovered, was that the practice of "these same people ... directly opposed their preaching" (172). While "scorning money," they "taught for pay, and underwent everything for the sake of money"; and "while almost all of them inveighed against pleasure, they privately devoted themselves to that alone" (172). Here, of course, the reader of keen judgment will ask, How might Menippus be acting in some way contrary to his own stated intent? Wisdom and self-knowledge are not possessions that the rich cynic has yet acquired.

So perplexed was he, Menippus reports, that he enlisted the help of the magician Mithrobarzanes[63] to bring him to Hades to consult blind Teiresias. After submitting himself for a month to Mithrobarzanes' ridiculous and degrading rituals (172–73), Menippus enters what is purportedly Hades where he discovers that each human being is "punished in proportion to his crimes," irrespective of wealth, position, or learning, although those are treated most harshly "who were swollen with pride of wealth and place," and who had failed "to remember that they themselves were mortal and had become possessed of mortal goods" (175). These discoveries lead Menippus to conclude that "human life is like a long pageant and that all its trappings are supplied and distributed by Fortune," and "when the time of the pageant is over, each gives back the properties and lays off the costume along with his body, becoming what he was before his birth, no different from his neighbour" (176). So why be vexed, when Fortune "asks her trappings back" (177)?

With this new perspective on earthly life, Menippus modifies his question when he finally comes to Teiresias: he no longer wants to know the way of life the most powerful choose; he asks only "what sort of

---

[61] "uita optima ... quanque sapientissimus quisque potissimum elegerit" (29/39–31/1) – that is, what Cicero, Seneca, and More would call *humanitas*.

[62] "uitae uiam simplicem ac certam" (27/35).

[63] In *Utopia*, Mithros is their god, and the original name of the "princeps" was "barzanes."

life he [Teiresias] considered the best" (179).[64] Teiresias, after laughing at Menippus's account of experience on earth, commiserates with him: "My son, I know the reason for your perplexity; it came from the wise men, who are not consistent with themselves" (179). Nonetheless, Teiresias says he is forbidden by Rhadamanthus to answer Menippus's question.[65] With coaxing, however, he does tell Menippus:

The life of the ordinary private citizen is best, and most prudent. You will act wisely if you stop speculating about heavenly bodies and discussing final causes and first causes, spit your scorn at those clever syllogisms, and counting all that sort of thing nonsense, make it always your sole object to manage well the present, to reject idle curiosity and anxiety, and to lead a life with as much laughter and cheer as you can.[66]

So important is the "life of the ordinary private citizen" to young More that, in a rare instance, he adds *priuatus* to Lucian's text, sharpening Lucian allusion to Plato's *Republic* 620c3–4, where Odysseus chooses for his next existence the "life of a private man who minds his own business."[67] To ensure this interpretation of Plato's and Lucian's *idiotarum*, More adds *priuatorum* to clarify that he is referring to a citizen and not a lone Achilles isolated from society.[68] As we will see, More continues to show the importance of "the ordinary private citizen" in his later works.[69]

---

[64] "quodnam optimum uitae genus putaret" (41/26).

[65] Rhadamanthus, judge of souls, could well have forbidden Teiresias to answer this question about the best life because each soul is ultimately responsible for its own choices, choices that require personal effort in discovering what is true and good – in bringing "truth and sound reason . . . to bear everywhere" (196).

[66] CW 3.1, 179: "Optima est, inquit, idiotarum priuatorumque uita, ac prudentissima. Quamobrem ab hac uanissima sublimium consyderatione desistens, mitte principia semper ac fines inquirere, & uafros hosce syllogismos despuens, atque id genus omnia nugas aestimans, hoc solum in tota uita persequere, ut praesentibus bene compositis minime curiosus, nulla re sollicitus, quam plurimum potes hilaris uitam ridensque traducas" (41/34–43/1).

[67] See Mary Pawlowski's article showing how More changes Lucian's text (in ways similar to how More changes Pico's text).

[68] CW 3.1, 179 correctly translates Lucian's Greek: "The life of the common sort is best, and you will act more wisely if you stop speculating about heavenly bodies." But CW 3.1 does not translate More's own Latin translation, which changes Lucian's text. More's translation – "Optima est, inquit, idiotarum priuatorumque vita, ac prudentissima" – makes clear what Paul Shorey brings out in his translation of Plato's "bios idiotou" whereby Odysseus looks for "the life of an ordinary citizen" (Loeb edition of *The Republic*).

[69] See especially the uses of *priuato* at CW 15, 334/19–26, 444/17–18 and Morus's statement at CW 4, 56/10 together with Cicero's *De Officiis* 1.124, along with EE 499/53 and the contradictory statements by Raphael at CW 4, 148/18 and 164/20 – as well

Why is the "life of the ordinary private citizen" the "best" and "most prudent" way of life? The reasons given here by Teiresias are the ability "to manage well the present" and to allow "as much laughter and cheer" as humanly possible. The prerequisites of this way of life are avoiding useless speculation and rejecting idle curiosity and anxiety (179).

More affirms this reasoning in the introductory letter to his Lucian translations. About *Menippus,* More says, "[H]ow wittily it rebukes the jugglery of magicians or the silly fictions of poets or the fruitless contentions of philosophers among themselves on any question whatever!" (5). He goes on to say, as we have seen, that the objective is to free ourselves "from foolish confidence and superstitious dread" (7) as shown through a life marked by a "simplicity, temperance, and frugality" (5) that lets "truth...stand by its own strength" (7). Such "foolish confidence" is clearly seen in the cynics' admiration of their own limited virtue; "superstitious dread" is seen in *Menippus* and in *Lovers of Lies.* All humorously display the extremes of "fruitless contentions of philosophers" – not the clear-sightedness of the private citizen dealing with and educated by the daily demands of ordinary life. All display the power of ungoverned appetites of which these "philosophers" are unaware.

As More explains in a letter of 1504, these daily, natural demands that make up "the steep path of virtue"[70] are precisely what educate the ordinary citizen when guided by the "most prudent counsel" (*prudentissimo consilio*)," "the powerful speeches," and the "most expert" skill of one like John Colet, who over a long time proved to More and to London the wisdom and integrity of his words and deeds.[71] The "very nod" of such a person,[72] says young More, he eagerly follows. What a John Colet did for More and London, Lucian does for the attentive readers of his dialogues; both exemplify the *aequo animo* needed for sharp-sighted judgment.[73]

These earliest works show that young More already by 1506 had thought deeply about the *libertas* of the city and the necessity for a skilled

---

as Morus's defense of legal protection for private citizens as a necessary dimension of "respublica."

[70] *Corr.* 7/19: "in arduum virtutis."

[71] *Corr.* 6/8–10, 7/45–48, 7/52–8/59 or *TMSB* 175/8–76/2, 176/36–37, 177/1–12.

[72] *Corr.* 6/11 or *TMSB* 176/3.

[73] Compare More's uses of this important frame of mind at *Corr.* 8/56 and *CW* 3.1, 2/11–12 and 8/1 with Cicero's frequent uses such as *De Oratore* 2.45 and 144 and *Tusculanae Disputationes* 2.39, 3.27, 4.60. It was a commonplace of Roman philosophy that clear-sighted, reasonable action depended upon maintaining a calm mind unperturbed by passions.

citizen-leader, a *princeps,* of proven experience and wisdom who has not been "captivated" by the Cynics' or Stoics' "ideal of endurance and hardness" nor by the Epicureans' "championship of pleasure."[74]

Did Pico della Mirandola share this view? Was Pico a wise and skilled guide whom More chose early in life, as many claim? In the next chapter, we will see that Pico della Mirandola was a wealthy philosopher and earl, richly endowed by Lady Fortune with what might seem to be all of her major gifts. Did Pico escape the dangers that Lucian dramatized in his comic dialogues? If the wealthy and privileged have a special capacity for self-deception because they have the means of removing themselves from the ordinary demands of nature and because their wealth and gifts invite flattery and self-indulgence, what does More's *Life of Pico* reveal as the means of escape? And did Pico escape?

---

[74] *De Oratore* 3.62–63, where Crassus explains that neither school of philosophy is "apt" for "the political leader of the nation, guiding the government and pre-eminent for wisdom and eloquence in the Senate, in the assembly of the people, and in public causes" (3.63); neither is "akin to the orator" (3.64).

5

More's *Life of Pico della Mirandola* (c. 1504–1507)

A Model of Libertas *and* Humanitas?

> Liberty above all things he loved, to which both his own natural affection and the study of philosophy inclined him; and for that he was always wandering and flitting and would never take himself to any certain dwelling....
>
> [Pico] to the end that, all the charge and business of rule or lordship set aside, he might lead his life in rest and peace,... all his patrimony and dominions... he sold.
>
> Thomas More, Life of Pico[1]

Well aware of the enticements of philosophic pleasure[2] and the difficulties of achieving that "true virtue" of the *princeps*,[3] Cicero gave his son the following advice in his last philosophic work, the work that More would later echo "almost word for word."[4]

> [M]y dear Cicero, while the whole field of philosophy is fertile and productive..., still no part is richer or more fruitful than that which deals with moral duties; for from these are derived the rules for living a consistent and good life.[5] (*De Officiis* 3.5)

---

[1] CW 1, 69/21–24, 63/22–64/2. For the dates in the title, see Parks 358–61.

[2] This is a frequent theme that Cicero develops. See, for example, *De Oratore* and *De Finibus* where Cicero points out that certain philosophies and ways of life, by choosing to withdraw from society, destroy the conditions needed for philosophy. See also Nicgorski 2002.

[3] See Chapters 1, 2, and 3.

[4] Referring to book 1 of *Utopia*, specifically to CW 4, 86, Skinner points out that Morus "echoes *De Officiis* almost word for word" (222) and that he sets forth "one particular set of humanist beliefs – those of a 'civic' or Ciceronian humanism" (223).

[5] The word Cicero uses that is translated here as "good" is *honestum*, the key term of his ethical theory meaning "moral or human excellence" that is "forged and fashioned" from all the human virtues. See the whole of book 1 of *De Officiis*, but especially 1.11–17.

Because his son was studying then in Athens with the best philosophers of the time "to purchase, as it were, . . . a store of *bonarum artium*," Cicero warns him that the intense effort involved may well be "work rather than pleasure," but that he had a "heavy responsibility" to succeed in doing so (6). When More translates the reference to this passage in the *Life of Pico,* he eliminates Cicero's name and substitutes "doctrine" for "good arts" (*bonarum artium*),[6] and although he translates *studia humanitatis* as "studies of humanity," More indicates in this early work that Pico's idea of *humanitas* is far different from Cicero's and his own.[7]

More's practical and demanding father also gave pointed advice to his philosophically inclined son. After a severe falling out with his father over irresponsibility, young More moved from (or was thrown out of) his comfortable home and took up residence with the Carthusians while completing his law studies and while beginning his work as a lawyer. During these years, he was also trying to discern his own calling and life's work. Erasmus explains the source of the conflict between More and his father:

A liberal education [*bonas literas*] he [More] had imbibed from his very earliest years. As a young man he devoted himself to the study of Greek literature and philosophy, with so little support from his father, a man in other respects of good sense and high character, that his efforts were deprived of all outside help and he was treated almost as if disinherited because he was thought to be deserting his father's profession, for his father is a specialist in English law.[8]

In trying to decide his path in life, More "made trial of himself" during his years with the Carthusians, applying "his whole mind to the pursuit of piety, with vigils and fasts and prayer and similar exercises"; he also deliberated with the help of counsel from learned and prudent teachers such as William Grocyn and John Colet.[9] Finally, at twenty-eight, More chose "to be a chaste husband rather than a licentious priest."[10] Time also showed that his father had judged well about his son's aptitude for law and public service.

---

[6] See note 7 in Chapter 1 for the different phrases used by More and Cicero for education in the liberal arts.

[7] CW 1, 59/28–29 and 302/36–7; 55/9, 12 and 296/26.

[8] TMSB 8; EE 999/141–46.

[9] SL 6. For an example and an explanation of his lifelong practice of seeking the "advice and counsel" of "more than one" known for "their wisdom and learning," see CW 6, 22/31–24/12.

[10] TMSB 8; EE 999/160–67.

By contrast, Pico della Mirandola's father died shortly after his birth, and his mother died when he was fifteen, leaving him very wealthy and "master of his own destiny."[11] Pico's mother had "longed very sore to have him priest,"[12] and she started him "on an ecclesiastical career so early in life that Cardinal Gonzaga granted him the title of apostolic protonotary" when Pico was just ten.[13] At fourteen, "by the commandment of his mother,"[14] he was sent to Bologna "to study in the laws of the Church" for two years.[15] "After this, as a desirous ensearcher of the secrets of nature, he [Pico] left these common trodden paths and gave himself wholly to speculation," especially the "secret mysteries of the Hebrews, Chaldees and Arabians" and "many other things strange and...not unknown only but also unheard of."[16] These adventurous new paths that Pico chose for himself were cabalistic and Neoplatonic studies as his means to achieve a grand synthesis of all ancient thought involving theories of liberty and happiness or *felicitas*.

Pico's favored nephew and admiring biographer[17] praises Pico for coming to this new knowledge "by himself with the strength of his own wit...without masters[,] so that we may say of him that Epicurus the philosopher said of himself, that he was his own master."[18] But as master of his own destiny, brilliant young Pico soon got into big troubles. By twenty-three, yes, he had acquired two university disciplines and working knowledge of six languages; he also had written "five volumes...of wanton verses of love"; and he had developed a taste for liberty: "Liberty above all things he loved, to which both his own natural affection and the study of philosophy inclined him; and for that he was always wandering and flitting[19] and would never take himself to any certain dwelling."[20]

[11] Borghesi 206.
[12] CW 1, 55.
[13] Borghesi 206.
[14] Compare with "the especial commandment of God" More adds to page 70 of this biography.
[15] CW 1, 55–56.
[16] CW 1, 57.
[17] The narrator of More's *Life of Pico* is the nephew to whom Pico sold his estate at such a bargain "that it seemed rather a gift than a sale" (CW 1, 63). In the original biography, John Francis begins with a long paragraph insisting that what he writes is not "prejudiced by favor or flattery" (CW 1, 295).
[18] CW 1, 62; the words here left out are the ones added by More: "for the love of God and profit of His Church."
[19] This "always wandering and flitting" is reminiscent not only of Ulysses' wanderlust, but also of Lucian's Cynic and *Utopia*'s Raphael. See the change that More makes in Lucian's use of Ulysses in *Menippus*, shown in Chapter 4. Raphael Hythlodaeus is himself compared to Ulysses at CW 4, 48/31.
[20] CW 1, 69.

This love for liberty also showed itself in Pico's being "desirous of glory" and in his "voluptuous use of women."[21] Desire for glory led him at twenty-three to challenge anyone in the world to dispute the 900 *Theses* he had formulated, offering to pay the expenses of contenders who would come to Rome to do so. The "voluptuous use of women" led to his being wounded, arrested, and disgraced on his way to Rome after abducting Margherita, the wife of Giuliano dei Medici, in May 1486.[22] Released through the help of influential friends, Pico continued to Rome for his intended intellectual triumph in November 1486.

Little did Pico expect the perilous situation that arose: "Coveting to make a show of his cunning and little considering how great envy [*inuidia*] he should raise against himself," he was charged with heresy, and the "fruits" of his learning were forbidden to be read. At this point in his *Life of Pico*, More adds a sentence quite similar to one that would appear later in his *Richard III*: "Lo, this end had Picus of his high mind and proud purpose, that where he thought to have gotten perpetual praise, there had he much work to keep himself upright, that he ran not in perpetual infamy and slander" (58).[23] Instead of being honored and respected, Pico had to leave Italy to avoid arrest even after he officially retracted his controversial theses in July 1487. Nonetheless, he was arrested and briefly imprisoned in France in January 1488 at the orders of Innocent VIII, and his official reconciliation was not until June 1493, the year before he died.

Looking back on that momentous year of 1486, Pico saw those events as the turning point whereby he changed his life, leading the narrator to claim Pico had a conversion.[24] As the narrator concludes: "Women's blandishments he changed into the desire of heavenly joys" (59).

But how completely, how successfully did Pico change? And when did he do so? Neither More nor the narrator makes the latter point clear,

---

[21] *CW* 1, 59.

[22] The dates in this chapter are based primarily on Borghesi.

[23] Compare this statement with those of Lord Hastings and of the narrator in *Richard III*. Just before Richard orders Hastings's execution, Hastings brags: "And lo how the world is turned: now stand mine enemies in the danger (as thou mayest hap to hear more hereafter), and I never in my life so merry, nor never in so great surety." The narrator immediately comments: "Oh good God, the blindness of our mortal nature: when he most feared, he was in good surety; when he reckoned himself surest, he lost his life, and that within two hours after" (*CW* 2, 52/10–16).

[24] Given his arrangement of materials, More seems to keep this claim open to question. Can Savonarola's reports, for example, be trusted? See also Black's recent study that questions John Francis's "claim that his uncle underwent a 'conversion'" (239).

but even the admiring narrator points out that Pico's high aspirations fluctuated considerably:

But in the inward affections of the mind[25] he [Pico] cleaved to God with very fervent love and devotion. Sometimes that marvellous alacrity languished and almost fell, and after again with great strength rose up into God. (70)

Pico's battles against such falls were not helped by his "soft" and privileged upbringing. The opening description of Pico in More's *Life* is important:

He was of feature and shape seemly and beauteous, of stature goodly and high, of flesh tender and *soft*, his visage lovely and fair, his colour white intermingled with comely reds, his eyes grey and quick of look, his teeth white and even, his hair yellow and not *too* picked [affected in style]. (55, emphases added)

Besides being temperamentally "of flesh tender and soft," Pico's "voluptuous use of women" (59) did not strengthen his self-mastery, although the indulgent narrator gives excuses for these youthful dalliances:

The comeliness of his body with the lovely favour of his visage, and therewithal his marvellous fame, his excellent learning, great riches and noble kindred, set many women afire on him, from the desire of whom he not abhorring... was somewhat fallen into wantonness. (59)

Unlike More, Pico refused to consider marriage as even an option to his wantonness because he saw marriage as a "servitude" impinging upon that "liberty [that] above all things he loved"; hence, "[w]edding and worldly business he fled almost alike" (69). At twenty-three, therefore, Pico decided he would father not children but books,[26] books that would give his grand synthesis of Neoplatonic, Aristotelian, cabalistic, and biblical views of *libertas* and *felicitas*.

This decision to father books Pico mentions in his Letter to Corneus, which More includes in his *Life of Pico* after changing the date from 1486 to 1492 and after eliminating any indication of Pico's running away with Margherita. More also excludes both Pico's denying any "blame of wrongdoing" for the "bad luck in his love affair" and Pico's creative excuses that included calling upon "great men as precedents to defend himself, especially David and Solomon, to say nothing of Aristotle, who forgot all about his moral precepts on those many occasions when he fell

---

[25] Consider the contrast with the frequent use of "heart" rather than "mind" in the second half of More's *Life*.

[26] Pico puns on *liberos / libros*, "children" / "books," as indicated in the commentary of CW 1, 87/27.

head over heels for some wenches or even whores" (355). For Cicero, forgetting about moral precepts under the influence of passion was no excuse for a *princeps*'s neglect of duty.[27] But Pico's philosophy, like those satirized by Lucian and rejected by Cicero, was not suited for guidance in practical duties.[28]

By contrast, More accepted the Ciceronian view that liberty, happiness, and duty are inseparable, and he showed in his life and writings a major struggle to harmonize these. When he was twenty-seven, for example, More wrote that he would have been brought "almost to the gates of hell" without the calm and expert advice of that "guide of my life,"[29] John Colet, who most likely introduced young More to the life and collected works of Pico della Mirandola in the early 1500s or late 1490s after Colet's return from Florence in 1496.[30] Eventually More published his shortened and strangely amended translation of Pico's life along with an unprecedented[31] but also very small[32] and strangely amended selection of Pico's most traditional instructions on how to wage "battle" to achieve the virtues needed for a good, happy, and consistent life.

During this emotionally tumultuous period of his mid- to late twenties, More chose the elements of what he eventually published as *The Life of John Picus Earl of Mirandola*.[33] From the title to the last line of More's amended translation of Pico's biography, Thomas More draws attention to Pico's civic position as "Earl of Mirandola."[34] The biography itself

---

[27] See especially his *De Officiis*. In *De Oratore* see the criticism of those talented individuals with "over-abundant leisure" and "unlimited command of unoccupied free time" at 3.57.

[28] For Cicero's rejection of Epicureanism as one such "inept" philosophy, see the references and arguments in Nicgorski 2002.

[29] More's Letter to John Colet, *Corr.* 9/1: "vitae meae magistro."

[30] *CW* 1, xli; on the date of Colet's return to England, see Gleason 47.

[31] Anthony Edwards points out that "there appear to be no precedents for the addition to the *Life* of selections from Pico's own works and for the translation of works in a variety of different forms – epistles, commentary, verse homilies, and a hymn" (*CW* 1, lv).

[32] From Pico's *Opera Omnia* (1496; reprinted 1498, 1504, 1517), totaling 531 folio pages, More chose what would become thirty-four folio pages in his 1557 *Workes* (Parks 352). Of these thirty-four folio pages, Pico's biography takes nine and a half, and the three letters take seven. Psalm 15 followed by Pico's only published psalm commentary (Black 9n) takes three and a half folio pages; More's own rhyme royal poetry takes the last fourteen pages.

[33] The most persuasive explanation for early composition is given by Parks 353–61, building on Reed in More's *English Works* 1, 18–20; see also Fox 28 and *CW* 1, xxxviii with notes 2 and 3, despite the comments of xxxix. No evidence, however, has yet determined with any certainty when More studied and translated Pico's work.

[34] *CW* 1, 49/1–2, 52/17–18, and 75/21.

shows that Pico failed significantly in specific duties, so much so that the work ends provocatively with Pico pleading for prayers supposedly from the fires of purgatory,[35] revealing that his life was cut short from its intended span because he failed to accomplish his duties in life – a life, though, said to be mercifully cut short,[36] because Pico did, in his last years, pray and do charitable deeds.

By eliminating well over one-third of the original biography, More changes the focus of the work from emphasis on Pico's extraordinary learning and intellectual gifts used for esoteric studies to an emphasis on issues related to Pico's virtue and responsibilities in life. The tension between learning and virtue holds first place in the work's opening lines as More amends them:

Earl of Mirandola, a great lord of Italy, an excellent cunning man in all sciences *and virtuous of living; with divers epistles and other works of the said John Picus, full of great science, virtue, and wisdom: whose life and works be worthy and digne to be read and often to be had in memory.* (49)

By adding the italicized lines of this title, More changes the focus from Pico's prestigious position and exalted learning to wise and virtuous living. All the "diverse epistles and other works" chosen to accompany this biography have the same focus on good living.

These opening lines reveal More's characteristic irony. Who or what, for example, is "full of science, virtue, and wisdom"? Is it Pico himself or the few "epistles and other works" that More selected and edited?[37] As the biographical account makes clear, Pico's life as a whole was not simply one of "virtue and wisdom." Significantly, More's last paragraphs emphasize the punishments Pico must suffer for his sins, not exemplary virtues as his source had done.

Contrary to his source, More's opening and closing lines of the biography in fact never indicate that Pico's life should be emulated. The opening lines end with the ironic statement that Pico's "life and works [are] worthy and digne [fitting] to be read and often to be had in memory" (49), but for *what* should they be read and remembered? As an extraordinarily talented person with every privilege in life who failed in his life's duties? That seems more likely than a hagiographic account inviting imitation, because More's abridged and altered account makes clear that Pico did

---

35   If the controversial figure of Savonarola can be trusted.
36   *CW* I, 74.
37   More chooses only three out of forty-seven letters (*CW* I, xlvii), and even those three are given distinct interpretations by More's introductions, omissions, and emendations.

not use his *libertas* to fulfill duties but to neglect them. Three times More adds the charge of negligence to the text he translates.[38]

More's *Life of Pico* can be divided into two parts:[39] one of prose, including the short biography of Pico and three of his letters; the other of poetry, forming what could be called More's compendium of spiritual principles. Although chosen in his youth, the principles set forth here are essentially those reiterated by More throughout his life up through his prison writings. Part 2 gives the measure to judge part 1; it also gives the first account of young More's distinctive Christian *humanitas*.

Part 2's spiritual compendium begins with Psalm 15, followed by a traditional and imitative commentary written by Pico shortly after his adventurous year of 1486,[40] as one small segment of his larger project of understanding the unique felicity and radical liberty of human beings. At the beginning of his *Oration on Man*, for example, Pico explains "why man has the greatest *felicitas* of any animal and is to be envied by all, 'not only by beasts, but by the stars and the ultramundane minds.'" The "unique ingredient of man's *felicitas*" is his liberty to choose what he will be:

The Father imparted to man at the moment of his birth seeds of all sorts and the buds of all kinds of life. The ones he cultivates will grow and bear their fruits in him. If [he cultivates] vegetable seeds, he will become a plant; if sensual ones, he will become brutish. If [he cultivates] rational ones, he will turn into a heavenly animal. If he cultivates intellectual ones, he will be an angel and a son of God.[41]

This "Protean" vision of human nature is far from Cicero's *humanitas* but is a necessary part of Pico's attempt to defuse differences between Christian, Muslim, and Jewish philosophers by "focusing on the higher, 'supernatural,' *felicitas* which he saw as transcending philosophies and their differences."[42] Psalm 15 was important for this philosophic project as shown by Pico's using this key term of *felicitas* eleven times in his short commentary. Although *felicitas* never occurs in the Latin text of Psalm 15 itself, Pico uses *felicitas* regularly as a fair translation of the full and happy life described in that psalm.[43] Why did Pico choose this particular psalm to study? Perhaps because it sets forth a traditional (and distinctively

---

[38] *CW* 1, 68/1 and 5, 75/7; compare these texts with the original at *CW* 1, 326 and 336.
[39] Parks 356.
[40] Dougherty 127n; Borghesi 217.
[41] Quoted in Black 191.
[42] Black 238.
[43] More himself uses "felicity" seven times to translate this term, but also "happiness" (twice), "goodness" (once), and "blessed" (once).

non-Neoplatonic) understanding of body, soul, and God, one in which "mind *and . . .* flesh *both* have joyed in the living God" (101/8–9, emphasis added). By selecting a text such as this uncharacteristic commentary,[44] More masks Pico's often daring Neoplatonic theories so that, especially in part 2, More can fashion clearly the features of his own distinctive Christian *humanitas.*

One example of the "radical surgery"[45] needed for this project can be seen in the one poem by Pico that More selects and amends as the final element of part 2. In the original poem, Pico opens by addressing a God "*terrible in the height* of your majesty . . . who *control[s] the world with your nod, by whose command the thunderbolts are thrown down*" and ends praying that "when my spirit has finished the tasks of mortal life and is brought before its lord, *coming to possess the happy lot [felici sorte]of the promised kingdom,* it may feel in you not a lord but a father" (379, 381). More changes the underlined words, eliminates the italicized words, changes Pico's epic hexameter to Chaucerian rhyme royal, and adds the qualifier, "a very tender loving," before the last word, "father." The force of this last qualifier is heightened by eliminating the phrase attributing *felicitas* to a place rather than to the company of a tender loving God (380/76). And in the last stanza More adds a parting humorous jab at Pico's cold and distant Neoplatonism by having the speaker lament that he "Departen must *without his fleshly wife,* / alone."[46] How better could a Lucian humorist respond to Pico's scorn for the "slavery" of marriage?[47]

Another example is the way More changes Pico's platonic interpretation of the standard list of Petrarchan properties of the lover. In Pico's list, the beloved is a man; in More's love ballad, we assume the beloved is

---

[44] All but the final prayer More selects from the "scattered personal items" that made up the "brief middle section of sixty-seven pages" of Pico's *Opera Omnia,* which "was labeled 'Epistolae plures' but included other things." The "verse prayer 'Deprecatoria ad Deum' of one and one-half pages was inserted after the *Heptaplus*" (Parks 352).

[45] In part 1, Edwards points out that "radical surgery" is needed to show "the necessity of the active life rather than the reclusive life of the solitary scholar/divine," and that Pico is "swiftly reconciled with Christian orthodoxy after his early excesses in a way that is at odds with the facts" (CW 1, xlviii, liv). In most of part 2, More can set forth a traditional view of Christian humanism by selecting only five short pieces from Pico's many works: a traditional and imitative psalm commentary, three conventional lists, and the verse prayer analyzed in part here.

[46] As Ben Beier explains, "More places particular emphasis on the physical body by inventing a metaphor not present in the Latin." See his analysis of More's addition of the soul's departing "without his fleshy wife" (40–42).

[47] See CW 4, 184–90 where the Piconean Raphael (who also shuns marriage and family) describes marriage in Utopia in the section titled "On Slavery," where selecting a spouse is compared to buying a colt.

a woman.[48] But in his ballad, More also eliminates the Petrarchan convention of a distant and unrequited love. More's "Twelve Properties of a Lover" expresses the mutual and ardent love of the "perfect lover," who not only "longeth for to be / In presence of his love both night and day" but who also "will his love obey" regardless of the suffering involved because "His joy it is and all his appetite / To pain himself in all that ever he may, / That person in whom he set hath his delight / Diligently to serve both day and night / For very love, without any regard / To any profit, guerdon [requital] or reward" (116, 119).

Young More breaks convention yet again by applying directly each property to the love of God in the second stanza in each of the twelve parts. Throughout, he emphasizes that perfect human lovers find joy in suffering or in diligent service for the sake of the beloved, and he ends this last and longest of his three poems with eight references to diligent "service." By contrast, what are we to think of Pico's earlier insistence that he and other philosophers "(as Horace saith) repute themselves king of kings; *they love liberty;*[49] . . . they cannot serve" (87)?

Here is a striking contradiction between the clear principle of service set forth in the spiritual compendium of part 2 and Pico's scorn for civic and marital service in part 1.[50] Even more strikingly mysterious in part 1 is Pico's refusal to serve even when given what he is said to understand as the "especial commandment of God" (70).

And what are we to make of Pico's invoking Horace as the authority for his un-Horatian views?[51] Here and in the only other use of Horace, Pico misses the humor in Horace's satirizing the very things that Pico praises.

[48] See the commentary of *CW* 1 at 113/13–25.
[49] More adds this italicized phrase.
[50] Consistency is largely present between the advice Pico gives in his two letters to Francis and the advice given in the second half, that is, in More's compendium. The most glaring inconsistencies arise when Corneus challenges Pico to apply principles to his own action. To heighten the inconsistency, More takes a letter from 1486, written before Pico's conversion and changes the date to 1492, the same year that Pico gives advice to Francis. Consider how More uses a similar technique in changing the age of Edward IV in the opening lines of *Richard III*. Consider also the end of Chapter 9's list of glaring contradictions in Raphael's account of Utopia.
[51] In doing so, attention is drawn to an example of More's fashioning what Horace called "living words," which are the "poet's office and duty." Horace was the first authority young More invoked in his opening line introducing the "first fruits" of his Greek studies, his translations of Lucian. Here in the first published fruits of his Latin translations, More depends upon his learned readers' appreciation of Horace's skill and wisdom, an appreciation that Pico did not have. See Horace's *De Arte Poetica*, especially lines 305–22. For an explanation of these "living words" and how they apply to Lucian's dialogues and to *Utopia*, see Wegemer 1996 84ff.

When Pico invokes Horace to defend the "kingly" liberty[52] of his philosophic way of life, he misreads the passage in which Horace makes fun of such individuals boasting of their supposed superiority and self-sufficiency. Pico refers to *Epistulae* 1.1.106–7, which is – contrary to Pico's reading – the humorous conclusion showing that, although philosophers may boast of godlike self-sufficiency, they are still all too mortal: "To sum up," Horace writes giving the philosopher's proud view of himself,[53] "the wise man is less than Jove alone. He is rich, free [*liber*], honored, beautiful, nay, a king of kings; above all, sound. . . . " But then Horace adds the final twist: "– save when troubled by the 'flu'!"[54]

In a similar way, the earlier reference to Horace (at *CW* 1, 69/14) also missed Horace's humor. There the reference is to *Epodes* 2.7–8 to justify Pico's hatred for "(as Horace saith) 'the proud palaces of stately lords.'" More undoubtedly noted the irony in that Pico had lived in just such a palace himself.[55] In this passage, however, Horace is not criticizing those he calls "citizens" (not lords); he is satirizing the speaker who gives a hyperbolic praise of country life and who, in this context, expresses the hypocritical desire to avoid "the Forum and the proud thresholds of more powerful citizens." The desire is hypocritical because the speaker is a usurer who lives in the city and is so successful that he has just recently bought a farm in the country and is at "the very point of *beginning* the farmer's life"; the satire ends with the speaker returning to the city to make his real living by lending money to those powerful citizens he has just condemned as proud (*Epodes* 2.67–70, emphasis added).

Pride, of course, is the "one peril" of special danger for the virtuous person – so begins the poetry section of More's *Life of Pico* (94); specifically, that special danger is pride in one's own virtue. The second great danger is "that thing taketh he for his chief good" because that chief good serves as "his god" (96). What was the chief good for Pico after his "conversion"? And why did he choose not to obey the "special commandment of God" that he insisted he saw clearly at least by 1492?[56]

---

[52] When Cicero refers to such "kingly" liberty at *De Officiis* 1.69, he, the Roman republican, is not giving praise as Pico does here and as Raphael Hythlodaeus does at *CW* 4, 56/1.

[53] This is the same view that Lucian's Cynic expressed about himself, as we have seen.

[54] As Horace here implies, if this special class of persons is so godlike and superior to other human beings, why do they get sick and need help (often unacknowledged) like everyone else?

[55] True, Pico does sell his large estate in 1491 but, as we will see, he buys another smaller one for "many thousands of gold coins."

[56] Or so Pico's nephew and biographer reports on the basis of his personal conversation with Pico (*CW* 1, 70 – as quoted later in the chapter), as does Savonarola (*CW* 1, 74).

If his conversion occurred after his arrest for heresy in 1488, then 1488 may have been the time he burned the five volumes he wrote of "wanton verses of love" in "detestation of his vice," but also in fear "lest these trifles might be some evil occasion afterward" (60). In 1489 Innocent VIII sent advice to Lorenzo de'Medici to encourage Pico to "write poetry rather than theological stuff, for that suits him better, since the Count lacks the foundations and hasn't seen as much as is needed for someone who writes on theology."[57]

In 1491 Pico sold to his nephew Francis his patrimony for the purpose of setting aside worldly entanglements,[58] but then spent "many thousands of gold coins" (321) for his new retirement property in Ferrara. Shortly afterward is the probable time that the following conversation occurred between Pico and his future biographer, Francis, who tells us about Pico's "especial commandment" from God:

[A]s he [Pico] walked with John Francis, his nephew, in an orchard at Ferrara, in the talking of the love of Christ, he broke out into these words, "Nephew," said he, "this will I show thee, I warn thee keep it secret; the substance that I have left, after certain books of mine finished, I intend to give out to poor folk, and fencing myself with the crucifix, barefoot walking around the world in every town and castle I purpose to preach of Christ." Afterwards, I understand, *by the especial commandment of God*, he changed that purpose and appointed [resolved] to profess himself in the order of Friars Preachers. (70)

Yet this "especial commandment of God" may not be what it seems, because More adds that phrase to his translation,[59] and the larger account is based on Savonarola's tale that Savonarola claimed to be "as true as the gospel of Saint John" (73).

If Pico saw his duty in life so clearly, why did he delay for two years?[60] It was this delay, we are told, that led God to end Pico's life before his allotted time. In this passage, Pico indicates his reason for delaying: he thought he must first finish writing "certain books" – books that, with

The nephew seems the more trustworthy source. More does not even identify Savonarola in his version although in the source material, Savonarola is highly praised. By the time More wrote, Savonarola was no longer in favor.

[57] Blum 37.

[58] *CW* 1, 63 reports that this occurs "[t]hree years before his [Pico's] death."

[59] Compare *CW* 1, 70/18–19, with the original text of *CW* 1, 330. Jeffrey Lehman's edition clearly shows how More alters the original text; see www.thomasmorestudies.org/docs/Picus.pdf.

[60] Francis reports that Savonarola said he had threatened Pico for "two years together that he would be punished if he forslothed that purpose which our Lord had put in his mind" (74).

characteristic hyperbole,[61] the narrator tells us that "every man by and by desired and looked after" (67).

But was this the real reason? Two others are given for this delay by the person who supposedly knew best Pico's conscience and character. The first set of reasons for Pico's disobedience is given as conjectures by the notorious Savonarola:[62]

[Pico] purposed oftentimes to obey this inspiration and follow his calling. Howbeit, not being kind [grateful] enough for so great benefices of God, or called back by the tenderness of his flesh (as he was a man of delicate complexion) he shrank from the labour, or thinking haply that the religion had no need of him, deferred it for a time; howbeit *this I speak only by conjecture.* (73–74, emphasis added)

That Pico did not value properly the gifts he had been given is likely, and we were alerted earlier to Pico's "softness," his wanderlust, and his idolatrous pleasures of books and secret studies.[63]

The second set of reasons is purported to be Pico's own:[64] "negligence and ... unkindness [ingratitude]"[65] (75). The negligence is undeniable according to the account given.[66] Earlier in the work, the narrator reported that Pico was "besprent [covered] with the freckle of negligence" and that his

friends oftentimes admonished him that he should not all utterly despise riches, showing him that it was his dishonesty and rebuke when it was reported (were it true or false) that his negligence and setting naught by money gave his servants occasion of deceit and robbery. Nevertheless, that mind of his (which evermore on high cleaved first in contemplation and in the ensearching of nature's counsel) could never let down itself to the consideration and overseeing of these base, abject, and vile earthly trifles. His high steward came on a time to him and desired him to receive his account of such money as he had in many years received of his:

---

[61] Or consider the narrator's hyperbolic description of Pico as "a perfect philosopher and a perfect divine" (56), followed shortly afterward by More's addition to the text that Pico's life was "full of pride and desirous of glory and man's praise" (57).

[62] Savonarola was at the height of his power in Florence when Francis published Pico's *Omnia Opera* in 1496. However, in 1497 Savonarola was excommunicated, and in 1498 he was hanged and burned by the government of Florence.

[63] See More's additions to his source about idolatry at CW 1, 77, 98–9/368–69, and compare these with what the narrator tells us about Pico's attachment to his books at 65.

[64] The account is based on what Savonarola told an acquaintance in More's version (CW 1, 75/5–7).

[65] "Unkindness" also meant "unnatural" as in anti-"kin." Pico's unmeasured study – a danger Cicero warns against – prevented the full flowering of Pico's humanity.

[66] But as seen earlier in this chapter, More adds the charge of "negligence" three times to the text he is translating.

and brought forth his books of reckoning. Picus answered him in this wise, "My friend (saith he), I know well ye might have oftentimes and yet may deceive me an [if] ye list; wherefore the examination of these expenses shall not need. There is no more to do: if I be aught in your debt I shall pay you by and by; if ye be in mine pay me, either now if ye have it, or hereafter if ye be now not able." (68)

Lucian would certainly have savored this paragraph for what it reveals in light of "truth and sound reason brought to bear everywhere,"[67] but the example given here clearly illustrates More's own charges of negligence, although the narrator in the original Latin text judged the fault as but a "mole of indifference" (*incuriositatis naevo*).[68]

So if negligence was one of Pico's faults according to More, was "unkindness" or ingratitude another? As More explains in his own introduction to the *Life of Pico*, gifts are signs of "love and friendship" (51). According to the spiritual compendium of part 2 all gifts are received from the "Creator of all" (95, 106, 123), and humble creatures should give "especial...thanks" (63/18) for all they possess; in fact, the one great peril is to "wax proud" of what has been received (94). In this light, "crime [is] the work of our uncourteous mind" (121), looking to find happiness in a gift rather than in the giver of that gift (96).

The commentary on Psalm 15 warns, as we have seen, that a human being often "taketh for his god" whatever he considers "his chief good," the gift without which he cannot be happy (96). This chief object of his desire or pleasure or passion becomes the "idol" to which "they run forth headlong unadvisedly," thus "forsak[ing] reason" and God (98–99).

What was Pico's "chief good" that blinded his reason and kept him from obeying his acknowledged calling and God's clear command? Perhaps John Donne, More's distant relative, put it best when he called it Pico's "concupiscence of inaccessible knowledges and transcendencies."[69] Pico said himself that only the loss of his books could upset him, but he rationalized that "since God is all good," and since Pico's intellectual labors are "only for the love of God," then God would "not suffer him" to have to give up his books (65). After these lines of self-deception, the unreliable narrator makes a comment Lucian could well have made:

O very happy mind, which none adversity might oppress, which no prosperity might enhance; not the cunning of all philosophy was able to make him proud, not the knowledge of the Hebrew, Chaldee and Arabic language, besides Greek

---

[67] CW 3.1, 77/25–26, 196.
[68] See note 38.
[69] Fox 32.

and Latin, could make him vainglorious; not his great substance, not his noble blood could blow up his heart, not the beauty of his body, not the great occasion of sin, were able to pull him back into the voluptuous broad way [and More adds:] that leadeth to hell. (65)

That "the cunning of all philosophy was [not] able to make him proud" – such delusion was seen in all the Lucian dialogues that More chose to translate about the proud and "uncivil" philosophers seen in Chapter 4.[70] Nowhere is Pico's "uncivil" or anti-Ciceronian outlook more evident than in Pico's Letter to Corneus, the letter that has led scholars such as Baker-Smith and Alistair Fox to show the similarity between Pico's and Raphael Hythlodaeus's "rejection of the *vita activa*."[71] When asked by a friend to put his philosophy at the service of a prince, Pico strongly refuses, arguing that it is "not princely, to make the study of wisdom... mercenary."[72] In response, Corneus says (with More adding what is italicized), "*I am content ye study, but I would have you outwardly occupied also.* And I desire you not so to embrace Martha that ye should utterly forsake Mary. *Love them and use them both, as well study as worldly occupation.*" Pico then justifies his actions by saying that it is "none error to decline" going from "contemplation [Mary] to the active living [Martha][73] – that is to say, *from the better to the worse*" and that he should not "be rebuked" for continually using his "pleasant ease and rest" for pursuing "virtue only for itself" and to study the "mysteries of God" and the "counsel of nature" (86).

More's additions are telling, especially the command: "Love them and use them both" – that is, love and live both the contemplative and active ways of life. The strength and importance of this conviction More expressed a few years later in his Letter to a Monk, a vigorous defense of Erasmus from the attacks of a monk whom More addresses as "my old, dear friend" but who is also shown to be proud and ignorant. After a long section praising the hardships and strains of Erasmus's "fruitful work" that is done "for the public benefit of everyone," as opposed to

---

[70] See CW 4, 98/4–11 and Chapter 9 for the charge that Morus makes against Raphael in book 1 of *Utopia*.

[71] Baker-Smith 137; he points out that Raphael, like Pico, gives up his patrimony (95). See also Fox 32.

[72] See the use of *princeps* at 352/8 and the preceding understanding of what Pico considered "princely" activities; see also 85/6 and 86/23 as compared to 350/16.

[73] The Martha and Mary allusion is to Luke 10:38–42. Martha represents the active life, immersed in the world's business; Mary represents the contemplative life, withdrawn from worldly involvement.

the misuse of monastic leisure by those who "arrogantly" and "grossly flatter" themselves of their own holiness, More writes these burning lines to a self-professed Mary:

[S]ince "All mortal justice is as the rag of a menstruating woman" [Isaiah 64:5], so that everyone has good reason to hold even his own good qualities suspect, it would probably be not unwholesome for you to feel inwardly doubtful and fearful lest either you do not share Mary's portion or you have chosen Mary's portion mistakenly, since you rank her function not merely above Martha's office, as Christ did, but even above that of the apostles. You should be afraid that, when you view yourself, too indulgently, as one who has retreated into holy solitude to escape harmful pleasures, the deeper scrutiny of God, who observes us with more penetration, who explores our own hearts more profoundly than we do, and whose eyes discern our imperfections, may find that what you have been doing is avoiding responsibility, dodging work, cultivating the pleasure of repose in the shadow of piety, looking for a way of out life's troubles. (CW 15, 301–3)

"Avoiding responsibility, dodging work, cultivating the pleasure of repose in the shadow of piety, looking for a way of out life's troubles" – this strong criticism of the monk's self-assured motives seems implied by More about Pico's motives as well – implied, that is, after weighing More's careful additions and edits to his *Life*.[74] In fact, by adding three times the charge of "negligence" to Pico's *Life*, More goes beyond implication.

In addition, Pico's eagerness to shun all public duty as the condition for his *libertas* stands in sharp contrast to the repeated call to service and sacrifice in the spiritual compendium of part 2;[75] it also stands in sharp contrast to the diligence, risk, vigilant care, and attentiveness to the gods that are entailed in the *libertas* spoken of repeatedly in More's *Declamation*. For the *Declamation*'s Orator, civic *libertas* is a condition of political order in which good laws are enforced by good magistrates who have the necessary clear-sighted prudence, vigilant labor, expert skills, Ulyssean resourcefulness, and respect for gods and law. Pico is a high magistrate, an earl, but one who ignores and even scorns his duties. True philosophers, Pico argues, "useth continually this pleasant ease and rest, seeking none outside thing, despising all other thing" (86). This view is similar to that of Lucian's Cynic, who boasted of his own virtue, of his self-contentment, of his refusal to serve, and of his contempt for all the

---

[74] This was also a criticism that More may have directed to himself, at a time when he may have seen the same motives operative in himself.

[75] See, for example, the many calls to serve that conclude More's "Twelve Properties of a Lover," and the emphasis on the joy that comes from imitating Christ's sacrifice in the care of others in the "Twelve Rules of Spiritual Battle."

normal ways of life so unlike his own.[76] When More summarizes Pico's position in the introduction to Pico's Letter to Corneus, he describes Pico's motives as studying philosophy "for pleasure of itself," and he then adds a motive that Pico never gives in his Letter to Corneus: "for the instruction of his mind in moral virtue."[77] More reinforces in his *Life* this second motive by his altered title, his introduction, and his many additions about the "profitable" character of learning,[78] and especially by his longest addition explaining the meaning of true nobility.[79]

As we have seen in earlier chapters, Cicero and Seneca and More agree that "true and refined philosophy" is that fruitful "art of living."[80] It requires an arduous training not only in the full range of liberal learning but also in the difficult work of knowing and governing one's own appetites to achieve virtue. This fruitful art involves a well-wrought idea of full human flourishing that cannot be achieved without a character adequately trained for the accurate perception needed to fashion that idea and for the endurance needed to govern oneself in achieving it. Cicero, Seneca, and More all included humor, charm, happiness, friendship, and civic service in their ideas of *humanitas,* of full human flourishing. Lucian and Horace did also, a factor that undoubtedly drew More's attention to them. While Pico had many of these qualities by nature,[81] his fashioned idea of *humanitas* did not.

What distinctive view of *humanitas* does More fashion in this book, his first published in English? Most succinctly and traditionally put: the view that "felicity is fulfilled in the vision and fruition of the *humanitas* of Christ" (103), a man-god of love who serves and suffers willingly and gladly, in the roles of both Martha and Mary. As Pico summarizes this biblical view in his commentary on Psalm 15, a person is "perfect when...not his soul only but also his flesh draw forth to Godward"

---

[76] See Chapter 4.

[77] CW 1, 85.

[78] The introduction to the *Life* that More adds argues repeatedly that the work is designed to be profitable and to bring a "gracious increase of virtue" to the reader (51–52). Even within the Letter to Corneus where Pico insists he will not use philosophy for "mercenary" purposes, More inserts the word "profit" (85 and 88).

[79] See CW 1, 52–53.

[80] See Chapters 1 and 2 and the end of Chapter 4.

[81] Young Thomas More would have recognized many similarities between Pico and himself. Besides sharing most of the "Five Causes that in so Short Time brought him to so Marvellous Cunning" (63), young More was famous for being "of cheer always merry and of so benign nature that he was never troubled with anger" (65). He was also strongly attracted to a life removed and to a life dedicated to study.

(101), when a person can say: "My mind and my flesh both have joyed in the living God" – a condition requiring voluntary training expressed in the "Twelve Rules" and "Twelve Weapons" of spiritual combat.[82] But lest this view be confused with a rigid Stoic self-mastery, More adds the longest and most original segment of his *Life of Pico*: "The Twelve Properties of a Lover" that shows the fundamental motive as intimacy with a "very tender loving" God who suffers and serves willingly and joyfully. Twice More points out that human beings are created in the image of this type of God,[83] not of a thunderbolt-wielding Jupiter or an impersonal force of Fate.

More's *Life of Pico* as a whole indicates powerfully both the difficulties of practicing genuine virtue and the ease of self-deception – especially for one as wealthy, brilliant, and gifted as Pico. As we saw in Lucian's comic dialogues, the wealthy and privileged have a special capacity for self-deception because they have the means of removing themselves from the ordinary demands of nature (and thus of citizenship) and because their wealth invites flattery and self-indulgence.

How would Henry VIII face such challenges when he assumed the throne of England at seventeen, as one of the wealthiest kings in English history?

---

[82] The same voluntary training is also expressed in traditional terms within the Psalm 15 commentary at CW 3.1, 98–99, and 101.

[83] CW 1, 77 and 111–12; for Cicero's similar view, see *De Natura Deorum* 2.78; *De Legibus* 1.25.

6

More's 1509 Coronation Ode

Artful Education of Eighteen-Year-Old Henry VIII?

Henry rejoiced to bear the name of his all-conquering predecessor....
[T]ales of Henry V's exploits...filled his ears as a boy and gave him his
ideal of kingship: he too, he resolved, would conquer France and make the
name of the king of England the most feared in Europe.

David Starkey, *Henry: Virtuous Prince*, p. 20

How tranquil the clemency that warms his peaceful heart, how far removed
from arrogance is his mind – these are the definite marks, marks that cannot
be counterfeited [*fingere*], that are displayed on the countenance of our
remarkable *princeps*.

Thomas More, Coronation Ode for Henry VIII, 19/78–81[1]

With good right was Socrates' look ever the same [tranquil and serene],
since his mind, by which the countenance is fashioned [*fingitur*], underwent
no change.

Cicero, *Tusculanae Disputationes* 3.31

The natural abilities of a *princeps* are cultivated by the liberal arts.

Thomas More, Coronation Ode for Henry VIII, 19/116–17

On 23 April 1509 Henry became king of England; on 28 June he turned
eighteen; by the end of the year, this young "king ever desirous of serving

---

[1] "Quam tranquilla fouet placidum clementia pectus, / Quam procul ex illo fastus abest
animo, / Principis egregii nostri (quas fingere non est) / Prae se fert certas uultus et ipse
notas" (CW 3.2). For famous sarcastic uses of *notas* or "remarkable" when applied to a
person's character, see Cicero, *Pro Caelio* 63; Virgil, *Aeneid* 6.523; and Tacitus, *Historiae*
1.33.

Mars,"² began diplomatic and military preparations for war and would go on to spend "roughly a quarter of his reign in open war with France."³ In doing so, he was imitating his "idea of man," his hero Henry V,⁴ his "conception and idea of a good person."⁵ Thomas More, in writing his coronation ode for Henry VIII, would try to give his young monarch an alternate idea.

As a gift for Henry's coronation, More wrote Epigrams 19–23 and sent them belatedly to "Princeps" Henry, whom he had known for at least a decade personally and through young Henry's most influential teachers.⁶ Epigram 19, the coronation ode, is a poem of praise, a panegyric that masterfully utilizes classical conventions to draw attention to the qualities that a new ruler should strive to embody. In classical usage, this type of poem is a "branch of epic" whose "real subject . . . is the *optimus princeps*."⁷ Throughout, the ode focuses greater attention on England and the English people than on Henry himself, but in a way that results in sustained reflection upon the nature of good government (*imperium*) and of a safe and healthy country.

The careful, overall plan of this poem is indicated by the marginal notes that set forth the traditional divisions of the classical epideictic poem:

8–57:	[Exordium or Introduction]
58–69:	LAVS A CORPORIS DOTIBVS (Praise for Bodily Gifts)⁸
70–91:	LAVS AB ANIMI VIRTVTIBVS (Praise for Virtues of the Soul)
92–115:	LAVS A REBVS GESTIS (Praise for Achievements)
116–19:	LAVS A LITTERIS (Praise for Learning)
120–57:	RES GESTAS PERSEQVITVR (Praise of Achievements Continued)
158–91:	LAVS REGINAE (Praise of the Queen)

---

² So Tudor historian Edward Hall describes Henry at the opening of Henry's third year of rule (30).

³ Gunn 28; Great Britain, *Letters and Papers of Henry VIII* 1, nos. 156 and 230.

⁴ For Henry's conscious imitation of England's most famous warrior king, see Scarisbrick 23; Gunn 36–37; Guy 2008 47 and 1988 41.

⁵ See the third and fourth epigraphs at the beginning of Chapter 1.

⁶ More's close friend John Holt served as Henry's tutor from 1502 to 1504; More's fellow humanist Lord Mountjoy was "Henry's companion of studies and the mentor of his teenage years, . . . perhaps the man who knew the young king best" (Starkey 173–79, 282ff.).

⁷ Garrison 82, 62.

⁸ These marginal notes in capitals are given only in the margins of the hand-illustrated copy presented to Henry VIII. See *CW* 3.2, 43–44 and the commentary at 19/56–58. Hereafter, page and line references for the coronation ode in text and notes are from *CW* 3.2.

Like the traditional form at its best, the content is full of surprises. Those few who know well that form have recognized how More follows it artfully so that what appears to be "uncharacteristic, unadulterated flattery" and "naive optimism" is in reality "subtly subversive."[9] As David Rundle perceptively points out, the "three methods used by More to create ambivalence within his poems" are "ambiguous Latin phrasing," the "equivocal use of classical examples," and "the barbed or double-edged comment."[10]

But more than writing an ingenious or ambiguous poem, Thomas More was presenting to young Henry the boldly subversive idea that "the *optimus princeps* [i]s a man of peace" rather than a man of war.[11]

The first surprise for the reader unaware of More's classical models is that, right from the opening lines, the major focus is on England, not Henry VIII, and the poem opens (as it will close) with direct address to "Anglia":

If ever there was a day, England, if ever there was a time for you to give thanks to those above,[12] this is that happy day.[13]

What causes such an outburst of joy addressed to England itself? The principal reasons are given next:

This day is a turning point [*meta*][14] of our slavery, the beginning of our liberty, the end of sadness, the source of joy.[15]

---

[9] Rundle 1995 67 and 1998 167. See also James Garrison's important study of the panegyric tradition; he points out that More's coronation ode marks "the beginning of the panegyrical tradition in England" (69–70).

[10] Rundle 1995 69.

[11] Garrison argues that this ode "indirectly defines the *optimus princeps* as a man of peace" (74) seeking "national reconciliation" (172–73).

[12] For More's characteristic invocation of *supera,* often ironic, see *Richard III:* as invoked by Edward IV at CW 2, 330/21, 334/8, 444/26; as invoked by Richard at 340/8, 480/21 (praying that heaven deprive him of his kingdom and his life if he stops thinking of the genuine commonwealth); as invoked by the cardinal and some bishops at 364/19 and 23; as invoked by the queen at 386/27, 388/3, and 396/6; as invoked by Stanley's servant at 416/5; as invoked by Hastings at 418/22; when Penker's hearers think *supera* punish Penker, 434/2; when the narrator says the queen was too dear to *supera* for her prayers to be answered, 448/3; as invoked by Buckingham at 464/12, 466/25, 476/16. More also uses the term repeatedly in his *Declamation in Reply to Lucian's* Tyrannicide, CW 3.1, 102/7; 122/6, 14, 21; 124/4, 28; 126/1.

[13] 19/8–10: "Si qua dies unquam, si quod fuit Anglia tempus, / Gratia quo superis esset agenda tibi, / Haec est illa dies. . . ."

[14] A *meta* is "a cone-shaped turning-post at either end of a race track" (*OLD*).

[15] 19/12–13: "Meta haec seruitij est, haec libertatis origo, / Tristitiae finis, laetitiaequa caput."

Liberty, happiness, and the end of slavery have begun. Why? Because this day "appoints to rule" (*in regem praeficit*) one who is "worthy of power" (*imperio dignus*).[16] In this first use of the word *imperium*, who does the appointing, and what is the extent of the power? Is it the heavens that appoint and give absolute authority? In other words, is the narrator assuming a view of divine right? Or what are the alternatives? The narrator of *Richard III* will state unambiguously[17] that the "absolute and supreme *potestas* in England is Parliament,"[18] although that narrator refrains from saying anything directly about *imperium*.

The coronation ode continues with its focus on the universal joy now present in England with the end of Henry VII's oppression. That joy has arisen because of the end of "our long distress" (19) and is experienced by every major segment of society: the general population is exuberant because it is now "free" (*liber*);[19] the "nobility . . . now lifts its head, now rejoices in such a king, and has proper reason for rejoicing"[20] (26–29); the merchants are also now happy, "heretofore deterred by numerous taxes" (30–31). Why are *all* happy? The laws are again in force (32–33); advantages are hoped to come (34–35); possessions are now safe (35–41);[21] fear of spies and informers is now gone[22] (42–45). Whatever the particular reason, joy and goodwill are universal and are not dependent on rank or condition. As a result, "the people gather together,

---

[16] The verb used here, *praeficit*, will appear again in Epigram 198, line 29, in the poem whose title is most closely tied to *Utopia's*; Epigram 198's title is "Qvis optimvs reipvblicae statvs." *Utopia's* actual title is "De optimo repvblicae / statv deqve / noua insula Vtopia libellus uere aureus, / nec minus salutaris quam festiuus, / clarissimi disertissimique uiri THOMAE MORI / inclytae ciuitatis Londinensis ciuis / & Vicecomitis" (*CW* 4, 1/1–7). To consider More's understanding of the term *imperium*, see www.thomasmorestudies.org/IndicesofLatinTerms.

[17] Or is the narrator stating a position so unbelievable that we are to see irony, as Kinney and Sylvester seem to suggest (*CW* 15, 320/22–23, commentary for *CW* 2, 6/14)?

[18] *CW* 15, 320/22–23: "Parliamenti cuius apud Anglos summa atque absoluta potestas est."

[19] This term will come up rather frequently in the poems seen in later chapters.

[20] What is that "proper reason"? We are not told directly.

[21] This reason that is given most emphasis is reminiscent of Cicero's statements that "it is the peculiar function of the state and the city to guarantee to every man the free and undisturbed control of his own particular property" and that "there is nothing that upholds a government more powerfully than its [financial] credit" (*De Officiis* 2.78 and 84). In *Utopia*, the character Morus will defend this position. See especially *CW* 4, 106/3–12.

[22] Compare with Tacitus, *Annales* 2.50, and Suetonius, *Nero* 10.1. As Rundle points out, "The poet forms a strikingly Tacitean image of the old order, where the wicked but unjust had control and the innocent feared informers" (1995 71).

every age, both sexes, and all ranks" (46) and shout enthusiastically
"on all sides" as Henry "undertakes, under happy auspices, the rule of
Britain" (49).

This new happiness comes in part from "weigh[ing] their earlier losses
against the advantages to come" (35),[23] and because they no longer have
to fearfully "lurk in their homes" (47). Instead of fear and suspicion
arising from the "bribery and tyranny" and the policies of "fiscal terror-
ism" that marked Henry VII's reign,[24] goodwill and love are the people's
attitude toward their new king. Therefore, they are eager to see him
(48–56) whom "nature has shaped [*finxit*],[25] to be lovable [26] (57). With
remarkable candor, this coronation ode sets forth at length the peoples'
complaints against Henry VII – so much so that More later feared for his
own safety and life when attention was drawn to those bold attacks on a
king by a subject.[27]

Unstated, in the midst of this outpouring of joy, is the important
question: even if nature has shaped or designed this young king to be
lovable, would he remain so? That Henry has an "inherent" *humanitas*
that is lovable at age eighteen does not preclude its degeneration into
immanitas.[28] As More's Epigram 198 observes:

A king in his first year is always very mild indeed, and so every year the consul
will be a like a new king. Over a long time a greedy king will gnaw away at
his people. If a consul is evil, there is hope of improvement. I am not swayed
by the well-known fable which recommends that one endure the well-fed fly lest
a hungry one take its place. It is a mistake to believe that a greedy king can be
satisfied; such a leech never leaves flesh until it is drained. (198/16–23)

Abruptly, wholly unexpectedly, these lines introduce an elected "consul"
as an alternative to the hereditary king; earlier the same poem showed

---

[23] See Epigram 113 for a development of the same idea.

[24] Starkey 246 and 264.

[25] For the importance of this term, see previous chapters and www.thomasmorestudies.org/
IndicesofLatinTerms.

[26] See Cicero's description of the ideal ruler as one who administers power in such a way
"that those under his rule desire no other power than his" (*Epistulae ad Quintum fratrem*
1.1.22).

[27] See the following lines, for example, that make allegations against Henry VII for slavery
(12–13), for harm to nobility, merchants, and laws (26–34, 100–15), for danger to
property (40–42), for using spies and informers (43–44, 96–99), and for causing fear to
have public assemblies (46–47).

[28] See earlier chapters for the necessary roles of love and friendship in a healthy body politic.
This focus on the lovable character of the ruler is also present in More's prefatory letter
to the coronation poems, which refers to young Henry's "inherent *humanitas*." Even in
Richard III one finds acknowledgments that the king needs the people's love (e.g., *CW*
15, 442/18–21, 448/15–16).

election to be the result of "sound deliberation" while heredity is the result of "blind chance" (Epigram 198/13).

But to sum up Epigram 19's unusually long exordium of fifty lines, over one-fourth of the poem: it focuses upon the joy of the English people arising from their newly regained *libertas* and their new hope of prosperity and protection arising from a new king's promises. These promises, together with painful memories of past hardships, are the reasons for the "new affection" for the new and untested king.[29]

If up to this point in the poem Henry VIII might be associated with an ideal king and Henry VII with the oppressive king, the next section immediately raises disturbing doubts about the young, inexperienced adolescent. It simultaneously continues to depict an alternate image of *humanitas*.

The second conventional part of this epideictic poem, the "Praise for Bodily Gifts," begins with an allusion to King Saul of the Old Testament – that handsome, most tall, and promising man who was consecrated king as a youth but who eventually rebelled against God.[30] This thought-provoking comparison is another reminder that young Henry VIII had yet to prove himself in serving God and country.

The next comparisons are to amorous Venus[31] (64) and then, jarringly unexpected, to the warrior-king Achilles, who "drag[s] Hector behind his Thessalian steeds" (68–69). Comparing youthful and handsome Henry with amorous Venus seems conventional enough, although the ode will later raise questions in the way it draws attention again to this aspect of Henry's character. But the second comparison is shocking: why link Henry with an action presented by Homer as so cruel, so vengeful, and so contrary to the ways of gods and men that the gods decide to intervene? This image of Achilles as the obsessed and inhumane warrior is reinforced by references to Henry's favorite pastime of battle games, such as jousting – charging "greedily [*auide*] with leveled lances"[32]

---

[29] Line 53 draws our attention to the people's *affectu nouo*. See More's reference to the dangers of being "inebriated with affection" (*Ebrius affectu*) in Epigram 224/5 on Herod and Herodias.

[30] 1 Kings 10:23, as noted in the commentary of CW 3.2, 19/58. By the end of More's life, King Saul becomes a favorite example of the unfaithful king. See, for example, CW 5, 336/19; CW 8, 50/15–21; CW 12, 62/7–31; especially CW 13, 112/10–113/10, 213/25–30 and CW 14, 153/5–155/2, 649/3–7, which indicate that More was thinking about Saul in a special way in connection with the English monarch.

[31] Consider the connotation of Venus in More's other epigrams: 8, 47, 54, 62, 65, 129, 253.

[32] The usual definition of this term is "greedily" with the connotations of "having an immoderate appetite" or "insatiable" (*OLD*). As Rundle points out, the poem establishes

(60–63) – or to Henry's "skilled hand" (60), which would require long practice to acquire.[33]

This emphasis on skills of war contrasts with the next section's emphasis on peace and the skills of ruling. Section 3 is a twenty-four-line "Praise for Virtues of the Soul" (70–93), which ends with another jarring and unexpected statement, followed by the most unbelievable statement of the poem, which is another strategic statement about *imperium*.

Central to this section is "the skill he has in the art of rule" (line 82). This skill is explained in the following list of qualities needed by the good king, a list that is not flattery but conventional epideictic praise ordered to instruct and to motivate:

Ah, if only nature would permit that, like his body, the outstanding excellence of his mind be visible to the eye. Nay but in fact his virtue does shine forth from his very face; his countenance bears the open message of a good heart, revealing how ripe the wisdom that dwells in his judicious mind, how profound the calm of his untroubled breast, how he bears his lot and manages it whether it be good or bad, how great his care for modest chastity. (70–77)

Modest chastity is, of course, a hope for youthful Henry – as are all the other virtues listed in this portrait of an ideal ruler. But Henry's "ripe wisdom" and "the calm of his untroubled breast" have clearly been questioned by the previous references to Achillean rage and Henry's avid interest in war games, an interest actively cultivated by Henry VII after his son Arthur's death.[34] With the image of revengeful Achilles in mind, we continue with a catalog of virtues culminating in justice (identified with the art of rule) and *pietas*:

How serene the clemency that warms his gentle heart, how far removed from arrogance of mind. . . . But his justice, the skill he has in the art of ruling, his sense of responsibility [*pietate*][35] in the treatment of his people – these can easily be

---

"choler to be Henry's dominant humour" and the comparison to Achilles is one of a "series of backhanded compliments" (1995, 70).

33 For an account of Henry's "jousting mania," which began in 1506, see Starkey 2008 221–23, 320–24, 346–55. See also Epigram 22. For King Henry's "passion for military games," which would eventually take place "almost every day of the week," see Graves, who also points out that Henry would enjoy "dressing up on various occasions as Hercules, St. George, and other heroic figures" (14).

34 For the personal role that Henry VII took "to train and mould his son" in light of Henry VII's "principal concern [of] security" and for the role of "martial sports," see Starkey especially 187–192 and 230–33. See also Epigram 22's statement that Henry's celebration of his coronation with the beautiful spectacle of dangerous war games "is appropriate to [Henry's] character."

35 The sovereign virtue of Virgil's Aeneas; see note 11 of Chapter 3 in contrast to note 62 of this chapter.

discerned from our faces, these must be perceived from the prosperity we enjoy. (78–79, 82–85)

The test of the ruler's art or skill is, as the English people have already indicated, their happiness and prosperity as well as their liberty and peace,[36] which these next lines emphasize:

In that we are treated thus and are gaining our liberty, in that fear, harm, danger, grief have vanished, while peace, ease, joy, and laughter have returned – therein is revealed the excellence of our distinguished ruler [*principis*]. (86–89)

Here we see that the "excellence of [the] distinguished *princeps*" is "proved" by criteria that focus, as do the opening fifty-seven lines, on the good of the people, not on the ruler himself. It is "proved" insofar as the English people "are gaining [their] liberty, in that fear, harm, danger, grief have vanished, while peace, ease, joy, and laughter have returned" (86–89) – clearly focusing on the entire body of the English people rather than the one now serving as its head.[37]

So far then, most important to *Anglia* seem to be "the prosperity we enjoy" (85), "gaining our liberty" (86), the vanishing of "fear, harm, danger, grief" (87), and the return of "peace, ease, joy, and laughter" (88) – all those things one would hope for in a "Golden Age," rather than England's usual Iron Age of war.

After this hopeful and demanding prescription for the good ruler comes the second jarring and unexpected statement. This surprising couplet gives a warning that would prove prophetic – or that would simply corroborate what More's other early writings will observe about history:

Unlimited power has a tendency to weaken good minds, and that even in the case of very gifted men. (90–91)

This two-line "interruption" and warning parallels the two-line "interruption" seen at lines 68–69.

Just as abruptly, this section turns again to an opening that is typically Morean in its thought-provoking twist, a twist that once again calls into question all that has been praised in young King Henry:

But howsoever dutiful/godly [*pius*] he was before, power [*imperium*] has brought to our prince a character worthy of power [*imperio*]. (92–93)

---

[36] Another way that author More seems to lead us to question these claims is by Epigram 21's misquotation of Plato in a therefore questionable prediction that Henry will bring a "golden age" of peace and prosperity.

[37] See Epigram 112.

How could power "bring" a character worthy of power? Character takes years to forge; Henry is young, and he has come to the throne quickly because of his older brother's early death and without the education that his brother received. For anyone with experience, these lines are simply unbelievable.[38] The experienced person would object with an opposite formulation: only a well-tested, proven character would make one deserving of rule.[39]

This expected objection is then "answered" by the opening of the next section, but in another unexpected – and dubious – way:

For he has provided promptly on his first day such advantages as few [kings] have granted in extreme old age. (94–95)

What are these "advantages" that the adolescent king has provided? He arrests and punishes those guilty of crimes, fosters trade, lightens the "overhard duties" imposed on merchants, respects the rights of nobles, and uses goodness or learning rather than money as the basis for getting public offices (96–107). Then comes a summary of these eleven lines of "advantages": "Our prince without delay has restored to the laws their ancient force and dignity (for they had been perverted so as to subvert the realm)" (108–9). That last parenthesis is another strong criticism of Henry VII, who in old age had no longer shown respect for England's laws, giving historical force to those lines of Epigram 198: "Over a long time a greedy king will gnaw away at his people" (18).

The "advantages" that young Henry VIII promises to bring are his plan to obey and execute England's laws. Why did Henry VIII change the policy of Henry VII, thus putting "his country [*patriam*] before his father [*patria*]" (115)? The reason is suggested in the shortest section of the poem that follows, "Praise of Learning" (116–19): Henry has had the advantage of natural gifts "enhanced by a liberal education" and "steeped in philosophy's own precepts." The surprising brevity of this four-line section leads one to wonder just how "steeped" in philosophy and liberal education the new and young warrior-king actually could be.

---

[38] Shakespeare's prodigal Prince Hal makes a similar claim to explain his astonishing reformation from merry wastrel to honored warrior king. But see Erasmus's *Instructions for a Christian Prince* to appreciate the rare occurrence of the good ruler even with the best of education. More's own awareness of this rarity is seen clearly at *CW* 5, 337/25–29, 14–16.

[39] For example, consider lord chancellor and Cardinal Morton's habit of testing character described in *Utopia*, *CW* 4, 58/23ff.

When the next section on "Praise of Achievements"[40] continues from line 120, the first achievement is put in an oddly negative way: the new king "could have inspired fear" like his father, and he "could have gathered from this source immense riches" like his father, but instead he did away with the "evil" that caused the "whole people" "distressing fear" (120–25).

After 127 lines explaining England's new joy, a joy "heretofore unknown since *Anglia* has never had such a king before,"[41] the narrator addresses Henry directly: "O *princeps*, terror to your proud enemies but not to your own people, it is your enemies who fear you; we revere and love you" (128–29). But of course, Henry is just eighteen; he is eager to be popular as a new ruler and, as a consequence, "in his first year is always very mild indeed" (Epigram 198/16). Up to this point in his sheltered life, there had been nothing whatsoever that would lead anyone to fear him.

In the following sentences, the narrator continues addressing Henry directly, advising or warning or instructing him of a political principle that will be seen repeatedly in *Richard III, Utopia,* and other *Epigrammata*:[42] "[Y]our people's love . . . will hedge you round in peace and safety" (132–33), not their fear, or Henry's force or wealth or might. Such is the power of the ruler who has his people's love, rather than their fear; such is the policy of the ruler who wishes to avoid the "common source" of civil wars.[43] Regarding threats from external neighbors, "no one is afraid, provided that *Anglia* is in concord" (135). What keeps *Anglia* in concord? "Most important" is the lack of controversy about Henry's "right and title" to rule (138–39) – an issue of enormous importance that More states in passing here but will explore at length in *Richard III*. As *Richard III* will reveal, English factions and civil wars most commonly involve competing hereditary claims to the throne.

---

[40] *Res Gesta Persequitur.*

[41] CW 3.2, 19.156–157: "nouo si gaudeat Anglia more, / Cum qualis nunquam rexerat ante, regat."

[42] See Epigram 120: "Not fear (accompanied by hatred), not towering palaces, not wealth wrung from a plundered people protects a king. . . . He will be safe who so rules his people that they judge none other would be more useful to them"; Epigram 112: "A kingdom in all its parts is like a man; it is held together by love [*amore*]"; Epigram 111: "The *pius princeps* . . . is father to the whole kingdom." At *Utopia*, CW 4, 94/16–30, 90/18–21, and 56/14–16, similar language is used explaining the relationship between peace, a prosperous and happy people, and the ruler worthy of "imperium." In *Richard III*, we come to appreciate the principle by seeing the tragic consequences of the opposite, that is, of fear, mistrust, and violence.

[43] In contrast to the advice given here and in the deathbed speech of Edward IV in *Richard III*, Utopia deliberately governs by fear, as we will see.

As if to hurriedly move on from this uncomfortable point, the narrator continues:

And anyway the anger of the people, common source of civil disturbance, a wicked thing, is even more remote from you. To all your citizens[44] you yourself alone are so dear that no man could be dearer to himself.[45] (142–45)

These lines use the same language that will appear in Epigram 112: the ruler as head of a united body of citizens, united by mutual affection and working together as one.

But what happens when angry outbursts arise from powerful warlords? (Such outbursts were continuous occurrences in England, given the factional centers of competing power.) The poem's answer draws attention again to Henry's youthful and untested stage of life:

But if perchance wrath were to bring powerful chieftains of war, your nod [*nutu tuo*] will promptly put an end to that wrath, such reverence for your sacred majesty have your virtues deservedly brought forth [*merito peperere*].[46] (146–49)

What tried virtues could this eighteen-year-old have shown to merit such reverence? He was an eighteen-year-old who had never been to war and had never ruled. To say that a "nod" from such a person would end the kind of wrath we will see in *Richard III* is ironic indeed, powerfully so.[47] Powerful too is the irony seen in *Utopia* when Utopian priests are said to have a similar power.[48] But the irony, heightened by the light shed by the issues raised in *Richard III* and *Utopia,* continues:

And whatever virtues your ancestors had, these are yours too, not excelled in ages past. For you, sire, have your father's wisdom, you have your mother's kindly strength, the devout intelligence of your paternal grandmother,[49] the noble heart of your mother's father.[50] (150–55)

---

44 The Yale translators have "your subjects" for *ciuibus*.
45 "Ast magis abs te etiam est populi procul ira, tumultus / Impia ciuilis quae solet esse caput. / Ciuibus ipse tuis tam charus es omnibus unus, / Vt nemo possit charior esse sibi."
46 "Quod si forte duces committeret ira potentes, / Soluetur nutu protinus illa tuo. / Tanta tibi est maiestatis reuerentia sacrae, / Virtutes merito quam peperere tuae."
47 See Chapter 11 for other "ruling with a nod" references in Homer, Virgil, Cicero, and More. This metaphor goes back to Homer who shows Zeus, Athena, and Odysseus as so ruling – because of their reputation for proven power and proven success.
48 See Chapter 9.
49 Margaret Beaufort.
50 "Quae tibi sunt, fuerant patrum quaecunque tuorum. / Secula prisca quibus nil habuere prius. / Est tibi namque tui princeps prudentia patris. / Estque tibi matris dextra benigna tuae. / Est tibi mens auiae, mens relligiosa paternae. / Est tibi materni nobile pectus aui."

Yes, sons often learn "whatever virtues" his parents and grandparents taught him. But how wise was Henry VII? The critical comments about Henry VII's rule in this poem are so great that they would, in the future, lead to serious threats to More's life and court career when public attention would be drawn to them.[51] And conspicuously absent from this particular list of ancestors is Henry VIII's grandmother Elizabeth Woodville, queen of Edward IV and leading protagonist of More's *Richard III,* a work begun not long after this poem. What qualities or traits did Henry VIII learn or inherit from her?

With these many questions in mind, we look again at the troubling couplet that concludes this section by giving two strong qualifications of praise:

What wonder, then, if England rejoices in a fashion heretofore unknown, since she has such a king as she never had before.[52]

If England has *never* before been able to rejoice this way and if England has *never* had such a king as this one now promises to be, how likely is it that Henry VIII will indeed be the first?

The final section of this epideictic poem is "Praise of the Queen," in which Catherine of Aragon is said to have the piety of the Sabine women (166), the chaste love of Alcestis, the good judgment of Tanaquil, the eloquence of Cornelia, and the loyalty (*fides*) of Penelope. But each of these examples has its dark side: "the rape of the Sabine women, the intrigue and assassination of Tarquinius Priscus, the revolt of Cornelia's

---

[51] In 1520, just two years after joining Henry VIII's court, Germanus Brixius accused More of disloyalty to the English monarchy. As the secretary of the French queen and supposedly a fellow humanist, Brixius received an international hearing when he strongly criticized "More's impudence in slandering the father as he sets out to praise the son" and in "defam[ing] and excoriat[ing] Henry's sire as one who bore no love for equity and the law, in whose reign England took on the yoke of servility" (*CW* 3.2, 493). That accusation was based on More's coronation ode, published in 1518 with More's collected epigrams. In self-defense, More wrote that Henry VII's "ill health was the cause of the failure for several years before his death" (641). Of course, there was not a hint of this reason in the coronation ode. When French patriot Brixius publicized his accusations in 1520, More recognized Brixius's actions as a genuine threat to his very life. More called Brixius's accusations "criminal," intended to bring "dire peril" upon More from Henry VIII (649). Upon consulting political friends, More was told he had to defend himself. If Brixius had been more attentive to More's characteristic irony, however, he would have found much more damning evidence in this collection than More's 1509 attack on King Henry VII.

[52] "Quid mirum ergo, nouo si gaudeat Anglia more, / Cum qualis nunquam rexerat ante, regat?"

sons, the slaughter of Penelope's suitors and the maidservants."[53] And
if Catherine is the loyal Penelope, is Henry the wandering Ulysses, ever
seeking new adventures and prizes?[54] After these disturbing allusions, the
poem ends with the hope that the crown can transfer to "their son's son
and their descendants thereafter" – drawing attention again to the ever-
present difficulty of the primitive transfer of power based on heredity.

To summarize, one could say that More's coronation ode sets forth an
alternate image of the good ruler for an adolescent king who has not yet
proved his character but who is enamored with war. That kings change,
More will make clear in Epigram 198, which points out, as we have seen,
that a "king in his first year is always very mild indeed," but that over "a
long time a greedy king will gnaw away at his people" and that it is "a
mistake to believe that a greedy king can be satisfied; such a leech never
leaves flesh until it is drained."

That Henry could become such a king was recognized by More as
shown by More's early writings, by his reluctance to join Henry's service,
by the letter More prefaced to the coronation ode – and by details we have
seen, such as More's comparison of Henry to Achilles. Having known
Henry at least since 1499,[55] More waited until 1518 before agreeing
to work for Henry, and only after assurances by many fellow English
humanists,[56] as well as by both Wolsey and Henry himself, that new
royal policies were in place promoting international peace.[57]

[53] CW 3.2, commentary on 19/176–79, which also points out the further "dark back-
ground" in the allusion to "Ariadne, who was cruelly abandoned by Theseus."
[54] See note 19 of Chapter 5.
[55] In 1499, on Erasmus's second visit to England, More walked with Erasmus to fellow
humanist Mountjoy's father-in-law's neighboring estate to visit nine-year-old Prince
Henry, and he played a practical joke on Erasmus with young Henry's help. See Scarisbrick 13–14 and Chambers 70. For Erasmus's account of this practical joke, which left
him annoyed and "slightly indignant with More," see CWE 9, Letter 299; EE 1341A;
Letter to Johann von Botzheim.
[56] In EE 855, Erasmus lists seven leading humanists in Henry's court of 1518: Thomas
Linacre, Cuthbert Tunstall, Thomas More, Richard Pace, William Mountjoy, John Colet,
and John Stokesley. Erasmus marvels to Paolo Bombace that "the men who have most
influence with [Henry VIII and Queen Catherine] are those who excel in the humanities
[*bonis literis*] and in integrity and wisdom [*integritate...prudentia*]" (CWE 6, Letter
855/36–37).
[57] For Henry VIII's early "Renewal of the Hundred Years War" and the boldness of
the humanists' "protest against the bootless, pestilential, and scandalous war among
European states," see Scarisbrick 21ff. For Henry's early "imperial" ambitions, see Guy
1988 105ff. More's awareness of these imperial ambitions is shown by his addressing
Henry in the 1509 coronation ode as the "Most Powerful King of Britain and France";
only in the presentation copy does More ever refer to Henry as king of France (CW 3.2,

More's clear recognition of the "serious risks" of tyranny with young Henry VIII came from a firsthand knowledge of his character,[58] along with a firm understanding of the perennial dangers of tyranny and power, as Tacitus pointed out about Emperor Tiberius's son: what hope was there for this youth tempted by the same "absolute power" that had "transformed and deranged" the man whom Augustus Caesar carefully selected and prepared?[59] As Starkey shows in his recent biography of Henry VIII, King Henry VII took over the education of his heir once his son Arthur died and redesigned that education in light of the realities of a rule based on usurpation and widespread concerns about Henry VII's tyranny.[60]

The prefatory letter of these epigrams, addressed to "Princeps" Henry, opens with "I fear"[61] and goes on to speak of "Princeps" Tiberius and his coldhearted attitude [62] toward citizens fearful of that emperor's tyrannical power.[63] More's ever-present awareness of the power exercised by tyrants typified by Tiberius would be evident throughout his life. Four years before writing this letter and the coronation ode, More had invited Erasmus to compete with him in writing disputations in response to Lucian's *Tyrannicida*.[64] In 1519, therefore, Erasmus would remark from

96/variant 1–4). In all publications of the epigrams and in both *Richard III* and *Utopia* author More refers to Henry as king of England alone. Tyrant Richard, however, in a context showing the independent sovereignties of both the English and French people, claims for himself "the government of the two realms of England and France" (*CW* 15, 480/15).

[58] *CWE* 7, Letter 999/236 and *EE* 999/215: "grauibus periculis"; consider also *Corr.* 111 (Letter 57: "To John Fisher) or *SL* 94.

[59] See Tacitus's *Annals,* a book More knew well: "If Tiberius, in spite of all his experience, has been transformed and deranged by absolute power [*vi dominationis*], will [the boy] Gaius do better?" (6.48). As we will see, More in Epigrams 243–44 sets forth Henry's Caesar-like "lust for power."

[60] Starkey especially 187ff.

[61] The opening words of this 1509 letter are "Vereor, illustrissime princeps" (*CW* 3.2, 96/5). The Tiberius reference occurs at *CW* 3.2, 96/17.

[62] Here More refers to Suetonius's *Tiberius* 52, where the emphasis is on the fact that Tiberius "had a father's affection neither for his own son Drusus nor his adopted son Germanicus" – nor for his own people. Throughout his account, Suetonius emphasizes Emperor Tiberius's "cruel and cold-blooded character"; see, for example, section 57.

See the fine analysis of this passage by Rundle (1995 68–69); he concludes: "Behind the facade of an uncritical attitude to Tiberius, there are darker implications of an emperor without *pietas*" (69).

[63] For a clear-sighted account of the power of fear, see the "Petition for Free Speech" that More gave while Speaker of the House of Commons in 1523 (Roper 12–16 or *TMSB* 24–25).

[64] Erasmus reports this contest just before giving his famous "explanation" of *Utopia:* "*Utopia* he published with the purpose of showing the reasons for the shortcomings of a

firsthand experience on More's "special hatred of tyranny" and love of *libertas*.[65] Most famously, fourteen years later, when invited by the English bishops to accompany them to the coronation of Anne Boleyn, Thomas More refused with a lengthy tale from the life of Tiberius. More said that their invitation reminded him of a beast fable concerning a certain emperor.[66] There was, he recounted,

an emperor that had ordained a law that whosoever committed a certain offense (which I now remember not) except it were a virgin, should suffer the pains of death, such a reverence had he for virginity. Now so it happened that the first committer of that offense was indeed a virgin, whereof the Emperor hearing, was in no small perplexity, as he that by some example [gladly] would have had that law to have been put in execution. Whereupon when his Council had sat long, solemnly debating this case, suddenly arose there up one of his Council, a good plain man, among them, and said, "Why make you so much ado, my lords, about so small a matter? Let her first be deflowered, and then after may she be devoured."

This story is from Tiberius's reign of terror, involving the imprisonment, rape, and murder of Sejanus's young daughter – which the learned bishops would have known. But lest any of them would miss the point, More continued:

And so, though your lordships have in the matter of the matrimony hitherto kept yourselves pure virgins, yet take good heed, my lords, that you keep your virginity still. For some there be that, by procuring your lordships first at the coronation to be present, and next to preach for the setting forth of it, and finally to write books to all the world in defense thereof, are desirous to deflower you; and when they have deflowered you, then will they not fail soon after to devour you. "Now my lords it lieth not in my power but that they may devour me; but God being my good lord, I will provide that they shall never deflower me." (*TMSB* 44)

More knew well the face of tyranny, and in this tale told at the end of his life, he linked the tyrant Tiberius with Henry VIII, as he did early in life.

In that same letter prefaced to Epigrams 19–23, More praises Henry for his "inherent *humanitas*"[67] and concludes the letter praising young

commonwealth; but he represented the English commonwealth in particular because he had studied it and knew it best." (Vtopiam hoc consilio aedidit, vt indicaret quibus rebus fiat vt minus commode habeant respublicae; sed Britannicam potissimum effinxit, quam habet penitus perspectam cognitamque) (*EE* 999/254–56 or *CWE* 7, Letter 999/277–79 or *TMSB* 11).

[65] *EE* 999/88–94; *CWE* 7, Letter 999/ 89ff.; *TMSB* 6.

[66] Tacitus, *Annales* 6.5.9. See also the beast fable of the tyrant-lion that Morton tells at the end of the English version of More's *Richard III* (*CW* 2, 93/1–10).

[67] *CW* 3.2, 96/13.

Princeps Henry[68] for a quality "strange and rare for kings": the quality of being "most beloved."[69]

---

[68] More uses the term *princeps* only three times in this letter: in his opening and closing address to Henry and in his reference to Tiberius.

[69] CW 3.2, 98/3: *amatissime.*

7

Political Poems of 1509–1516

Proposing Self-Government by "Sound Deliberation"

WHAT IS THE BEST FORM OF THE RESPUBLICA?

A senator is elected by the people to rule; a king attains this end by being born. In the one case blind chance rules; in the other, sound deliberation.

Thomas More, Epigram 198/1, 12–13[1]

THE GOOD "FIRST CITIZEN" IS A FATHER NOT A MASTER

The godly first citizen [*pius princeps*] will never lack children/freemen.[2] He is father to the whole realm. Therefore the most successful first citizen abounds with as many freemen as citizens.

Thomas More, Epigram 111[3]

In every human being, "reason ought to reign like a king,"[4] and in every *respublica*, "sound deliberation" is the best way to rule.[5] But every human

---

[1] "Qvis optimvs reipvb. statvs. / ... Alter ut eligitur populo, sic nascitur alter. / Sors hic caeca regit, certum ibi consilium" (*CW* 3.2).

[2] *Liberos* means both "children" and "freemen."

[3] "BONVM PRINCIPEM ESSE PATREM / NON DOMINVM / Princeps pius nunquam carebit liberis. / Totius est regni pater. / Princeps abundat ergo felicissimus, / Tot liberis, quot ciuibus" (*CW* 3.2).

[4] So More wrote in his last work, after an unusually active life: *CW* 14, 509/2–3, but this classical principle appears throughout his works, even from his earliest. It is a commonplace in Plato, Aristotle, and Cicero; see notes 34–36 of Chapter 2 and note 35 of Chapter 3.

[5] That "certum consilium" is a deliberately provocative phrase, consider Aristotle's, Cicero's, and Quintilian's positions that *consilium* can be probable but not certain (*Nicomachean Ethics* 1112a19–1113a14, 1140a–1145a12; *De Finibus* 2.43–44, *De Officiis* 2.7–8; *Institutio Oratoria* 6.5.3). In this context, nonetheless, the sense of *certum* can

being is free[6] and can "tak[e] counsel [*consilium*] of . . . desire"[7] and thus
freely "take from desire" a "plan . . . reckless and shameless,"[8] so reckless,
so shameless that fratricide and generations of civil war have occurred
since the beginning of recorded history.

For reason to reign, art must help, or so Lucian shows through his skillful use of humor. More does the same in his collection of 260 epigrams.[9]
Though intended to be published with the first edition of *Utopia*,[10] the
epigrams were actually published only with the second, thus providing
another level of dialectical engagement for the attentive reader of More's
puzzling masterpiece.

The 260 epigrams display the wide and humorous and all-too-familiar
range of human irrationality. Many are comic sketches translated from
the *Greek Anthology*, and More's original poems are often reminiscent
of Terence, the Roman comedian he loved. Within this large collection,
however, is a smaller one of distinctively political epigrams,[11] the only

also be translated as "sound," "genuine," or "reliable" – yet see note 79 of Chapter
1 and More's own English translations of *certum* as "sure" at CW 2, [English] 67/32
or 52/13ff., and Aquinas's explanation of the sense in which *consilium* can be *certum*
(*Summa Theologiae* 1–2.15.6c and 1–2.57.4).

[6] So important is this principle to More that, after resigning from public life, he wrote
a commentary on Genesis showing that human beings "were left in the hand of their
own free will and liberty" (CW 13, 4/17–18) and that human beings were not given
"dominion" over each other but, through reason, were to "give . . . good counsel" (21/6).
These issues of human nature and the roles of reason, will, and freedom became major
points of disagreement with Luther and his followers.

[7] "[T]aking counsel of his desire" is More's English version (CW 2, [English] 61/28) of the
Latin version(s), "amorem consulens suum" at CW 15, 440/3 or "ab amore consilium
mutuatus" at CW 2, [Latin] 61/28. Cicero also cautions that the cause of error is often
judging with desire and not with "ratio atque consilium" (*De Finibus* 2.115).

[8] In the Latin version of CW 2, 61/28 ("ab amore consilium mutuatus"), More is alluding to the famous scene in Livy 30.12.19 where Roman commander Scipio deals with
Masinissa who, "reckless and shameless" and contrary to agreement and expressed
orders, marries the wife of captive Syphax. This story of Masinissa, captive of love
("amore captivae," 12.18), is similar to Xenophon's account of how Cyrus deals
with lovestruck Araspas, who similarly violates his oath (*Education of Cyrus* 5.8–
18 and 6.31–35). Livy's portrayal shows the superiority of Scipio's art of free rule
and of friendship to that of tyrant Cyrus's extraordinary skill. As Cicero reminds us
at the beginning of his *Dream of Scipio*, Masinissa had changed because of Scipio
and remained loyal to Rome and to the Scipio family for the rest of his life (*De Re
Publica* 6.1).

[9] More has "281 extant Latin poems" (CW 3.2, 11), but 260 appear in the 1518 editions.

[10] CW 3.2, 3–4.

[11] Damian Grace's 1985 listing of "explicitly political epigrams" is CW 3.2, Epigrams
19–23, 32, 39, 45, 80, 107, 109–115, 120, 121, 142, 162, 183, 184, 198, 201, 206,
224, 226, 238, 243, 244 (although Grace gives the numbering of the earlier edition of

such collection known to exist in sixteenth-century literature.[12] This collection is not only unique but extraordinarily daring, for it does set forth a view of self-government in harmony with Cicero and not with hereditary monarchy.

Epigram 198, for example, clearly favors a senate chosen by "sound deliberation" (*certum consilium*) rather than the "blind chance" of hereditary kingship.[13] Epigram 121 declares outright that "The Consent of the People Both Bestows and Withdraws Sovereignty" and ends with the caustic questions: "Why are impotent kings so proud? Because they rule merely on sufferance?" And throughout the other major political poems in his collected Latin verse, we discover that the status of kings is repeatedly deflated, sometimes in surprisingly irreverent and humorous ways.[14]

The poem "On the King and the Peasant" (Epigram 201) gives the candid reaction of the "forest-bred peasant" who sees for the first time a king, one "resplendent with gold, escorted by a large company, and astride a tall horse." In contrast to the "rapt" attention of the "roaring crowd,"

The peasant cried out, "Where is the king? Where is the king?" And one of the bystanders replied: "There he is, the one mounted high on that horse over there." The peasant said, "Is that the king? I think you are making fun of me. To me he looks like a man in fancy dress."

This stress on the equality of human beings Erasmus considered intrinsic to More's view of *humanitas*.[15] This emphasis on equality is humorously seen in poems such as "A Funny Story about a Prince and a Peasant from Zeeland" (Epigram 206), presenting in Lucianic style the pretentions of not only kings but also those who surround him:

A prince, as he gazed at the water, sat down on a bridge, and his nobles [*primores*][16] stood respectfully about. A peasant sat down, too, but not near by, and thought himself polite because of the distance he kept. A certain courtier

---

     More's epigrams published by the University of Chicago Press). This chapter suggests
     that Epigrams 180, 181, 227, and especially 271 should be added.
[12] Editors Bradner and Lynch point out the "refreshing new range of subjects" treated in
     More's collection. "Among these topics, the most original for an epigrammatist was
     kingship [and tyranny]. In fact, we know of no other sixteenth-century poet who used
     this theme for short poems" (CW 3.2, 62). They conclude that "More's *Epigrammata*
     [is] incomparably the best book of Latin epigrams in the sixteenth century" (63).
[13] CW 3.2, Epigram 198/12–13.
[14] CW 3.2, Epigrams 39, 201, 206, 243, 244.
[15] EE 999/88 or TMSB 6.
[16] See Chapter 8 for the significance of More's names for "nobles."

got him up and said, "Peasant, do you dare to sit on the same bridge with the prince? Aren't you ashamed?" The peasant answered, "Is it wrong to sit on the same bridge? What if the bridge were ten miles long?"

The pride of courtiers and kings – and the foolish blindness accompanying that pride – is cleverly represented in More's three epigrams on lions (from the Latin for "king"). One is addressed directly "To a Courtier" (Epigram 162):[17]

You often boast to me that you have the king's ear and often have fun with him, freely [*libere*] and according to your own whims. This is like having fun with tamed lions – often it is harmless, but just as often there is fear of harm. Often he roars in rage for no known reason, and suddenly the fun becomes fatal.[18]

This simple but convincing beast fable, a genre More loved to use, moves next into the motive for such dangerous fun: the pleasure that comes from the pride beneath the boasting. As the concluding couplet puts it:

The pleasure you get is not safe enough to relieve you of anxiety. For you it is a great pleasure; for me, let my pleasure be less great – and safe.

As these playful epigrams show, More is keenly aware of the dangers in dealing with kings and tyrants. Not playful, however, are More's three epigrams on King Herod. The cruel horror of a king-turned-criminal, of a person powerful enough to act on the counsel of his unchecked desires, is set forth graphically in Epigrams 224 and 226, while Epigram 227 puts such action in the context of classical mythology:

The king's table bears a severed head and a saint's countenance dripping with hideous gore. So too King Atreus, King Thyestes' brother, served as food to Thyestes the bodies of his two sons. Similarly, to the Thracian king his queen, a loyal sister but a treacherous mother, served their murdered son, Itys.

---

[17] The other two are Epigrams 180 and 181. Compare these with More's famous words addressed to Thomas Cromwell shortly after More resigned from King Henry's service: "Master Cromwell, you are now entered into the service of a most noble, wise and liberal prince. If you will follow my poor advice, you shall, in your counsel giving unto His Grace, ever tell him what he ought to do, but never what he is able to do. So shall you show yourself a true faithful servant and a right worthy Councillor. For if a lion knew his own strength, hard were it for any man to rule him" (Roper 56–7 or *TMSB* 43).

[18] The Latin text of these last two lines recalls the alarm often repeated by English courtiers, "The indignation of the king is death": "Infremit incerta crebra *indignatio* caussa / Et subito *mors est*, ut sit secura uoluptas" (emphasis added). See, for example, Roper 71 or *TMSB* 50.

These royal horrors were best known from Seneca's *Thyestes* and Ovid's *Metamorphoses,* but the understated conclusion More draws in the final couplet is one More expresses elsewhere in his own works:

Such delicacies as these mark the tables of kings; I assure you this is not a poor man's fare.

The wealth and power that come with rule pose a positive danger, a fact of life More presents in his earliest poems on fortune and throughout his later writings. That Utopia would favor the poor garb of Franciscans and their simple fare should, therefore, be no surprise.

Despite the cruelty and horror of unchecked kings and tyrants, More has several epigrams showing powerful rulers to be ultimately equal with powerless slaves, as seen in the Greek epigram More chose to translate in his Epigram 45:

ON A DEAD SLAVE

While he lived, this man was a slave. But now, in death, he wields no less power than you, mighty Darius.

This proverbial view of the common humanity shared by all, from poor beggar to mighty ruler, is expressed in another Greek epigram More chose to translate:

Almost half of life is sleep. During that period the rich and the poor lie equal. And so, Croesus, wealthiest of kings, for almost half a lifetime Irus the beggar was your equal. (Epigram 107)

More's original variation on this theme (Epigram 114) differs from Epigram 107 in that "sleep causes the tyrant to lose not only his supposed happiness but also his personal power":[19]

THAT THE TYRANT WHILE HE SLEEPS IS NO DIFFERENT FROM THE COMMONER

Well, then, you madman, it is pride which makes you carry your head so high – because the throng bows to you on bended knee, because the people rise and uncover for you, because you have in your power the life and death of many. But whenever sleep secures your body in inactivity, then, tell me, where is this glory of yours? Then you lie, useless creature, like a lifeless log or like a recent corpse. But if you were not lying protected, like a coward, unseen indoors, your own life would be at the disposal of any man. (Epigram 114)

This bold address to the tyrant, calling him a madman and a coward, demonstrates the tone of many of these epigrams. Others, such as Epigram

---

[19] CW 3.2, 364, commentary on Epigram 114/1-12.

238 "On the Anxious Life of Rulers," dispel any illusions of bliss imagined by those thirsting for power. And as usual, More shows the essential human equality of the powerful and the commoner.

That essential equality is seen most in death, as elaborated in another original epigram by More, one in which the speaker argues that "Death, touched by pity" is the great "defender of liberty." Epigram 80 begins in this way:

DEATH UNASSISTED KILLS TYRANTS

You who have been cruelly persecuted at the hands of unjust men, take hope. Let kindly hope alleviate your sufferings. A turn of fortune will improve your state – like the sun shining through scattered clouds. Or the defender of liberty, Death, touched by pity, will put forth her hand, while the tyrant rages, and rescue you. Death will snatch him away too (the more to please you) and will lay him right before your feet.

This notion that the higher powers favor human *libertas* was also seen in More's *Declamation in Reply to Lucian's* Tyrannicide.[20] As that work did, this epigram goes on to give essential characteristics of the tyrant:

He who was so carried away by his great wealth and his empty pride, he who once upon a time amid his thronging henchmen[21] was so bold, O, he will not be fierce, will not wear an expression of pride.

These fleeting characteristics are put in perspective by the wise – and comic – vision of the poet:

He will be an object of pity, cast down from his high place, abandoned, helpless, penniless. What gift has life ever given you to compare with this gift? The tables are turned: the man once so fearsome deserves only a laugh.

Few poets have summed up tyrannical aspirations as "deserv[ing] only a laugh," but the narrator of *Richard III* will also adopt this unsettling comic tone and attitude.[22]

---

[20] CW 3.1, 124/22 and 126/3.
[21] See the frequent use of this term "satellites" in *Richard III,* in his Latin *Declamation in Reply to Lucian's* Tyrannicide, and in epigrams such as 19/132, 80/11, and 120/1. As Sylvester points out in his commentary at CW 2, 40/23, More uses the term "with a somewhat sinister connotation," imitating Cicero, where the term "frequently means 'assistant in crime,'" and Tacitus. See note 71.
[22] See Chapter 8 and such passages as CW 2, [English] 84/14–15. The same tone is evident in Epigram 39.

Most daringly – even dangerously[23] – More suggests that Henry VIII himself has the tyrant's "lust for power" as shown by his imperialistic invasion of France in 1512–13, discreetly indicated by More's silent juxtaposition of the following epigrams:[24]

ON LUST FOR POWER

Among many kings there will be scarcely one, if there is really one, who is satisfied to have one kingdom. And yet among many kings there will be scarcely one, if there is really one, who rules a single kingdom well.[25] (Epigram 243)

ON THE SURRENDER OF TOURNAI TO HENRY VIII, KING OF ENGLAND

Warlike Caesar vanquished you, Tournai, till then unconquered, but not without disaster on both sides. Henry, a king both mightier and better than great Caesar, has taken you without bloodshed. The king felt that he had gained honor by taking you, and you yourself felt it no less advantageous to be taken.[26] (Epigram 244)

As Tudor historian John Guy points out, Epigram 244 compares Henry's "pointless war" to the "notoriously wasteful and bloody battle of Julius Caesar."[27] To write that Henry VIII *felt [sensit]* that he had gained honor" is much different from saying that he actually gained honor. Quite strikingly, this epigram also identifies Henry VIII as king only of England, not of the customary "England and France,"[28] thus reinforcing the main point of the preceding epigram.

Written in the same year as Epigrams 243 and 244, another series – Epigrams 183, 184, 271 – focuses on the king of Scotland's invasion of England while Henry VIII was away invading France. This grave and predicted danger was one of the reasons given by royal counselors for

---

[23] Consider note 51 of Chapter 6.

[24] Grace 1985 120; Adams 76.

[25] "DE CVPIDITATE REGNANDI / Regibus e multis regnum cui sufficit unum, / Vix Rex unus erit, si tamen unus erit. / Regibus e multis regnum bene qui regat unum, / Vix tamen unus erit, si tamen unus erit."

[26] "DE DEDITIONE NERVIAE HENRICO VIII. / ANGLIAE REGI. / Belliger inuictam domuit te Neruia Caesar, / Non tamen extremis absque utriusque malis. / Te capit Henricus, capit et sine sanguine, princeps / Magno tam maior Caesare quam melior. / Sensit honorificum sibi rex cepisse, tibique / Vtile sensisti non minus ipsa capi."

[27] Guy 2008 48–49.

[28] This abridgment of sovereignty is also present not only in *Utopia's* introductory materials but also in all other copies of the coronation ode except for the presentation copy given to Henry in 1509. Consider also the irony – and the implications – of Richard III's argument that England belongs wholly to the people and that he, assuming that France could not belong to its people, will invade France. (See note 55 and the next chapter.)

Henry's not leaving the country.[29] The first epigram in this series More would exclude from future editions. Why exclude that one and not the others? Epigram 271 begins by contrasting *pius Henricus* with *impius Iacobus*, but for actions that are quite similar: both invade a sovereign country;[30] both go against their own treaties; both go against "good faith" or *fides* with an ally; and both do so at the cost of "the slaughter of [their own] men."[31]

One of the longest series of epigrams,[32] entitled "On Two Beggars: One Blind, One Lame," points to qualities essential to More's plan of reform. The two Greek poems that More translates for this series represent two approaches to the universal experience of human limitations,[33] which makes clear our need to cooperate with one another. Or put differently: this ordinary and pressing experience of limitation makes clear our political nature.

The first Greek poem is marked by noble simplicity and a rather matter-of-fact description of considerable hardship: "A blind neighbor carries a lame man about; by an *artful* combination, he borrows eyes and lends feet."[34] This short poem represents a clear-sighted and constructive approach to our flawed and incomplete condition: because it is obvious that we are all limited, we use art to borrow and lend from each other. More gives three other translations of the same Greek poem but, instead of art, he gives other similar clear-sighted approaches: using prudence,[35] working cooperatively,[36] and finally "ruling" with an eye to utility.[37]

---

[29] Scarisbrick gives a clear account of the danger posed and of the superior victory that Queen Catherine achieves in her "immense and consequential... victory" in routing this northern attack, as compared to Henry's "slender" achievement in gaining Tournai (37–38).

[30] See Chapter 8 for the explanation in *Richard III* that each country belongs to the people who compose it – not to a person who happens to rule, or to invade.

[31] See especially Epigram 271/8 regarding the *foedera* or treaties and the contrast made between "pius" Henry (271/2) and "impius" King Jacob (271/5). Compare this with the treatment of treaties and good faith in *Utopia*, as seen in Chapter 9.

[32] For other interconnected series of poems in More's collection, see the analysis of More's twelve poems on paintings and art's difficulty in representing the reality it depicts (Wegemer 1996 80).

[33] See Epigrams 13a and 11 of book 9 of *The Greek Anthology*.

[34] "IN CAECVM ET CLAVDVM MENDICOS./ Claudipedem gestat caecis uicinus ocellis, / Conducitque oculos arte, locatque pedes" (Epigram 27, emphasis added).

[35] Epigram 28: "prudenter."

[36] Epigram 29: "opera ... eadem."

[37] Epigram 30: "utile ... regit."

The first three use the language of primitive barter,[38] and only the fourth, as if following historical progression,[39] introduces the concept of formal governing (*regere*).[40]

The fifth in the sequence is the translation of a different Greek epigram.[41] This second Greek poem represents another distinct attitude towards human limitations, an attitude marked by unhealthy self-pity:

Very sad misfortune overtook two unhappy men and cruelly deprived the one of his eyes, the other of his feet. Their common misery united them.[42] (Epigram 31/1–3)

In this poem, the barter arrangement continues but without a positive perception on our needy condition. In contrast to this pessimistic attitude of cynical self-pity and in contrast to the primitive barter represented in this poem, More concludes his series with two poems giving distinct alternatives but building upon the first four poems of this sequence.

Epigram 32 is the longest poem in the sequence and the only one that introduces dialogue. It has no classical models for the elements added and is clearly More's original composition. It goes beyond the matter-of-fact and the ingeniously utilitarian; instead of cynical self-pity, it invokes magnanimous friendship and the positive role of law:

There can be nothing more helpful than a faithful friend, who by his own efforts [*officio*] assuages your hurts. Two beggars contracted an alliance[43] of firm friendship – a blind man and a lame one. The blind man said to the lame one, "You

---

[38] As the editors of CW 3.2 point out, the many variations are "made possible by the fact that the ideas of borrowing and lending, expressed by one verb in Greek, are divided between two words in Latin (*conducere* and *locare*)" (338).

[39] This progression from primitive barter and informal cooperation to a developed legal order becomes clear in poems six and seven of this series.

[40] Cicero uses this verb in distinct ways: "It is a difficult art of *guiding* a commonwealth in the right way" (*Atticus* 7.25); "the inexperience of youth requires the prudence of age to strengthen and *guide* it" (*De Officiis* 1.122, emphasis added); "by their counsel and wisdom, [they] can *guide* and govern [*gubernare*] the commonwealth" (*De Oratore* 1.8, emphasis added). Cicero claims he can "guide" Cato, who is fashioned for *honestas*, with the help of *studiis humanitatis* (*Pro Murena* 60–61). *De Oratore* 1.214 describes Scaurus as a man most knowledgeable about guiding the commonwealth.

[41] Epigram 11 of book 9 of *The Greek Anthology*.

[42] "Tristis erat nimium miseris fortuna duobus, / Huic oculos, illi dempsit iniqua pedes. / Sors illos coplat similis, ..."

[43] "foedera contraxere," both are legal terms; cf. CW 4, 198/4–6.

must ride upon my shoulders." The latter answered, "You, blind friend, must find your way by means of my eyes."[44]

Friendship is explicitly mentioned twice in these few lines, reflecting the importance given that human reality by Plato, Aristotle, Cicero, and Seneca; significantly, law in the form of a contractual agreement is also given a privileged and positive place in making firm that friendship; and equally significantly, duty (*officio*)[45] arises in the opening sentence following upon "faithful friend." Going further, the concluding couplet (unlike any other sixteenth-century epigram) turns explicitly to the political:

The love that unites, shuns the castles of proud kings and rules [*regnant*] in the humble hut.[46]

Ruling in humility with love brings concord, and giving *amor* the place of greatest rhetorical emphasis contributes to the strikingly amiable tone of the entire poem.

As a whole, this epigram indicates that a politically harmonious life – that is, one that is happy, "expedient,"[47] and peaceful – depends upon a clear-sighted and positive response to our flawed and therefore dependent condition. Such a response is presented here through the voice of a loving and humble and freely dutiful friend who invites mutual service, a voice said to be impossible for a proud king set apart in his castle.

Epigram 33, the seventh and last poem in More's sequence, at first appears to be only another variation of Epigrams 27–30. Looking more closely, however, one notices that, instead of the primitive economy of informal lending and borrowing, the language of contract, law, and justice in the first line introduces the more formal language of rule in line 2,[48] thus pointing again to an evolutionary development within the sequence, culminating in the natural role of law characteristic of developed political life based on "sound deliberation."

---

[44] "Vtilius nihil esse potest, quam fidus amicus, / Qui tua damna suo leniat officio. / Foedera contraxere simul mendicus uterque / Cum claudo solidae caecus amicitiae. / Claudo caecus ait, collo gestabere nostro. / Retulit hic, oculis caece regere meis."

[45] Consider Cicero's arguments in his last work, *De Officiis*.

[46] "Alta superborum fugitat penetralia regum, / Inque casa concors paupere regnat amor."

[47] For the importance of *utile*, and its significance in Cicero's project of translating Greek philosophy for Romans, see Nicgorski 1984.

[48] "Cum claudo caecus sic lege paciscitur aequa, ut / Hic ferat illum humeris, hunc regat ille oculis."

Of More's other "directly political epigrams,"[49] Epigram 112 presents the function of king (*rex*) as but one important part of the larger body that must "be held together by love" if the king is to be considered "good."[50] Instead of *rex*, Epigram 111 uses the term that will have such prominence in Utopia: *princeps*. As Epigram 111 ("That the Good *Princeps* Is a Father Not a Master") shows, the true first citizen of a country is not looking for dominion over his fellow citizens; he is looking for their good as seen in their ability to act as free citizens. As More would humorously put it while in prison, quoting Boethius: For "one man to be proud that he bears rule over other men is much like as one mouse would be proud to bear a rule over other mice in a barn."[51] When we consider the actions of the *principes* in *Utopia*, we will see a very different attitude toward citizens because they depend on fear rather than love[52] and because there is no sense of equality between rulers and those they treat as subjects.[53]

Epigram 111, like Epigram 112, emphasizes in a way similar to Cicero and Aristotle the attitude of friendship within the good city – the very quality that is conspicuously absent from *Richard III* and from *Utopia*. Another poem that will echo loudly in *Richard III* and *Utopia* is Epigram 243, which was seen earlier in this chapter; it expresses the wish that kings would rule one country well instead of letting unreined their ambition to rule many. This same idea is stated four times in the text of *Utopia*[54] and twice in *Richard III*.[55] It is stated again at the end of More's life, in

---

[49] Grace 1985 116.
[50] "De Bono Rege et Popvlo. / Totum est unus homo regnum, idque cohaeret amore" (112.1–2). For the full text, Latin and English, and for a commentary of the body-politic metaphor, see Chapter 3.
[51] *Corr.* 519 or *TMSB* 324/5–7.
[52] See *Utopia*, CW 4, 220/25, where we are told that fear is the motive for obeying law, and 234/6–7, where fear of God is said to be the "greatest and almost the only stimulus to the practice of virtues" (compare with 222/3, 228/4–7, and 232.31).
[53] Rulers in Utopia are chosen from a separate class of people, the so-called intellectual class, who actually achieve and maintain its position by conformity rather than intelligence.
[54] CW 4, 57/25–30, 89/27–3, 91/12–17 and 21–28.
[55] Once positively at CW 15, 444/5–7, and once ironically in tyrant Richard's claim at 481/6–20. Notice that Richard raises the essential question of true ownership and sovereignty by the people: "Though I personally regret your unbending resolve not to tolerate this king any longer, I consider it to be neither possible nor proper for anyone to rule unwilling subjects. For my own part, at least, though I know that there is no other to whom the crown rightly [*iure*] belongs by inheritance, I consider your desires [*voluntates*] more important than any number of laws, which derive all their efficacy from you; and since I see that your solid consensus supports me, lest I should seem either timid about laboring for the commonweal or unmindful of your goodwill toward me,

his prison writings, where More laments in Anthony's voice that "much trouble to many people and great effusion of blood" is caused by the king who looks "to reign in five countries, who can not well rule one."[56]

The issue of ruling well is addressed especially in Epigram 198, "What Is the Best Form of *Res Publica*?" which we have already briefly seen. This daring epigram shows that term limits for officials elected by the people are superior to having kings with neither term limits nor accountability, and it boldly introduces the option of the Romans' limited and elected office of consul. These lines, for example, are powerful indictments of kingship:

A king in his first year is always very mild indeed, and so every year the *consul*[57] will be like a new king. Over a long time a greedy king will gnaw away at his people. If a *consul* is evil, there is hope of improvement. I am not swayed by the well-known fable which recommends that one endure the well-fed fly lest a hungry one takes its place. It is a mistake to believe that a greedy king can be satisfied; such a leech never leaves flesh until it is drained.[58] (198/16–23, emphasis added)

In the previous lines of this poem, More weighed the benefits of a senate over a king, but clearly showed the superiority of the senate. In the section just quoted, More compares a king with a consul – that is, he compares a hereditary monarch with a head of government elected for a limited term[59] – and graphically emphasizes the dangers of kingship.

here on this day I take upon myself the government of the two realms of England and France, the one to protect and extend and the other to subdue for England, bringing it back into your power and making it submit to those it should obey; for I regard only the management of these realms as my own, but the title and the profit and the ownership as totally your own – as a genuine commonwealth." Notably, this section is in the Latin edition only. One glaring issue of special importance is raised by this odd formulation: If England belongs to the English people, why would the separate "realm of . . . France" not belong to the French people? And why would the desires of one people be the basis for ignoring legitimate laws? Are laws only an arbitrary expression of changing will?

[56] *CW* 12, 224/26–28.

[57] Unannounced and unprepared, this invocation of the Roman consulship abruptly invites the reader to consider one of history's most famous options to hereditary monarchy.

[58] "Rex est in primo semper blandissimus anno, / Omni anno consul rex erit ergo nouus. / Rex cupidus longo populum corroserit aeuo. / Si consul malus est, spes melioris adest. / Nec me nota mouet quae pastam fabula muscam / Ferre iubet, subeat ne male pransa locum. / Fallitur, expleri regem qui credit auarum, / Nunquam haec non uacuam mittet hirudo cutem."

[59] See line 12: One "is elected by the people to rule"; the other "attains this end by being born" (*Alter ut eligitur populo, sic nascitur alter*).

In the next section the speaker returns to weighing the advantages and disadvantages of a senate compared with those of a king, only to abruptly interrupt his argument:

But, you say, a serious disagreement impedes a senate's decisions [*patrum consulta*], while no one disagrees with a king. But that is the worse evil of the two, for when there is a difference of opinion about important matters –. But why are you asking such a question?[60]

If the interrupted sentence would have been finished, this decisive reason would have been given: when there are important differences of opinion, these very differences will require consultation, serious discussion, and further study and debate, all serving to bring out the principles and issues involved, and therefore enhancing the understanding and consensus of all – at least such was the decisive reason More would give in 1523 when he argued for freedom of speech in the House of Commons.[61]

Why, however, is this line of thought broken and left incomplete? The literary answer to this question will be suggested in the next chapters, but for now we turn to the poem's unexpected ending:

But why are you asking such a question? Is there a people anywhere to whom you can assign a king or a parliament [*senatus*] just as you choose? If you can, you rule them already. But do not consider to which one you should give the power to rule. The more basic question is: "Would it work?"[62]

Sallust in his *Catiline* answers yes to these three questions, in what became his most famous passage for those aspiring to self-government. He reports that not only did the ancient Romans choose to get rid of monarchy, but Rome achieved its greatness only when they did.[63] But how did the Romans do it? What made it work? Sallust answers these questions also.

---

[60] "At patrum consulta grauis dissensio turbat, / Regi dissentit nemo, malum hoc grauius. / Nam quum de magnis uaria est sententia rebus, / Quaestio sed tamen haec nascitur unde tibi?"

[61] See Chapter 11 for a summary of the argument. For the full text of this speech, see Roper 12–16 or *TMSB* 23–25. In considering the authenticity of this speech, see Roper's comment that an earlier oration to the king was "not nowe extant" (12/14), mentioned just before quoting More's speech in full. Also see the summary of this speech in Hall 279, which corresponds to the speech as given in Roper.

[62] The translation of these lines is Clarence Miller's, *CW* 3.2, 50. "Quaestio sed tamen haec nascitur unde tibi? / Est ne usquam populus, cui regem siue Senatum / Praeficere arbitrio tu potes ipse tuo? / Si potes hoc, regnas: nec iam cui, *consule*, tradas / Imperium: prior est quaestio, an expediat" (emphasis added).

[63] *Catiline* 6.6–7.

The change worked only when the Romans had developed enough to have "a constitution founded upon law" and only when "a chosen few, whose bodies were enfeebled by age but whose minds were fortified with wisdom, had taken counsel [*consultabant*] for the welfare of the state [*rei publicae*]."[64] So honored and well respected were these first or leading citizens that they "were called Fathers."[65] With these elements in place, a deliberative and peaceful change then became possible:

> Later, when the rule of the kings, which at first had tended to preserve freedom [*libertas*] and advance the state [*rei publicae*], had degenerated into a lawless tyranny, they altered the form of government and appointed two rulers with annual power, thinking that this device would prevent men's minds from growing arrogant through unlimited authority. (*Catiline* 6.7)

The condition for this major political change was having a group of leading citizens respected enough and capable enough of effective consultation,[66] of "sound deliberation" about the common welfare. The precipitating cause of that change was a clear national crisis – a crisis similar, perhaps, to the one More perceived in *The History of King Richard III*.

More himself recognizes the importance of deliberation by leading citizens and the laws that result. In Epigram 109, for example, law is the determining factor in showing "The Difference between a Tyrant and the *Princeps*."[67] The two-word first line sets forth the difference in stark and dramatic terms: "*Legitimus immanissimis*" – "Lawful" versus "most savage" – the terms that Cicero used to distinguish *ius* from *vis*, *humanitas* from *immanitas,* a civilization of dignified peace from a life of constant discord.[68] And in his *History of Richard III*, More states clearly what is presented in Epigram 121 and what he would say at the end of his

---

[64] *Catiline* 6.6.

[65] *Catiline* 6.6.

[66] Hence, as Cicero and Augustine agree, arose the term "consul." See Cicero, *De Legibus* 3.8 and Augustine, *City of God* 5.12. Cicero points out in *Verrine Orations* 2.1.107 that magistrates of the Roman Republic consult *ius* and *lex*. The *Oxford Latin Dictionary* reports the common understanding that *consilium* ("deliberation, debate") evolved from *consulo*.

[67] "QVID INTER TYRANNVM ET PRINCIPEM. / Legitimus immanissimis / Rex hoc tyrannis interest. / Seruos tyrannus quos regit, / Rex liberos putat suos." Notice that the poem concludes by contrasting the tyrant's treatment of his people as slaves and the true *princeps*'s treatment of his people as his own children/free citizens.

[68] *Pro Sestio* 92 as seen in Chapter 3.

life:[69] that in England, Parliament has the ultimate authority (*potestas*) to make or depose kings.[70]

Epigram 115 shows the difference between the *princeps* and the tyrant briefly and simply: one is the watchdog and guardian protecting his flock from the wolf; the other is the wolf. Epigram 110 shows that the tyrant can never be happy, never at peace, and that "the tyrant does not rest more comfortably on any soft bed than the poor man does on the hard ground." In contrast to the unhappy tyrant, the *"bonum princeps"* of Epigram 111 is "most happy" being surrounded by citizens who love him as their father. The love between good leaders and their people is developed in Epigram 112 by comparing, as we saw in Chapter 3, the leader to a body united by love; such love will lead the people to risk their lives to protect their head.

Epigram 113 reveals that history – that is, judgment over time – is needed for accurate assessment of any particular *princeps,* especially because human nature is such that "[a]lmost all of us recognize our advantages by losing them." History also shows, as articulated in Epigram 120, that the ruler's virtues are a much stronger protection than fear, wealth, or armed power:

A KING IS PROTECTED NOT BY HENCHMEN[71]

BUT BY HIS OWN VIRTUES

Not fear (accompanied by ill-will), not towering palaces, Not wealth wrung from a plundered people will protect a king, Nor stern henchmen, hired for a pittance and willing to serve a new master as he served the old. He will be safe who so rules his people that they judge none other would promote their interests better.[72]

As we will see in the next chapter, the England of *Richard III* is dominated by fear, ill will, and armed power, not trust, goodwill, and virtuous friends. Utopia is also dominated by fear, but not – we are told – by ill will (*inuidia*).

---

[69] See More's conversation with Richard Rich, as reported by Roper and by the official Indictment (Roper 85; Harpsfield, appendix 3, 274).

[70] CW 15, 320/22–24.

[71] As seen in note 21, "satellites" is used repeatedly by More in his earliest published work "with a somewhat sinister connotation," in imitation of Cicero and Tacitus.

[72] "REGEM NON SATELLITIVM SED / VIRTVS REDDIT TVTVM / Non timor inuisus, non alta palatia regem, / Non compilata plebe tuentur opes, / Non rigidus uili mercabilis aere satelles / Qui sic alterius fiet ut huius erat. / Tutus erit, populum qui sic regit, utiliorem / Vt populus nullum censeat esse sibi."

8

Richard III

Diagnosing the Causes of England's Plague
of Civil War

[W]ell aware of the old vying factions at court (factions that he had even done all that he could to foment), . . . [Richard] supposed it would further his plans a great deal if he secretly served his own interests under a pretext of partisanship.

Thomas More, *Historia Richardi Tertii* 328/10–12, 14–15

If I as a private citizen [*priuato*] had been able to foresee and anticipate [this wicked ardor for glory's] ill effects . . . , I would never have sacrificed so many men's heads to see men on their knees doing me honor.

Thomas More, *Historia Richardi Tertii* 334/22–24

When everyone tries to ingratiate his own faction with the prince, the result is that his favor, more than truth and expediency [*vero atque vtili*], determines how people advise him: and thus . . . drag the kingdom to ruin.

Thomas More, *Historia Richardi Tertii* 332/9–12

On his deathbed, King Edward IV comes to recognize the extreme danger of factions as well as his own misguided choice that heightened those factions. Before recounting this classic deathbed speech with its dramatic revelations,[1] the narrator of *Historia Richardi Tertii* gives a rare endorsement of what Edward will reveal:

[T]hough [King Edward IV] feared nothing less than what actually happened, he foresaw that the dissension of [his sons'] friends could do them great harm, since their naturally frail and improvident youth would be stripped on its one source of strength, their friends' counsel [*consiliis*]. For when dissension and discord

---

[1] Compare Edward's speech with King Micipsa's in Sallust's *Jugurtha* 10.1–8.

polarized the supporters, they would pay more attention to partisan interests than to stating the truth, and would advise what was pleasant, and not what was profitable, in order to advance their own faction in the favor of the prince.[2]

Counsel ordered to truth and the country's good is the "one source of strength" King Edward and the narrator see for England, but as King Edward will explain to the nobles he assembles, such sound deliberation depends on the nobles' "mutual love" (*amore mutuo*) and a nation (*patria*) of peace and not of "internal sedition" (336). Or, as we saw in Chapters 1 and 7, the healthy body-politic is united by love, not divided by *inuidia*, that is, by ill will or envy.

In looking back over his life, King Edward reveals in his deathbed speech what "fate" allowed that has brought so much deadly strife to England, but first he marvels that such strife should be possible, given "our common humanity and our sworn allegiance to Christ, who gave his soldiers one and only one watchword, that of charity" (332). How then could these warring factions be "my kindred by blood and the other my kindred by marriage," all of whom should take "Christ's precepts as seriously as Christians ought," thus "joining hearts" more effectively than "actual blood-tie" (334)? What "evil fate" (*malo fato*) could account for breaking all bonds human and divine to result in such factious hatred? King Edward immediately gives the answer as that "odious monster" of "pride and the lust for supremacy"[3] who has "crept into illustrious noblemen's hearts" and "has drenched all in slaughter and bloodshed." But he then becomes unexpectedly personal in confessing his own misguided desire to "excel and surpass" all others:

Would that God would as readily forget as we personally remember what a great conflagration this wicked ardor for glory has ignited and how much slaughter it has provoked in this kingdom within these last few years; and if I as a private citizen [*privato*] had been able to foresee and anticipate its ill effects as distinctly in thought as I later experienced them in deed, with less pleasure than pain, on my life I would never have sacrificed so many men's heads to see men on their knees doing me honor. (334)

This stunning insight about the superiority of the life of the "private citizen" to that of the tyrant is quickly passed over – because "evil fate"

---

[2] CW 15, 328/29–330/8. Hereafter, page and line references in the text and notes for *Historia Richardi Tertii* are from CW 15.

[3] The narrator identifies the "odious craving for power" (*execrabilis imperandi sitis*) as the reason Richard will "rupture all bonds of human society . . . in defiance of man's law and God's" (320/11–12). Cicero identifies the same motive operating in Caesar at *De Officiis* 3.83. Surprisingly, this motive is absent from the Utopians.

is responsible – and yet Edward does admit that he made a deliberate choice, uninformed as it was. Now at the end of his life, however, he then goes on to instruct the assembled nobles that the prosperity of England depends upon their concord and mutual love (336).

The English version[4] of *Richard III* is explicit about the cause of England's civil wars: "[T]he sure ground for the foundation of all" was faction,[5] factions that Edward and Richard fostered.[6] The Latin version of *Richard III* has at least eight terms for faction and at least seven terms for fear,[7] emphasizing England's "state of affairs" whereby "you could not tell for certain whom you should trust and whom you should fear."[8] This complete erosion of trust or *fides* marks one of the greatest contrasts between a once healthy Roman Republic and the sickly English *regnum*.[9] More uses *fides* well over thirty times,[10] habitually in the context of a critical decision. By doing so, he repeatedly calls to mind what was for the Romans the basis of society and of all justice.

Fides or *bona fides* – the quality of trust or reliability – was the first virtue in ancient Rome to become a divinity. The great lawgiver Numa built the temple of Fides near the temple of Jupiter "and taught the

---

[4] More wrote two versions, apparently simultaneously: one in English and one in Latin. At that early stage of his writing career, More was experimenting with both English and Latin in his poetry and in his prose. As that experimental period came to a close – that is, when he began writing *Utopia* and the most polished version of *Richard III* – he turned to Latin, just as he would do again at the end of his life when writing his final book, *De Tristitia Christi*.

[5] CW 2, 10/1–3; repeated at 14/18–19: "[T]heir division should be (as it was in deed)...a sure ground for the foundation of all [Richard's] building." In this English version, More is using an English proverb explained by Hosington at n. 19 and p. 21.

[6] CW 2, 14/16–15/30. The Latin version gives abundant proof to make this same conclusion, but the Latin narrator does not give readers such a straightforward assessment. The Latin edition at CW 15, 338/10–11, presents faction as one element, but note the difference in emphasis. This is but one example of how More refines the Latin version to demand more judgment and greater attentiveness – as well as more comparisons with classical predecessors – than the English version. See the remarks of editor Daniel Kinney about the Latin version's "unusual compactness" and "elaborate rhetorical structure" (CW 15, clii).

[7] See www.thomasmorestudies.org/IndicesofLatinTerms.

[8] CW 15, 398/18–20; the term for trust here is *confidere*. This assessment is restated at CW 15, 432/7–8: "neque sciret...cui consilia crederet."

[9] That England is more of a "kingdom" than a republic is seen in many ways. Notice the few uses of the term *res publica* in this work as compared to *Utopia*, and notice how every use is in an ironic or highly significant context: for example, CW 15, 342/26, 348/13, 394/7, 478/12, 480/3.

[10] In More's English text, the most frequently used equivalent of *fides* is "trust" and sometimes "special trust" (e.g., 45/22 and 31), but More also uses "faith" or "good faith."

Romans that the name of Fides was the most solemn oath that they could swear."[11] *Bona fides* remains an indispensable element of law in our own day, "implying the absence of all fraud and unfair dealing or acting."[12] In fact, all experienced citizens and friends know the importance of establishing the trustworthiness or *bona fides* of those they choose as leaders or as friends.

Cicero explained that *fides*, understood as "truth and fidelity to promises and agreements," is the very "foundation of justice" and a clear sign that human beings are meant "mutually to help one another . . . , to contribute to the general good by an interchange of acts of kindness."[13] "Charity" (*caritas*) is the term Cicero uses for the ideal societal bond,[14] and most famously, he idealistically wrote that as long as Rome is ruled by justice and *fides*,[15] it "could be called more accurately a protectorate [*patrocinium*][16] of the world than a dominion [*imperium*]."[17] Such *fides* is so important, Cicero went on to write, that the very bond of humanity requires it[18] and that "all the transactions on which the social relations of daily life depend" presuppose it.[19] For Cicero, the famous general and consul Regulus is the Roman hero who best illustrates *bona fides*, that *princeps* who was willing to counsel his own death, undergoing the cruelest torture for the good of the country he loved.[20] Such a character is strikingly absent from *Richard III*, except for the silent Londoners who refuse to capitulate to both Buckingham's and Richard's enticements to their self-interest, and for Chief Justice Markham, who loses his position as chief justice rather than go along with the king's illegal actions.

How *fides* and its corollary friendship affect civic life is seen vividly in the character of Lord Hastings.[21] When his fellow nobleman Lord

---

[11] Reported in Plutarch's life of Numa and in *De Officiis* 3.104.

[12] William Smith 207.

[13] *De Officiis* 1.22–23.

[14] *De Officiis* 1.54–57.

[15] *De Officiis* 2.27: "aequitate et fide."

[16] This legal term, of such importance to the Romans, is used in most provocative – and somewhat humorous – contexts at *Utopia*, CW 4, 160/25 and *Richardi Tertii* at 462/4.

[17] *De Officiis* 2.27. As we have seen, More uses "imperium" in his 1509 coronation ode, and we have yet to see how he uses it in the contexts of *Richardi Tertii* and *Utopia*.

[18] *De Officiis* 3.69.

[19] *De Officiis* 3.70.

[20] Cicero's most extensive treatment of Regulus is in book 3 of *De Officiis*.

[21] See Cicero's *De Amicitia* for the important connection between *fides*, *amicitia*, and good political life. The passage 14.49–15.55 uses the example of King Tarquin as the type of character who could not "procure . . . true friends," and it quotes Tarquin's complaint that he was unable to distinguish *fidos amicos* from *infidos* (15.53); 14.50 points to

Stanley expresses grave concern about the secret council Richard has set up, Hastings boasts that he has no fear because he has a lawyer-friend of "special trust [*fides*]" who attends that council and supposedly reports everything to Hastings. This lawyer

was Catesby, who was of [Hasting's] near secret counsel and whom he very familiarly used, and in his most weighty matters put no man in so *special trust*,[22] reckoning himself to no man so dear, since he well knew there was no man to him so much beholden as was this Catesby, who was a man well learned in the laws of this land, and by the special favor of the Lord Chamberlain, in good authority and much rule bore in that county of Leicester where the Lord Chamberlain's power chiefly lay. But surely great pity was it, that he had not had either more truth or less wit. For his dissimulation *only* kept all that mischief up. If the Lord Hastings had not put so *special trust* in Catesby, the Lord Stanley and he had departed with diverse other lords and broken all the dance.[23]

Only misplaced *fides* in Catesby "kept all that mischief up." Blindly, Hastings could not see that, instead of *fides*, Catesby "trusted"[24] that by Hastings's death he could "obtain much [more] of the rule." Once again the narrator draws our attention to the effects of unrestrained desire for power, which was the "only desire . . . that induced [Catesby] to be partner and one special contriver of all this horrible treason."[25] The narrator then describes Hastings as a person "especially dear to the king on account of his trustworthiness [*fidem*], . . . a man trusty [*fidus*] enough, trusting too much [*fidens nimium*]."[26] This inability to trust wisely characterizes not only individuals like Hastings but England at large during this period: "For the state of things and the dispositions of men were *then* such that a man could not well tell whom he might *trust* or whom he might fear."[27] As in the case of the counsel given by Catesby, the counsel given by each faction is dictated by personal desire and narrow self-interest, not the good of friend or country.

Queen Elizabeth (1437–92) embodies this problem of not knowing whom to trust more prominently and more mysteriously than any other

---

pride (*superba*) as an especially debilitating character trait. Other passages of special significance for *fides* and *amicitia* are 17.64–18.65 and 23.86–25.96. For an excellent commentary on *De Amicitia*, see Nicgorski 2008.

[22] The Latin version uses *fides* here; see CW 15, 404/1.

[23] CW 2, 45/19–46/1, emphases added. Compare the Latin at CW 15, 404/1–16.

[24] This pun at 46/23 draws attention in yet another way to the importance of *fides*.

[25] CW 2, 46/22–26.

[26] CW 15, 420/4–5, 7–8.

[27] This English version seems to place greater stress on this period as a unique period of time: CW 2, 43/26–28 emphasis added; compare with CW 15, 398/18–20.

character in the *Historia*.[28] How could the queen be trusting enough
to hand over her sick son to their greatest enemy? She has had thorough experience in English ways for forty-six years, nineteen of those
as queen. As she points out, her last stay in sanctuary saved her life
and the life of her eldest son, now king at thirteen. She knows that the
safety of the younger son is the best safeguard of the older. How then
could she be so trusting, right after she has just eloquently and persua-
sively invoked recent and past history, English law, church law, natural
law, and her personal experience? Quite significantly, *fides* is invoked
before, during, and at the end of this most dramatic scene of *Historia
Richardi*. A closer look at this unusually long section of More's history is
revealing.

Richard begins his ploy to gain control of the second prince by asking
the English leaders for help in getting the right intermediary: "I think
we should send some venerable and influential emissary to the mother,
someone who cares about the king's honor and the reputation of our order
but who also commands some love and trust (*cui sit amoris nonnihil . . . et
fidei*) from the queen."[29]

Once the cardinal has deliberately chosen to do Richard's bidding,[30] he
introduces himself to the queen as her "trustworthy and loving friend"
who comes to appeal to her about "the realm's public interests, her
friends' mutual interests, and her own private interests."[31] After a spirited
debate, and "when the cardinal saw that his arguments were getting
him nowhere," he changes tactics, and along with his threat that he
and his friends would "leave right away" – abandoning her into the
hands of her greatest enemy, the enemy who just recently imprisoned her
brother and son – he concludes with a short statement invoking *fides*
four times, pledging by oath his and his fellow nobles' trust for her son's

---

[28] This theme of trust is dominant in Shakespeare's plays. For example, shortly before King
Duncan is murdered by placing too much trust in Macbeth, he complains that there is
no way to judge those we can trust: "There is no art / To find the mind's construction in
the face: / He was a gentleman on whom I build / An absolute *trust*" (*Macbeth* 1.4.11–
14, emphasis added). This inability to judge, that allows the tyrant Macbeth to arise
in Scotland, seems to be the same as what allows the tyrant Richard to arise in More's
account of England. Or is it possible that More agrees with Duncan's tragic view of
human intelligence? As this book indicates, More follows his greatest classical teachers
in positing the opposite view – and not only positing that view but in devising literature
that exercises and develops the very art that Duncan did not believe to exist.

[29] CW 15, 362/24. See Cicero's explanation of the relationship between *amor* and *amicitia*
in *De Amicitia* 8.26–9.32; see also Nicgorski 2008.

[30] Consider CW 15, 358/25–26, where the narrator comments on how "the lamb was
deliberately entrusted to the wolf."

[31] CW 15, 378/17–18.

safety,[32] ending by scornfully saying that the queen "seemed to doubt either their prudence or *good faith* in the matter, their prudence if she thought they were dupes of another man's perfidy, their *good faith* if she thought they were knowing accessories."[33] "Upon these words," the narrator tells us, "the queen entered into a long, thoughtful silence."[34]

Here the narrator invites his reader to do the same: to enter into a long, thoughtful reflection. In reviewing the evidence the narrator has given, what do we conclude? Is the cardinal trustworthy? Or is he a dupe or even a knowing accomplice of Richard? And at this climactic moment of decision, why will Queen Elizabeth so readily capitulate? She has just brilliantly and powerfully set forth not only the extreme dangers but also the many protections available to her son. Is the queen simply *deceived*, as Hastings was, by an appearance of *fides*?[35] Does she give in because of *fear*?[36] Does she suffer from *poor judgment*, something she has already lamented in letting herself be convinced to send a much too small guard for her elder son?[37] Is she *momentarily blinded* in a pressured moment of haste? Or what else might be at work here? These are questions that the narrator leads us to ask, inviting us to probe deeply the motives at work.[38]

The greatest puzzle of *Richard III* is why Queen Elizabeth decides to turn over her son to Richard – "the lamb ... to the wolf"[39] – but such puzzles and this issue of *fides* run throughout the entire history.[40] Significantly, the queen sees clearly that her action could well "inflict an incurable wound on ... the commonwealth [*rei publicae*],"[41] but she does it nonetheless. Why?

---

[32] The cardinal pledges his soul at CW 2, [English] 40/14; compare this English account with the Latin at CW 15, 392/4–5: "fidem ipsos suam in eius incolumitatem obstricturos."

[33] CW 15, 392/3–8.

[34] CW 15, 392/9: "longius deliberabunda conticuit."

[35] In his deathbed speech, King Micipsa advises Jugurtha to "prove virtuous" by fidelity (*fide*) with his fellow Numidians because "neither armies nor treasure form the bulwarks of a throne, but friends" who are won "by duty and trust" (*officio et fide*; *Jugurtha* 10.4–6).

[36] CW 15, 354/1.

[37] CW 15, 350/27.

[38] In ways that Shakespeare does in each of his plays.

[39] CW 15, 358/25, and the English version of CW 2, 24/30.

[40] Early on, for example, the narrator asks us how it is that Richard was able to triumph over all the bonds of nature and society, of loyalty, good faith, and law to achieve his will, when "every prompting of either nature, fidelity [*fides*], or gratitude should have moved [Richard] to lay down his own life to thwart any enemy of" these young princes (CW 15, 320/8–10).

[41] CW 15, 394/7.

The technical name of the literary device at work here is "dialysis" or, more popularly called, "the dismemberer." In using this classical trope, the narrator sets forth a series of alternatives but leaves it to the reader, on the basis of the many clues given, to decide which is actually correct, or left out. The effect of this technique is a deep and powerful engagement of careful readers, leading them to appreciate the great difficulty of accurately discerning true motives by grappling with the full complexity and often obscurity surrounding human action.

In various ways and at every stage, this literary masterpiece challenges and engages the thoughtful reader to exercise careful observation and "sharp-sighted" judgment.[42] This compelling and mysterious engagement is evident from the first sentence, which asserts that "King Edward... succumbed to fate," and then goes on to insist that "fate" (*fatum*), "fortune" (*fortuna*), and "chance" (*sors*) are the causes of this history.[43] Yet later, right after the nobles unanimously consent to make Richard "the sole protector" of the young thirteen-year-old king, the narrator poses the question whether this important event in history came about through ignorance or through fate (*siue... inscitia... accidit fato*), only to go on immediately to say, "what is certain is that the lamb was *deliberately* entrusted to the wolf."[44] Curiously, the nobles base their trust on Richard's perceived "integrity."[45]

Why open a history attributing the major action to fate or fortune? – a view opposed by any Christian historian or classical author such as Sallust, whom More imitates closely, a view later opposed in the same work by the narrator himself, who seems to have the same stance as Sallust: that fortune changes with character.[46]

That opening sentence of *Historia Richardi* goes on to declare that King Edward IV "succumbed to fate"[47] when he was fifty-three years,

---

[42] See More's letter explaining how the *Utopia* should be read, especially CW 4, 248/23.

[43] CW 15, 314/5, 10, 12, 17.

[44] CW 15, 358/24–26 (emphasis added): "Itaque siue id inscitia factum siue accidit fato agnus certe consulto in lupi fidem creditus."

[45] CW 15, 358/23. For the importance of Sallust's use of "integrity," see Batstone, who argues that Sallust gives a "subtle and sophisticated" and "disturbing meditation on the late Republic" centered upon the meaning "complete virtue."

[46] Sallust's *War with Jugurtha* opens with an argument for virtue as the only way to overcome the fickleness of fortune "since fortune can neither give to any man honesty, industry, and other good qualities, nor can she take them away" (1.3). In *The Catiline*, Sallust argues that "fortune changes with character" (2.5) – a common idea expressed centuries earlier by Heraclitus (see fragment 119).

[47] As we will see, this narrative perspective that attributes all to fate is not the narrator's but the narrator's representation of Edward IV's self-understanding.

seven months, and six days old. In fact, Edward died at forty, and from "over liberal diet"[48] and immoderate living, rather than mere fate.[49] In Edward IV's case, perhaps character did have some influence on fate, and on English history. After all, this "mistake" draws attention to the fact that his age at death was of immense importance historically and politically because if Edward IV had lived thirteen additional years, his two sons would have been twenty-six and twenty-four rather than thirteen and eleven, and therefore not such easy prey to Richard's manipulation.

Another mysterious aspect of *Richard III* is the artful complexity of the narrator's voice. What is the narrator's point of view? Is it dark and pessimistic about human nature and the possibility of justice? If so, is the tone sarcastic and even bitter? Or is the narrator wise, detached, even humorous? Is the narrator reliable or unreliable? For example, does the narrator really believe the following report he gives on the second page?

[F]rom early youth throughout his life, whenever business did not call him away, [Edward] was particularly given to dissipation and wantonness, *like virtually everyone else*; for you will hardly persuade anyone in good health to restrain himself when his fortune permits great extravagance.[50]

Does the narrator really believe that human beings will be dissolute and wanton whenever good fortune allows?

To appreciate the narrative subtlety and sophistication at work, one could look to Thucydides, whom More imitated as a great master.[51] What Plutarch said of Thucydides could be said of More: "Thucydides aims always at this: to make his reader a spectator.... [The events] are so

---

[48] CW 2, 4/18, but see especially 8/29 where we find out that Richard "looked that evil diet should shorten" his brother's life. In the Latin version, Richard is not directly accused; there is only mention of Edward IV's "rather loose living and fleshly indulgence" (*CW* 15, 316/26–26) and "a hope [for Edward's early death] by the king's frequent feasts and immoderate eating" (*CW* 15, 326/10–11).

[49] In a similar way, the opening paragraph claims that "Elizabeth . . . by the guidance of fate became the consort of Henry VII and the mother of Henry VIII." In fact, Richard III made great efforts to marry Elizabeth, and Thomas More's own mentor, as More's English *History* tells us, was the careful architect of Elizabeth's marriage to Henry Tudor – thus finally ending the War of the Roses. In the English version of *Richard III*, the narrator raises this issue of fate not in the opening lines but in different ways. For example, after "the lamb was given to the wolf to keep," the narrator of the English version also asks if the murder of the innocent princes was caused by fate or folly, at CW 2, 24/30.

[50] CW 15, 316/27–318/3, emphasis added. This is again the narrator's representation of Edward IV's own view.

[51] As Sylvester points out, "More had studied the classical historians with typical thoroughness. . . . [I]t was the works of Thucydides and Livy, Sallust and Tacitus, that taught him how the best history should be written" (*CW* 2, lxxxii).

described and so evidently set before our eyes that the mind of the reader is no less affected than if he had been present in the actions."[52]

Another master of narration who had special importance to More was Sallust.[53] As Richard Sylvester observes, More must have known Sallust "almost by heart." Sallust was required reading in More's school, and his histories are "significantly echoed in [More's] *Historia*.[54] More probably lectured at Oxford on Sallust in 1513 or shortly afterward, and we know that Sallust held an important place among the English humanists,[55] just as he did among those in Florence.[56]

Promoted by Julius Caesar, Sallust was the experienced general and senator whose long reflections led him to conclude that Rome grew "incredibly strong and great in a remarkably short time" only "once liberty was won" – that is, only once wise, experienced "fathers" [*patres*] of Rome changed its government from a monarchy to a republic, with the explicit intent to "prevent men's minds from growing proud [*superbia*] through unlimited authority [*per licentiam*]"[57] (*Catiline* 6.7–7.3).

In Sallust's two histories, each focuses upon one specific event of the late war-torn Roman Republic,[58] just as More focuses upon one three-month event of war-torn England. Sallust's two histories, when considered together, give an interpretation of what caused the rise and fall of the great Roman Republic and, implicitly, of Roman civic health understood as just and peaceful self-rule. More's *Historia* reveals England's strengths and weaknesses, and it points, as we will see, to an understanding similar to Sallust's of civic health.

More's narrative technique could be compared to what today would be called a limited narrative point of view, a narrative strategy that expresses what a particular character would think himself. At different

---

[52] From Plutarch's "Were the Athenians More Famous in War or in Wisdom?" 347a (in vol. 4 of *Moralia*), but drawing upon the translation of Hobbes, as this passage appears in his prefatory letter "To the Readers" of his translation of Thucydides' *Peloponnesian War* (xxii).

[53] Sallust also imitated Thucydides.

[54] CW 2, lxxxvii–lxxxviii.

[55] Nelson 154.

[56] The great leader of Florence Leonardo Bruni – a classical scholar and a chancellor like More – based his history of the Republic of Florence on Sallust's in his dangerous task of recovering and strengthening republican rule in an age of tyranny. See Osmond 1995 and 1993.

[57] 6.7: "eo modo minume posse putabant per licentiam insolescere animum humanum."

[58] Sallust's *War with Jugurtha* takes place around 118 B.C. when the Roman Republic is already in decline, while *The War with Catiline* focuses upon the famous conspiracy against the Roman Republic in 63 B.C. just a short time before the republic's actual fall and before the rise of Rome's hereditary emperors.

times, the narrator portrays a particular character's self-understanding[59] –
as we saw in the early descriptions of Edward IV. At crucial points
in *Richard III*, the narrative perspective changes according to circumstances and character – which readers are meant to observe and
which is part of the reader's education in "sharp-sightedness" and good
judgment.[60]

More's artful ways of engaging our minds as if we were actually present
and involved can be seen by analyzing a few of the most striking rhetorical
devices.

The most obvious is the ironic use of "Protector," a term used almost
one hundred times referring to the very person planning the murder of
the two boy-princes.[61] But less obvious is More's use of *princeps* in the
same way and with the same effect – for anyone familiar with Cicero's
understanding of *princeps*.[62] When Buckingham's theatrics lead him to
say to Richard in front of the assembled faction-ridden nobles that "they
could easily find some other candidate [to be *princeps*] who cared for the
respublica,"[63] we are meant to smile – at Buckingham's audacity, and
at the absurdity of the claim given the diseased state of this faction-torn
regnum so devoid of wise and courageous leaders. Another example is
the narrator's calling Richard the *pius princeps*[64] for his punishment of
Jane Shore; we give a sarcastic guffaw, feeling disgust for Richard and –
as most of the London people did – great pity for poor Jane. The same
sarcasm is elicited by the rant of King Edward's mother, who is aghast
that the "sacrosanct majesty" of the *princeps*'s blood[65] would "spawn
mongrel, degenerate kings" through marriage to a commoner. Because the
only reputable people in this history turn out to be the commoners, here
is powerful irony indeed – another of More's masterful and humorous
uses of "praising of the unworthy."[66]

---

[59] For More's own explanation of such change of narrative perspective, see CW 6, 336/14–
28.

[60] These terms More uses in his letter explaining how to read *Utopia*. See especially CW 4,
248–51.

[61] Shakespeare most famously uses this same technique when Mark Antony repeatedly
calls Brutus an "honorable man" in *Julius Caesar*.

[62] Especially toward the end of his life, Cicero shows an acute awareness of the *fides*, the
rare mastery of the arts of rule, and the fullness of *humanitas* required to lead a nation
toward greater *humanitas*.

[63] CW 15, 480/2–3.

[64] CW 15, 424/8. Consider also the contrast with Epigram 111's treatment of the same
subject along with *Utopia*'s sarcastic use of the same phrase at 92/3.

[65] CW 15, 440/27; here the queen identifies "princeps" with hereditary royalty.

[66] In his *Art of Rhetoric* Thomas Wilson praises More for his "excellent gift" for this type
of irony (175).

The absurd misuse of *princeps* is perhaps most dramatically seen in the role given to the boy Edward as *princeps* of Wales:

[S]ince that country was far from the king and thus carelessly governed, so that it had begun to revert to a sort of wild savagery, with evil men freely and safely [*licenter impuneque*] engaging in robbery and murder, the younger Edward was sent there with a military command so the authority of the prince's [*authoritate Principis*] presence would check the audacity of wrongdoers.[67]

Without his mother or father, Edward is sent as a young child to Wales "where he lived during his father's lifetime." Describing this child – as yet uneducated, untried, and unskilled – as a *princeps* among savage criminals is meant to ellicit horror rather than humor. Cicero had described the role of the *princeps* in savage society, but he had presented that person as the rarest of the wise, the most persuasive of the eloquent, and the most trusted of leaders because of tried virtue and faithful, proven service.[68] Not only is having child Edward in Wales a perversion of the *princeps,* but it is also a perversion of the bond between parent and child and another sign of the brutality, the *immanitas,* of this country. That parental bond should be one of tender love and personal care, at least as described in the writings of More,[69] and of Cicero.[70]

This political perversion of the parent-child relations prepares us for the perversion of another foundational bond, that of husband-wife relation. With humorous irony,[71] the narrator has lecherous Edward IV make the case – a case that ends up being all the more powerful given the source. The setting is Edward IV's argument with his mother as to why

[67] CW 15, 336/27–338/3.
[68] See *De Inventione* 1.1–3; *De Oratore* 1.30–33; *De Officiis* 1.12.
[69] Compare, for example, Epigram 264/20–23 with the "liberos meos, naturae primum iure charos" of *Corr.* 123/117 (More's letter to tutor William Gonell). See also *CW* 12, 182/14–183/20. That More, throughout his life, conceived of God as a "tender loving father," see *CW* 1, 123/11 (More's translation) and *SL* 223 and 226, where More uses this same phrase before his signature. See also *CW* 12, 318/20.
[70] Cicero explains the parents' "strangely tender love for offspring" as one of the most important fonts giving rise to society in *De Officiis* 1.12 and 54 and *De Finibus* 3.62–65.
[71] The narrator has a distinctive voice of irrepressible comic irony. What the last line of Epigram 80 says of tyrants could have been said by the narrator of *Richard III:* the tyrant, snatched away by Death, who was "once so fearsome [now] deserves only a laugh." More undoubtedly learned many techniques from Lucian, but they shared the same irrepressible comic vision. The most famous example of comic irony More excluded from the Latin version, that is, the "bathroom humor" of *CW* 2, 84/14–15. And who could forget Edward IV's "holiest harlot" (56/8)?

he intends to marry for love a supposedly virtuous woman,[72] rather than marry for money and power an unknown and unloved foreign princess. His mother, as we have seen, is aghast at such an idea. It would be more "honorable and useful,"[73] she insists, to stabilize his claim to the throne and to increase his wealth by establishing "a marriage alliance with some foreign king."[74] Then follow her rant against contaminating royal blood with the degenerate blood of commoners and her warning that Edward's action will anger "the Earl of Warwick, the most powerful man in your realm besides you."[75]

Edward IV responds in a dismissive and jesting tone that angers his mother and hardens her opposition to his marriage plan.[76] The first part of his argument, however, is based on God and God's order:

Holy sacrament that it is, marriage ought to be contracted in the interests of virtue, not wealth – when, that is, God inspired mutual love and fidelity [*amorem fidemque mutuam*] in both partners, as I am sure that he has in our own case.[77]

Proceeding to the next argument based on "utility [rather] than sanctity,"[78] Edward observes that the love of his own people is more important than alliances with foreign powers, especially since he can make alliances by using his kinsmen for such marriages.

As for family connections with foreign princes, which your motherly affection represents as supremely desirable, but which we have seen often give rise to a torrent of troubles, they can still be established, with less hardship for me, if it happens that some of my kinsmen can bear to be wedded to strangers.[79]

---

[72] In the English version, however, the narrator says that Edward IV makes his decision to marry Elizabeth Woodville after "taking counsel of his *desire*" (CW 2, 61/28, emphasis added) rather than love – alluding to the famous scene from Livy (see notes 7 and 8 of Chapter 7).

[73] CW 15, 440/9–10: "honorificentius illum vtiliusque rebus consulturum." Undoubtedly More wants us to think of Cicero's famous identification of *honestas* and *vtilitas* with the requirements of truth, *fides*, and the bonds of society as seen throughout *De Officiis*.

[74] CW 15, 440/10–12.

[75] CW 15, 440/12–442/8. Her warning proves true: Warwick becomes so angry that he starts another civil war, deposes Edward IV, and reinstates Henry VI. During that civil war, Elizabeth takes refuge in sanctuary and gives birth to the son who will briefly become Edward V.

[76] CW 15, 446/5–7.

[77] CW 15, 442/12–15.

[78] By invoking *vtilia* (CW 15, 442/17) again, the narrator recalls again Cicero's famous argument in *De Officiis*, whereby true utility can never be separated from right action.

[79] CW 15, 442/21–24.

With powerful dramatic irony, the narrator has Edward acknowledge the "torrent of troubles" that political marriages have created, but then, because "useful" power and wealth can be achieved in ways that involve "less hardship for me," Edward happily lets others continue the practice. He never thinks that what is odious to him might also be bad as a public policy and bad for everyone. So odious is politicizing marriage to Edward that he swears:[80]

I would rather be a free private citizen than a king in a state of such servitude that a wife should be forced on me at another's direction without my consent.[81]

These appeals to *libertas* and to consent and to the privileged state of the "free private citizen," along with the complete rejection of servitude, point to those fonts or foundations of healthy social life that Cicero emphasized.[82] So strong among the Londoners is their desire for *libertas*, for example, that Richard and Buckingham must also appeal to it in their arguments to the English citizens.[83]

Perhaps the most frequently used literary device,[84] at least in the Latin text, is allusion. As we have seen earlier, More uses Roman terms such as senate, forum, *senatusconsultum*, *res publica* or commonwealth, *patria* or fatherland, *patrocinium*, and *bona fides*.[85] Without saying so directly,[86] More invites a comparison between the Roman Republic and England's hereditary *regnum* with its faltering parliament. But More broadens this comparison by bringing in London's sturdier institutions of self-government refined over three centuries of self-rule.[87] Why else does More refer habitually to the aldermen of London as the *senate* of London, meeting in the *forum* of London where the *recorder* is present,

[80] CW 15, 444/13; he swears again in this way at 334/23. Buckingham does the same at 366/7. In the English version, the cardinal did the same at CW 2, 40/14, but see the significant change where the Latin of 392/3–4 has the cardinal promise to pledge or bind by oath his *fides* and the other nobles' as well, for the boy's safety.

[81] CW 15, 444/17–19: "quin disperam ni priuatus esse liber quam rex hac seruitute vellem vxor vt inuito mihi alieno arbitratu obtruderetur."

[82] *De Officiis* 1.11–17.

[83] The strength of this desire was also revealed in More's coronation ode.

[84] Others are More's much loved assonance and consonance and, of course, puns.

[85] See www.thomasmorestudies.org/IndicesofLatinTerms for references to these and other terms.

[86] Morus, the character and narrator in *Utopia*, advises and uses the same "indirect approach."

[87] Already in 1215 London had annual elections for its mayor, a right written into the Magna Carta. For Londoners' struggle for independent self-government against the English kings, see both Williams and Barron. The significance of More the Londoner is well explained in James McConica's "The Patrimony of Thomas More."

a legal official whose task is to present new proposals to the London citizens so that all decisions are informed by the law?[88] Yes, the *History* shows a corrupt mayor, and the aldermen go along with corruption, but the *History* also shows a good number of wise London citizens who refuse to accept Richard's and Buckingham's offers to prostitute their freedom for personal advantage. And the Londoners' tears and heartfelt sorrow move us to pity at the "tragedy" of these "kings' games . . . played upon scaffolds,"[89] which they – and we – witness. Besides, Mayor Shaa has a one-year term, and the aldermen are elected officials. Given the people's response to the "performance" of the mayor's brother Fr. Shaa, the narrator is clear about the fatal consequences of such action in London.[90]

But how does London compare to Rome, a republic so defective that it fell? How did England's and London's institutions of self-rule differ from Rome's? Would they also fall? These were the types of questions More would have discussed with an unusually learned and talented circle of humanists from England and the continent. More's answers could not be given overtly, as the dangers to his life in 1520[91] and as his execution in 1535 would reveal, because overt criticism of the monarch was considered treasonous. Nonetheless, many of the problems that More faced in Henry VIII's war-loving empire were those faced in Rome's.

More seems to reserve special criticism for England's "noble" leaders as indicated by consistently ironic use of four different terms for these leaders encountered in *Richard III*. The first, *patres,* is used only twice in *Richard III*,[92] but with such a biting irony that one must ask, Are there

---

It must also be remembered that England, early in its history, was conquered by the Romans, as the remains of the Roman roads, walls, forums, etc., indicate. Shakespeare also draws attention to this dimension of English culture in such plays as *Cymbeline*.

[88] Notice how carefully the role of this official is explained at CW 15, 470/7–9: "Appellant recordatorem Londinenses ibi eum qui prefecti assessor est eruditus patrijs legibus ne quid in reddendis iudicijs imperitia peccetur" (The Londoners use the title "recorder" for a mayoral assistant well trained in the laws of his country who prevents any erroneous judgments from being given through ignorance of the laws). A few lines earlier we are told that he alone presents new proposals to the London citizens.

[89] This phrase appears only in the English version, at CW 2, 81/6–7, although the Latin version does use the theatrical metaphor and refer to the "tragic games of kings" (*tragicos esse ludos regum*) at CW 15, 482/20–21.

[90] CW 15, 448–454. Note the role (and power) of the truthful London friend at 454/9–12 – an important point brought to my attention by Stephen W. Smith.

[91] See note 51 of Chapter 6 regarding More's concern about the "dire peril" caused by Brixius's "criminal" attack on More.

[92] CW 15, 478/21, where Buckingham says that the *patres* will not be ruled by Edward IV's bastards. The first use is at 316/7, which is the narrator's representation of Edward IV's perspective.

any real fathers – or mothers – of this country? A mother such as Queen Elizabeth, for some mysterious reason, does not even act as a mother would,[93] and the nobles we see in *Richard III* do not act as fathers of their countries would.

Proceres and *nobilitas* are the terms most frequently used, and *nobilitas,* the general term, seems to be used, as the editor suggests, as an alternative for *proceres*.[94] Throughout *Richard III,* however, these faction-ridden leaders are clearly a major cause of England's disease. The narrator's sarcastic comment that "even a few of the leaders of the country [*proceres*] began to wake up"[95] to Richard's absurdly obvious "games . . . played upon scaffolds"[96] seems to hold true for all the *proceres* that we meet in this history.

Purpurati is a fourth term used in *Richard III* for English leaders, and every occurrence appears in a context that satirically exposes these "royal officials dressed in purple." For example, we are told that cruelty in the *purpurati* is euphemistically called "warlike";[97] and after "a quite insignificant knight" proves such cruelty by cooperating in murder, the narrator tells us that he is "now one of the highest nobility [*purpuratorum*]."[98] In such actions, these "noble" leaders routinely foster factional hatred, personal profit, and civil war.

If the leaders seem to be corrupt almost without exception in this history, the same uniform judgment could never be made about the people. As the narrator repeatedly indicates, the good and wise citizens refuse to cooperate, seeing Richard and Buckingham's actions for what they are: "intolerable flattery . . . , blasphemous adulation."[99]

Significantly, the English people are never called "subjects" in More's Latin history.[100] More never uses "subject" in his poetry either; instead,

---

[93] It is strange indeed that the queen never even thinks, You will take my sick child from me over my dead body. She never thinks about using her life to protect her son's. Her extraordinary rhetorical powers seem to be used in a measured and politically calculating way. And her calculation does work in that her daughter will marry Henry VII.

[94] See note at variant of *CW* 15, 420/20. What is said of this one instance seems to be a pattern throughout. "Proceres" are "leading men of a country, society, . . . profession, art, etc." (*OLD*).

[95] *CW* 15, 402/15.

[96] This phrase is used only in the English version: *CW* 2, 81/6–7.

[97] *CW* 15, 322/22–23.

[98] *CW* 15, 416/15ff.

[99] *CW* 15, 482/2–7, 432/27–434/2.

[100] As seen earlier, "subject" is used only once in the English version, ironically, when Edward IV's mother objected that "it was not princely to marry his own subject" (*CW* 2, 62/9).

he consistently uses "citizen" or "people."[101] That self-government by the people – genuine *respublica* – is at the heart of the work is indicated in many ways. For example, Richard and Buckingham make concerted efforts to win (with transparent deceptiveness)[102] the English people's consent. Richard recognizes that he cannot govern the people without their consent;[103] he also finds it necessary to say that "the title and profit and the ownership [of England is] totally [their] own – as a genuine commonwealth."[104] As one critic put it in speculating about More's overall project in this work, "the most vital issue of his history" is Richard's effort to win over the people.[105] Richard's winning over the nobles and clergy proves to be easy because both interest groups show themselves accustomed to taking "counsel of [their] desire."[106] The people of London, however, prove to be seasoned in their "everyday forms of resistance"[107] – constituting a formidable and enduring force against Edward IV as well as Richard III. Edward and Richard,[108] both violent usurpers of the throne, acknowledge the absolute necessity of winning over the people, although neither succeeds.[109] Throughout *Richardi Historia,* both are constantly judged by the people and by a narrator who

[101] Grace 1988 133–36 and 1985 115–29. As seen in Chapter 1, More states explicitly that wise and prudent rulers are not "swayed by the fact that they would not have many under them as subjects [*subiectos*], as the term is now used by kings to refer to their people [*populum*], who are really worse off than slaves [*seruos*]; for it is a much higher honor to rule over free people [*liberis*] . . . " (*SL* 80).

[102] *CW* 15, 454/6–12, 470/15–17, 472/15–16, 472/25–474/2, 484/15–22. That the narrator agrees with the prudence of this silence by the wise, consider *CW* 15, 482/20–24. More used the same strategy at important times in his own political life.

[103] *CW* 15, 480/7–8, 19–20; 484/1–5.

[104] *CW* 15, 480/19–20.

[105] Heath 15.

[106] *CW* 15, 440/3.

[107] Herman 1997 260.

[108] Catiline is presented – as is More's Richard III – as "an evil and depraved nature" who from "youth up . . . reveled in civil wars, murder, pillage, and political dissension" (5.1). Instead of being restrained by public virtue, he – like Richard III – was "spurred on . . . by the corruption of public morals" (5.9). Catiline is for Sallust an exemplum of the disease threatening Rome just a short time before the republic's fall. Sallust identifies Catiline and the corrupted public that fostered his rise as characteristic of "the worst and most vicious" in the history of the Roman Republic. Catiline's lust for power, Sallust observes, "was spurred on" not only by his own "haughty spirit" and guilty conscience (*conscientia scelerum*) "but also by the corruption of the public morals, which were being ruined by two great evils of an opposite character, extravagance and avarice" (*Catiline* 5.6–8) – both of which are major factors in More's *History.*

[109] Although the narrator, adopting the perspective of King Edward, claims that Edward did win over the English by the end of his life, this claim is undermined by statements made later in the work – and by the actual historical record. Consider the example of *CW* 15, 319/24–32: Who but the king himself would think that the game from

speaks as someone strongly independent of royal interests. The narrator of *Richard III* also shows the virtue and the "sharp-eyed" perspective of those people he presents as wise.[110]

This history is more forthright than Sallust's about political sovereignty belonging to the people.[111] In the Latin version of this *History*, More's narrator says explicitly that Parliament's "authority in England is supreme and absolute."[112] This perspective proves true within the text because "kings' games played upon scaffolds" come and go, accentuating by contrast the stability of the laws represented by London institutions such as the recorder, the *senatus* of aldermen, and the *forum* of the Guildhall where Buckingham pleads for Richard's "ludicrous election." In both the English and Latin versions, this history acknowledges that the kings of England must be elected by the English people[113] – even if the "ludicrous election"[114] is transparently manipulated. Significantly, however, only the Latin version states that "the title [*ius*] and the profit and the ownership" are "totally" the people's "as a genuine commonwealth"

"the pleasure of [his] hunt" would win the "widespread and hearty goodwill" of the Londoners?

[110] Herman 1997 263.

[111] One important reason Sallust gives for choosing the topic of *The War with Jugurtha* is that "it marked the first successful resistance [by the Roman people] to the insolence [*superbiae*] of the nobles" (5.1). As we will see, More's history has a similar intent. But what power did or could the Roman people have over the wealthy and politically domineering patricians and senators? Sallust and More agree that the source of power of the Roman and English people is the same: popular sovereignty based on rule by law. Especially considering that Sallust wrote during the time of the emperor Augustus Caesar, Sallust seems at first surprisingly forthright about political sovereignty belonging to the Roman people (*Jugurtha* 8.2, 14.7, 31.9, 17, 20, 22–25), a sovereignty that necessarily involves rule by law (*Jugurtha* 21.4, 31.9, 17, 18, 20, 33.2, 35.7; *Catiline* 6.6), which in turn is protected by the internal law of virtue (*Jugurtha* 1.1–3; 4.5–6; 14.19; 85.4, 17, 20, 31–2; *Catiline* 1.4; 2.1, 5, 7; 52.21, 29; 54.4). I say "at first surprisingly forthright" because, as Tacitus makes clear, Emperor Augustus was able to consolidate his centralized power only by making public appeals to the Roman tradition of republican self-rule – just as Richard and Buckingham do in *Richard III*.

[112] *CW* 15, 320/22–23. In his commentary on these lines, editor Kinney interprets this statement as an "overstatement." In his commentary at *CW* 2, 6/14, Sylvester observes: "More's observation is striking in that it was not even true *de facto* in the early sixteenth century. *De jure* it has never been valid" – until much later in England's history. This same position, however, More expresses in Epigram 121, at *CW* 13, 21/2–6, and in More's conversation with Richard Rich as recorded by Roper and the trial documents (Roper 85; Harpsfield 274). It is also the view assumed by most of More's political epigrams, and by *Richard III* and *Utopia*.

[113] *CW* 2, [English] 74/33, 79/23–32 implied, 83/3, 82/9; *CW* 15, 468/12, 470/24, 472/3, 18–19, 480/1.

[114] *CW* 15, 484/22; *CW* 2, [English] 82/9.

and not the king's[115] – the same view expressed in Epigram 121 and implied in Epigram 198.

In their effort to win support from the "honest citizens" of London,[116] Buckingham and Richard know they have to address the Londoners as "citizens" and "the people," and to promise rule by law. Buckingham ironically presents Chief Justice Markham as a hero for defying Edward IV's orders to make a ruling against English law,[117] and Richard ironically insists on being crowned in Westminster Hall "where the king himself sits and ministers the law," because he considered "that to carry out the laws and to act as their servant was the essence of kingship."[118]

Richard also recognizes the self-governing temper of the English people when he says – again with dramatic irony – that "no earthly man can govern [the English] against their wills,"[119] a principle recognized by Sallust in his history of the Roman Republic[120] – and by Cicero,[121] whom Sallust discreetly presents as the "best of consuls."[122]

Considering the work as a whole, More's *Historia Richardi* shows that the cause of civil war was faction, which in turn was caused by ambitious and "noble" leaders such as Lord Hastings who help Richard come to power even though they are aware of Richard's cruel and ambitious character. Hastings, for example, knowingly collaborates in the murder

---

[115] *CW* 15, 480/19–20: "fructumque ac proprietatem vtriusque omnem vestrum haud dubie publicam." In *City of God* 2.21 and 19.21 and 24, Augustine quotes Cicero's definition of *res publica* as *res populi* (*De Re Publica* 1.39 and 3.43). To stress the point that *res publica* refers to the good of the people as a whole, Augustine offers this explanation: "rem publicam, id est rem populi, rem patriae, rem communem" (*City of God* 5.18). Nonetheless, the definition of *populus* becomes a major point of disagreement between Augustine and Cicero. In *City of God* 2.21 and 19.21, Augustine gives Cicero's definition of *populus,* "multitudinis coetum iuris consensu et utilitatis communione sociatum esse" (*De Re Publica* 1.39, 3.43), but strongly disagrees with it, redefining it in terms of *concordia,* not *ius* and *utilitas*: "an assembly of the rational multitude united in fellowship by a harmonious agreement as to the objects of its love" (*rationalis multitudinis coetus rerum quas diligit concordi communione societus*), *City of God* 19.24). As seen earlier, More as a young man lectured in London on *The City of God.*

[116] Note the distinction that Buckingham makes at *CW* 15, 472/15–16.

[117] *CW* 15, 458; *CW* 2, [English] 70.

[118] *CW* 15, 484/4–5.

[119] *CW* 15, 480/8; *CW* 2, [English] 79/31–32.

[120] See, for example, the speech that Memmius makes to the Roman people at *Jugurtha* 31 and 23–29.

[121] *De Officiis* 2.23–25.

[122] *Catiline* 43.1: "optumo consuli." Consider how Sallust's history as a whole assumes but never draws much attention to Cicero's principal role in saving Rome from Catiline's treachery.

of Richard's political opponents; he knowingly and maliciously lies,[123] prostituting his reputation to do Richard's will. Jane Shore is not alone in her willingness to sell her services; she, however, as the narrator so movingly portrays, was abused both by her society's custom of loveless marriage[124] and by the very fathers of her country. The king himself used his position to seduce her; Hastings did the same. What a tragedy, the narrator seems to conclude.[125]

But what is the cause of this tragedy? Why is good leadership so egregiously lacking in England? The narrator, who gives voice to thirty-five of the English text's fifty-nine proverbs,[126] artfully poses this question with the voice of a father of his country – of his *patria*.[127] He shows that institutional changes are desperately needed.[128] But what changes?

---

[123] CW 15, 356/3–5: "Hastings offered his word of honor [*fides*] (which everyone trusted)" – before lying. The narrator than comments: "This speech had a considerable influence because of the speaker's honorable reputation" (*Hec oratio ob creditam viri fidem magnam habuit vim*).

[124] Consider how the narrator presents Jane's marriage: "This woman...was joined in a marriage which was otherwise promising enough but contracted too early. For though her husband was honorable, fashionable, prosperous, and youthful, since she married before she was ready, she never cherished her husband at all, having gotten him before she desired him" (CW 15, 424/23–426/2).

[125] CW 15, 482/15, 20; in the English version, compare the wording of CW 2, 81/6–7 with 82/13–20 and with 24/30.

[126] See Hosington's "More's Use of English Proverbs in *The History of King Richard III*." No comparable study of the Latin text has been done.

[127] CW 15, 336, 378, 470, 476.

[128] To prevent *superbia* from corrupting the powerful leaders and therefore bringing about "lawless tyranny," Sallust similarly reports that the old and experienced "fathers" of Rome "altered their [monarchical] form of government and appointed two rulers with annual power, thinking that this device would prevent men's minds from growing arrogant though unlimited authority" (*Catiline* 6.7–7.3).

9

Utopia

A Model Respublica of Peace, Liberty, and Self-Government?

> [W]ell and wisely trained citizens you will hardly find anywhere.
>
> Morus's introduction to Raphael's story, *Utopia* 52/30–54/1[1]

> No force of rule is strong enough to be lasting if it labors under the weight of fear.
>
> Cicero, *De Officiis* 2.23, 25[2]

> You have either no image [of a true commonwealth], or a false one. But you should have been with me in Utopia.
>
> Hythlodaeus to Morus, *Utopia* 106/13–14[3]

Raphael's passionate appeals for *humanitas*, justice, and peaceful free government are among the most powerful in world literature. So urgent and so vivid are they that many identify them completely as author Thomas More's. Are they? How do we know? And can we ever know if author More agrees with his character Morus?

Raphael's appeals to *humanitas* in *Utopia* are usually made while showing Utopia's superiority to the inhumane practices of other countries, especially England itself. Raphael vividly describes such practices as starving veterans maimed while fighting loyally for war-mongering kings

---

[1] "[O]missa interim inquisitione monstrorum, quibus nihil est minus nouum . . . at sane ac sapienter institutos ciues haud reperias ubilibet" (CW 4). The translation, however, is from *CUP Utopia* 49.

[2] "[O]diis nullas opes posse obsistere. . . . Nec vero ulla vis imperii tanta est, quae premente metu possit esse diuturna."

[3] "Tibi . . . eius imago rei, aut nulla succurrit, aut falsa. Verum si in Vtopia fuisses mecum . . ." (CW 4).

but left with no means of livelihood; starving citizens hung for stealing grain needed for survival; war-bent kings hoarding gold needed by citizens for trade; and citizens "eaten by sheep" because of get-rich-quick schemes by callous sheep-barons. Such images show us a country stratified by wealth and poverty, by corrupt power and desperate need – the very conditions that Aristotle presented as the major causes of factions and civil war.[4] Like *Richard III*, *Utopia* focuses a great deal upon the social and political conditions of civil unrest, leading careful readers to wonder how Utopus could so quickly bring about Utopia's transformation from bitter factions to the height of *humanitas*.[5]

Despite Raphael's attractive promises of *humanitas,* Thomae Morus completely disagrees with Raphael's proposed solutions for England's political and economic problems. When Raphael first proposes the elimination of private property as the cure to injustice and inhumanity, Morus immediately disagrees, with the bluntest language he uses in the entire book: "I am of the contrary opinion," and he goes on to say that, without legal protection (*tueri lege*) for the profit of one's own labor, the only result could be unending murder, sedition, and an insufficient lack of goods.[6] Raphael responds by saying that Morus is understandably mistaken, not having an "image" of a *respublica*.[7] Then, after presenting Morus with his own detailed image in the course of book 2, Raphael gives his famous peroration praising Utopia as not only the best *res publica* but the only one deserving that name. Raphael concludes with the promise that there will be no sedition or murder and no lack of life's necessities wherever Utopia is imitated.[8]

How are we to judge between these two opposed positions? Morus argues that legal protections such as private property are necessary; Raphael argues that only by eliminating all private property and all lawyers and all complex laws will social ills be eliminated.[9] What are we to make of the fact that the book is written by a lawyer and judge who was strongly convinced that laws were a natural expression and

[4] On this point, see Aristotle's *Politics* 1303b15–17, but see all of book 5 for the causes of factions and internal war.
[5] CW 4, 112/1–6. Page and line references in the text for *Utopia* are from CW 4.
[6] CW 4, 106/3–12.
[7] CW 4, 106/13: "imago rei."
[8] CW 4, 242/3, 14–16.
[9] The same would be true in Shakespeare's first utopia: In *2 Henry VI*, the rebel Jack Cade "vows reformation" whereby "All the realm shall be in common" (4.2.65, 68), "there shall be no money," and all will be dressed "in one livery" (72–74). To bring this new order about, Cade insists that "first thing we do, let's kill all the lawyers" (76–78).

necessary development of reason, as confirmed by "the judgment of all learned men, . . . all good men," by "the public agreement of the whole world," and by God himself?[10]

The fictional character Morus not only insists on the necessity of legal protections but also is represented four times as the "sheriff [*vicecomitis*] of the city of London."[11] The *vicecomitis* of London was definitely a position of enforcing the law, although "sheriff" is not an adequate translation.[12] For almost four hundred years, Thomas More's London had been electing its own sheriff,[13] and for three hundred years its own mayor[14] – all serving one-year terms, all responsible to the people who elected them, and all accountable to the law.[15] Its historically devised trade guilds (also regulated by law) became so effective that London prospered enormously. Furthermore, these trade guilds became a way that cycles of poverty and class were broken by allowing apprentices to achieve status of "freeman" (*liberi*).[16] London eventually became so prosperous that it could demand its liberties even from powerful kings.

Utopia has nothing comparable to these London fashionings because the Utopian *princeps* serves as judge, lawmaker, and law enforcer.

---

[10] CW 5, 277–81.

[11] The 1518 edition of *Utopia*, which More corrected before publication, identifies Morus in this way in four different places (1/6–7, 46/6–7, 110/6, 246/9); he also draws attention to his legal and judicial duties at 38/24–26. The 1565 and 1689 Latin versions we have of *Richard III* also identify the author as "Londinensis Civitatis jam tum Vicecomitem"; see CW 15, 314/22–23.

[12] For the complexity of this word's meaning, consider Maitland's commentary in *Domesday Book and Beyond*: "If we render *vicecomes* by *sheriff* we are making our sheriff too little of a *vicomte*. When *comes* is before us we have to choose between giving Brittany an *earl*, giving Chester a *count*, or offending some of our *comites* by invidious distinctions. Time will show what these words shall mean" (8). Genius of language that he was, More must have had a reason to identify himself repeatedly as a *vicecomes* instead of what was actually his position of *subvicecomes*. See the next note and Harpsfield 312, 313. In the interpretation developed in this book, I take More as identifying himself as the legal officer of (*vice* meaning "instead of, in place of") the people (drawing upon the *comitia* which was the legal assembly of the people in ancient republican Rome, and which is the term used in *Utopia* at 124/1, 5).

[13] London and his legal profession were so important to More that the first sentence of his tombstone epitaph of 1532 mentions both: "Thomas More was born in the city of London of a family not famous but honest, . . . and after spending some years of his youth as a pleader of cases in the forum, he dispensed right in his city for the Sheriff" (*Thomas Morus vrbe Londinensi familia non celebri sed honesta natus . . . quum et causas aliquot annos iuuenis egisset in foro, et in vrbe sua pro Shyreuo ius dixisset . . .*)."

[14] Since the Magna Carta of 1215.

[15] See Barron, Williams, and Brooke.

[16] Nightingale, especially 565–70.

Furthermore, unlike in London and Rome,[17] leaders of Utopia generally serve for life.

The American Founders, having studied Rome and England carefully, agreed with Polybius and Cicero on the need for a division of powers, limited terms, and a mixed form of government. Alexander Hamilton had also read *Utopia*, but faced with Raphael's federation of fifty-four *principes* living in peace and harmony, Hamilton concluded that *Utopia* was a foolish work indeed: "A man must be far gone in Utopian speculation who can seriously doubt that . . . [they] would have frequent and violent contests with each other." He went on in *Federalist Papers* no. 6 to explain why such harmony among fifty-four major cities was simply impossible:

[M]en are ambitious, vindictive, and rapacious. To look for a continuation of harmony between a number of independent, unconnected sovereignties situated in the same neighborhood would be to disregard the uniform course of human events, and to set at defiance the accumulated experience of ages.

Of course, the situation is impossible for more reasons than Hamilton indicates because Raphael leaves out the factor in London's history that played an enormous role in its development: the English kings, who played a major role in transforming a warring federation into a somewhat united country, yet also posed one of the greatest points of contention in London's development as a free and self-governing society.

King and Conqueror Utopus is the only factor given in Raphael's account that could explain how all fifty-four Utopian cities have the very same laws. What are those laws and what are the reasons for Utopia's alleged success? Answering those questions is, of course, a major part of the intellectual game that Thomas More has created, inviting readers to be attentive to the many clues he has given. Eventually, attentive readers have to ask: is it good for the average Utopian citizen to have no lawyers or independent judicial system and for all the power of the city to be in the hands of twenty-one highly privileged officials with virtual lifetime terms?[18] More's London and Cicero's Rome developed various professions, such as lawyers and different kinds of judges and avenues of appeal,

---

[17] Just as much as Rome, London is also present throughout Utopia as a point of comparison and contrast. Like London, every Utopian city is surrounded by a wall, has pleasant gardens – and is even as large and prosperous as London. The description of the Utopian city of Amaurotum is so similar to London in rivers, bridges, harbor structure, and encircling walls that the marginal gloss draws attention to this striking correspondence (CW 4, 118/15).

[18] The only grounds for the *princeps*'s loss of position is tyranny, and the tranibors "are not changed without good reason" (CW 4, 122). But because these twenty-one seem

to assist in the difficult task of justice; both had several courts of law along with hard-won protections for citizens, and both took special care to limit power and to limit the terms of those who exercised most power.

Utopia has caused great confusion ever since its publication. Even in 1516 there was such perplexity that More wrote a letter to Peter Giles, which was published with the 1517 edition of *Utopia*.[19] This important letter humorously explains how a book like *Utopia* should be read, and it draws attention to the issue of Morus's trustworthiness or *fides*[20] as reporter of Raphael's tale in contrast to Raphael's *fides* as teller of the tale.[21] At the end of this letter, distinguishing between his own and Raphael's *fides,* Morus suggests that unbelievers seek out Raphael and "inquire the truth from him or, if they like, dig it out of him with questions (*questionibus exculpant*)" (252/3–4). Of course, this is just what lawyer Morus did not do at any point in his Sunday afternoon visit with old Raphael. But what if he did? What would happen if Raphael were cross-examined by a well-trained lawyer? Could Raphael's story hold up in court? Of course, the whole ironic structure of this work and the odd ending of book 2 invite the attentive reader to do just that, to "cross-examine" Raphael and his claims. An examination of this kind reveals many blatant contradictions or impossibilities such as the examples that follow.

Utopia's size: Raphael gives us two accounts of Utopia's size: the first makes Utopia the size of Wales (31,000 square miles),[22] the second makes Utopia the size of all of Great Britain.[23] Which is it?

Utopia's change from peninsula to island: Really? How would it be possible to cut a fifteen-mile-wide channel with primitive tools, at

---

to oversee and judge most everything, would they also supervise charges made against themselves, or their own elections by secret ballot?

[19] CW 4, 248–52, gives the whole of this letter.

[20] More discusses the same issue at length in his 1520 Letter to Brixius. See CW 3.2, 577–88, 600ff. Notice that Budé in his letter claims to have "full faith" *(fidem plane)* in More (CW 4, 14/1).

[21] CW 4, 250/16–22. See also R. S. Sylvester's classic article "'Si Hythlodaeo Credimus': Vision and Revision in Thomas More's *Utopia*." Sylvester notes how "[t]wice Budé hedges his praise for Utopian institutions with the words 'if we may believe Hythlodaeus' (*si Hythlodaeo credimus* or 'if we may believe the story'" [CW 4, 10/30–12/1 and 10/3].

[22] Heiserman 171, Kinney 62: fifty-four cities of 645 square miles each. As Kinney points out, Morus is "in the fictional presence of his close friend Cuthbert Tunstall," who is a famous arithmetician. Tunstall had dedicated his book on arithmetic to More; both served in treasury and government positions that required talent for numbers. See Chambers 197, 216–17.

[23] See note to CW 4, 110/8.

"incredible speed" (112/6–15)? The marginal gloss on this "incredible" accomplishment reads: "This feat was greater than digging the Isthmus of Corinth." Attempting to dig that channel across the Corinthian isthmus involved so many futile attempts that the project became proverbial as an impossibly difficult – and unaccomplished – task.[24]

Utopia's cities: Raphael tells us that his small island supports fifty-four cities, each the size of London. Could there be fifty-four Romes in central Italy or fifty-four New York Cities in the northeast United States? Why this is economically impossible would lead to a fascinating lesson on the nature of real economics.[25] This alleged equality of cities parallels the alleged equality of citizens.

Equality of all: Repeatedly Raphael praises the equality of all Utopians, and he denounces money as the source of all evils. How are we to take the offhanded revelation, then, that certain Utopian leaders called *quaestors* live abroad "in great style and . . . play the part of magnates"[26] (214/25–26)?

Words versus reality: Raphael makes sweeping statements that are initially inviting, but then we discover they are not true. Examples include the attractiveness and ease of travel in Utopia's harbor when that harbor is treacherous; supposed ease of travel within Utopia when travel requires many difficulties; insistence that everyone shares the farming duties when

---

[24] Here the gloss is certainly playing upon the well-known adage whereby building a Corinthian canal meant foolishly trying the impossible, as the marginal gloss indicates. A similar "incredible" excavation project is reported in the story of Atlantis in Plato's *Critias*. As suggested by *CW* 4's commentary at 112/8, this may be More's "Gargantuan humor pictur[ing] the English Channel as man-made."

[25] See economist Samuel Bostaph's analysis. In More's time, the most popular text on economics was based on Aristotle and translated with commentary by the Florentine humanist and Lord Chancellor Leonardo Bruni. That text begins by asserting what Utopia denies: that family and commonwealth differ substantially, indeed essentially.

When Aristotle begins his treatment of the best regime, he turns immediately to questions about size of cities and the quality of the territory that supports a particular city, be that city large or small (*Politics* 1325b40 ff.). Beginning in this way reveals the immense practical experience Aristotle has in economic and political matters. He devotes an entire chapter, for example, on positive and negative features of cities that have good harbors – showing in specific ways that some cities have greater resources and capacities than others and that each has unique characteristics.

How then could anyone with experience believe Raphael when he tells us that all fifty-four cities of Utopia, having the same enormous populations, are "identical in . . . traditions, customs, and laws," and "even in appearance" "as far as the nature of the ground permits" 112/15–19)? Then, after stressing their similarities, Raphael calls Amaurotum the "princeps" of all (112/27)?

[26] In Rome, *quaestores* were junior magistrates. Thomas More was appointed *proquaestor* (see his epitaph, *EE* 2821, line 80) or under-treasurer in 1521.

in fact the scholar class does not; and insistence that free speech exists, yet it is a capital offense to "take counsel on matters of common interest outside the senate or the popular assembly."[27]

The root of all evil: If money and property are the root of all evils as Raphael argues in his own name, what are we to make of his opinion that he has "performed [his] duty" to his relatives and friends by giving them his money and property (54/19–25 and 50/3)?

All killing is wrong: In book 1, Raphael's strongest tirade is against those who change the law of God to support their own misguided interpretation of killing. How then are we to respond in book 2 when Raphael approvingly reports the Utopians' frequent use of capital punishment and their pride in being "the greatest benefactors to the human race" in wanting to exterminate the entire nation of Zapoletans (208/10–13)?[28] Even in book 1, however, Raphael praises the *humanitas* of the Polylerites' punishment of criminals, punishment that includes death[29] – thus raising questions of the consistency of Raphael's thoughts and actions.

Misuse of Scripture: Raphael misquotes Scripture to support other positions. In referring to God's alleged biblical command against all killing, he does not distinguish between murder and killing, failing to recount that capital punishment is "fully approved" in the Old Testament itself and that the biblical term "*rāsah* means to kill a human being *illegally*."[30] A similar misrepresentation occurs when Raphael strongly

---

[27] CW 4, 124/1–2.

[28] By contrast, Cicero denied legal protection to only one category of rational creatures: those who chose to become tyrants set on oppressing other rational creatures. Here is Cicero's argument in *De Officiis* 3.6.32:

> [W]e have no ties of fellowship with a tyrant, but rather the bitterest feud; and it is not opposed to Nature to rob, if one can, a man whom it is morally right to kill; – nay, all that pestilent and abominable race should be exterminated from human society. And this may be done by proper measures; for, as certain members are amputated, if they show signs themselves of being bloodless and virtually lifeless and thus jeopardize the health of the other parts of the body, so those fierce and savage monsters in human form should be cut off from what may be called the common body of humanity.

> Later on, Cicero says, "Our tyrant [Julius Caesar] deserved his death...for he justifies the destruction of law and liberty" and was guilty of "the most horrible and hideous of all murders – that of the fatherland" (3.82–3). Significantly, More and Erasmus wrote competing declamations on tyrannicide in 1504.

[29] At 78/10 Raphael praises the Polylerites' *humanitas*; at 76/30 he off-handedly mentions their use of capital punishment.

[30] Emphasis added. See the commentary on Exodus 20:13 in the *Anchor Bible* (New York: Doubleday, 2006), 179, also on Exodus 21:12–17, Deuteronomy 20:1–14, and Matthew 19:18.

rebukes Morus for advocating a tact and prudence that Raphael calls lying.[31] In support of this extreme position,[32] Raphael invokes the New Testament, supposedly quoting Christ as saying that "what He had whispered in the ears of His disciples He commanded to be preached openly from the housetops."[33] This quote could refer to two passages in Scripture. The first occurs when Christ is advising his twelve newly selected apostles to be "prudent as serpents" but "innocent as doves" (Matthew 10:16). Even with such shrewdness and virtue, however, Christ warns them to expect persecution and only "[w]hen they deliver you up," then "[w]hat you hear whispered, preach it on the housetops" (Matthew 10:27–8). The second source is Christ's discourse on the Last Judgment, when "what you have said in darkness will be said in the light; and what you have whispered in the inner chambers will be preached on the housetops" (Luke 12:1–3). When considered in context, the sources of Raphael's quotations work against Raphael's dismissive position toward prudent and tactful action in the world.

Location of Utopia: We are never told where it is because, Morus mistakenly claims,[34] Raphael "forgot to say" (42/1). We are, however, told that Raphael circumnavigated the entire world in 1503 to get there, when in fact Magellan was the first to do so years later, in 1519–22.[35] Well-trained lawyers and judges notice such discrepancies.

Raphael's travel to Utopia: After being compared to Ulysses rather than Palinurus, Raphael claims to have gone on the "last three of those four voyages which are now universally read of, but on the final voyage he did not return with" Vespucci and then proceeded to Utopia. But Vespucci never made a fourth voyage, and the book everyone was reading contained fabricated stories about activities of naked natives that would appeal to readers because Vespucci's accounts were much too uninteresting.[36]

---

[31] CW 4, 100/6.
[32] Cicero praises "my masters, the schools of Plato and Aristotle, men who do not hold violent or extreme views" (*Pro Murena* 63).
[33] CW 4, 100/17–27.
[34] Giles humorously insists that Raphael *did* address "More's difficulty about the geographical position of the island," but unfortunately while "Raphael was speaking on the topic, one of More's servants had come up to him to whisper something or other in his ear," and Giles himself was prevented from hearing this crucial bit of information because someone coughed loudly at just that moment (CW 4, 22/21ff.). Budé also humorously draws attention to this omission at 12/1–5.
[35] Other dates are also incredible, such as Raphael's claim to have brought Hesychius's Greek dictionary to Utopia in 1503, when its first printing was not until 1514.
[36] Pohl 154.

Other Utopian impossibilities: These include uprooting whole forests by hand and transplanting them from one region to another (178/26–30); securing slaves with chains of gold, the softest of metals (152/8–9); using durable armor that does not make swimming the least bit awkward (212/25–29); saying that with their well-built but very old buildings, there is "scarcely anything to do" to maintain them (132/25–29); and possessing books that had not yet been printed (182/1).

Other contradictions: Raphael speaks passionately in book 1 against any form of slavery for himself, but he is completely undisturbed by the widespread slavery in Utopia – even of citizens.[37] He reports that there are no fixed penalties except for the few crimes related to marriage (190), but in the same paragraph he notes that there is death for slaves who rebel and elsewhere he reports other severe penalties (124/1–2, 146/9, 192/24-, 29–30) for behavior that is hardly criminal. He speaks about the importance of governing free citizens, without recognizing how unfree his Utopians actually are, even in an activity as common as the travel that Raphael passionately loves.

In light of such blatant contradictions and impossibilities, a reasonable judge could conclude that Raphael is not a trustworthy narrator. If Plato's *Republic* boasts openly that its "best republic" is based on a noble lie (414b-415d), *Utopia* is based on lies of another kind. But of what kind? And what possible advantages would there be in creating an unreliable narrator with a last name that means "Speaker of Nonsense"?[38] The advantages are many.

Of greatest practical importance, author More gains protection because Hythlodaeus is the one who openly criticizes kings, flawed institutions, and all-too-familiar abuses of power.[39] When, for example, the Anchorian people "humanely" (90/8) require their king to choose one kingdom to rule after his invasion of a second, what informed reader would not think of King Henry VIII's invasion of France at the cost of his citizens' blood, wealth, and peace? So artful and indirect is More's

---

[37] The Roman people devised specific protections to prevent enslavement of citizens. Cicero argues that the human "thirst" for liberty is one of the strongest drives in human nature and that "in defense of liberty a great-souled person would stake everything" (*De Officiis* 1.68).

[38] For the etymology of "Hythlodaeus," see CW 4, 301–2.

[39] By creating a long-winded lead-character named Hythlodaeus, "Speaker of Nonsense," More imitates Erasmus's success with Folly as the loquacious lead character in that classic which More inspired and which Erasmus dedicated to More. In the prefatory letter in *Folly*, addressed to More, Erasmus recalls that More's last name means folly in Greek, even though More is "as far removed from it as possible."

literary approach that even an enemy set on destroying More did not find sufficient evidence to do so.[40] After all, fictitious Morus is simply reporting what Raphael, "speaker of nonsense," claims to have seen during his world travels.

Other advantages are artistic and humorous, as the earliest commentators observed:[41] an unreliable narrator gives the author a grand field for irony, allusion, and great wit.[42]

Most importantly, overall, are the philosophical advantages: by the richly ironic and allusive designs of his text, More engages those most active readers who are willing to exercise and develop the "sharp-sightedness" that prudent leadership and true philosophy require.[43] Why would this dimension of the work be the most important? Because according to Cicero, Seneca, and young More, philosophy is the "art of living" that everyone needs in piloting one's own life and one's own ship of state.

Sharp-sighted readers must ask, for example, the question presented as having greatest interest to *princeps* Morus,[44] and arguably to all those fashioned in Ciceronian *humanitas*: are the Utopians "well and wisely trained citizens"?[45] *Utopia* is so designed that attentive readers must also ask: how has this supposedly peaceful and prosperous society been educated and what kind of laws and rhetoric have fashioned this unusual political order?

As we have seen, the role of the *princeps* is so important in Cicero's account that peace in a society can begin only when one arises. That word *princeps* is used more than sixty times in *Utopia*. But Cicero's artful and dedicated *princeps* brings peace by convincing warring individuals and factions to come together on the basis of a shared consensus about justice and mutual advantage. As shown by Cicero's own attempts, such a leader is also needed to deepen or at least continue that consensus and hence that

---

[40] See note 51 of Chapter 6 for the account of Brixius's dangerous attack on More.

[41] See Budé's comments at *CW* 4, 12/14–20, for example.

[42] Jonathan Swift imitates More in *Gulliver's Travels* by having as the narrator Gulliver, who, only at the end of the book, clearly reveals that he is mad. Like Hythlodaeus, Gulliver ends his narration with a proud tirade against pride.

[43] This quality of sharp-sightedness More points out in his Letter to Giles, *CW* 4, 248/23.

[44] That Morus and Giles were not interested in much of Raphael's "long tale," see *CW* 4, 52/24–27. What they "most eagerly inquired of him" were "those wise and prudent provisions which he noticed anywhere among nations living together in a manner suited to citizens [*quae apud populos unquam civiliter conuiuentes*]" (52/27–29).

[45] *CW* 4, 52/33; see the opening quotation in this chapter. That More was one who was recognized as "first" among city leaders can be seen by the many offices in London he was asked to assume. See Peter Ackroyd's *Thomas More*.

peaceful and prosperous condition of his society. Such talented, virtuous, and skillful leaders of the free use education, law, and rhetoric to fashion the happiness and peace of their country.

Cicero names specific history-making leaders of this kind, showing how they made the difference between war and peace, greatness and mediocrity.[46] The most famous that Cicero mentions are Julius Brutus,[47] Scipio, Regulus, Cato, and Cicero[48] himself. In Cicero's account, each of these individuals made important contributions to Roman life and left the culture and the nation better and a different place. So difficult were their challenges that they all required heroic efforts, often culminating in death.

In the entire work, Raphael names only two leaders who could be called a *princeps*: Lord Chancellor and Cardinal John Morton in book 1[49] and Conqueror Utopus in book 2.[50] The first ultimately disappoints Raphael,[51] but the second receives unqualified praise for founding the only society that deserves the name of *respublica*, the only society that is truly just. Raphael also praises unqualifiedly those unnamed scholars elected to be the *principes* of Utopia's fifty-four Londons.

By contrast, within the opening paragraphs of book 1, Morus names and describes four *princeps* worthy of imitation; three are with him to negotiate a new treaty for international trade: his fellow ambassador from England, Tunstall, known for proven competence, popularity, integrity, and learning; the mayor of Bruges, who is the *princeps* and head of the Flanders' delegation with whom Morus and Tunstall have been sent to negotiate a new trade treaty; the "chief speaker and guiding spirit" of that delegation, Georges de Themsecke, a lawyer-orator of such exceptional education and practical experience that he is said to be a greater "chief and guide" than the one actually serving as *princeps*

---

[46] As Sallust put it: "After long reflection I became convinced that it [the greatness of Rome] had all been accomplished by the eminent virtue of a few citizens" (*Catiline* 53.4).

[47] Who helped end the rule of kings and begin the Roman Republic.

[48] Who defeated – without war – Catiline's conspiracy against Rome.

[49] Forced to defend his position, Raphael gives three historical examples: Morton in England, "some" French king, and a hypothetical king in a hypothetical country.

[50] The only other individuals whom Raphael names are Vespucci (50/26) and a fellow companion with as strange a name as Hythlodaeus's own: Tricius Apinatus, his companion who brings along medical books (182/6).

[51] At 84/24–30 Raphael expresses his judgment that the cardinal allowed himself to be flattered, and Raphael interprets the whole event as evidence of "what little regard courtiers would pay to me and to my advice." At 58/19–60/5, however, Raphael praises him as a prudent, virtuous, effective leader and expert of laws. Morton is, in fact, willing to try out Raphael's suggestions, and by Raphael's own account, he has been of great benefit to the English *Respublica*.

or head of his delegation.[52] Morus is himself a learned lawyer and
"orator."[53] Henry VIII is called a *princeps*, but in a way reminiscent
of the epigrams: this "most invincible King of England" is presented as
"richly adorned with skills for an outstanding *princeps*."[54] The longest
and greatest praise of any civil leader, however, is given to Morus's
coauthor, so to speak, of *Utopia*, Peter Giles[55] – whom Morus describes
as a model civic humanist and "the perfect friend": honest, loyal, learned,
of proven character and effective public service, prudent and innocent,[56]
witty and charming. Although Morus does not himself directly give high
praise to John Morton,[57] all the *princeps* he names are real individuals
who influenced history by rendering services to specific cities facing great
political difficulties.

How, then, do Raphael's ideal Utopian *principes* compare when measured by Cicero's and Morus's criteria?[58] For example, are the fully educated Utopian leaders and citizens disdainful of pleasure, as Cicero insists
that his must be? Clearly not, because maximizing pleasure is an often-
mentioned objective of the Utopian order.

Or measured by Cicero's leaders of "great souls," of *magnanimity*,
how do Utopian leaders compare? In all of *Utopia*, the concept is conspicuously absent, as it is in *Richard III* as well.[59]

---

[52] CW 4, 46/24–26: "[T]heir chief speaker and guiding spirit was Georges de Themsecke,
Provost of Cassel, a man not only trained in eloquence but a natural orator – most
learned, too, in the law and consummately skillful in diplomacy by native ability as well
as by long experience."

[53] At CW 4, 46/12, Morus identifies himself as being "sent as an orator" (*oratorem me
legauit*) by *princeps* Henry VIII.

[54] More does not recognize Henry as king of England *and France*; see Erasmus's comments
on the absurdity of the title "Invincible" (*Education of a Christian Prince*, 59). And how
is one "most invincible"?

[55] Giles contributes an introductory letter, the Utopian alphabet and poem, and marginal
notes that serve as an often-humorous commentary on the work. See CW 4, 20–24, 277,
280–81.

[56] CW 4, 48/10 – "simplicitas inest prudentior" – alludes to "prudent as a serpent, innocent
as a dove" of Matthew 10:16. See Chapter 1.

[57] Morus may not praise Morton for the reason the narrator gives in *Richard III*. Morton
is only mentioned in passing twice in the Latin version of *Richard III*; in the English
version he has a major role at the end, but the narrator draws attention to his darker
and questionable side in these words: Morton ended his days "so godly that his death,
with God's mercy, well changed his life" (CW 2, 91/16–17).

[58] See Logan's important study as well as Skinner 2002, where he points out that Morus
"echoes *De Officiis* almost word for word" (222) and that he sets forth "one particular
set of humanist beliefs – those of a 'civic' or Ciceronian humanism" (223).

[59] See www.thomasmorestudies.org/IndicesofLatinTerms. The closest that either work
comes to mentioning the concept of magnanimity is the praise that the lawyer at

Or measured by Cicero's leaders of *libertas*, are Utopians willing to "stake everything" – even life – for freedom under law?[60] Utopia boasts of few laws – and no independent judiciary. When measured by Cicero's and the Roman Republic's experience, the Utopian people have *no* liberty because liberty requires specific protections based on strong consensus and time-tested institutions historically fashioned and embodied in law. In Cicero's famous words,

Law is the bond which secures these our privileges in the commonwealth, the foundation of our liberty, the fountain-head of justice. Within the law are reposed the mind and heart, the judgment and the conviction of the state [*civitas*]. The state without law would be like the human body without mind – unable to employ the parts which are to it as sinews, blood, and limbs. The magistrates who administer the law, the jurors who interpret it – all of us in short – obey the law that we might be free. (*Pro Cluentio* 146)

"Law or violence," *ius* or *vis*, peace or war, *humanitas* or savagery – that was the fundamental alternative offered by history, as presented by Cicero in his last public speech before being effectively silenced by Julius Caesar.[61] In that speech, Cicero set forth what he considered to be the landmark that should guide citizens and "first citizens":

What then is the mark set before those who guide the helm of state, upon which they ought to keep their eyes and towards which they ought to direct their course? It is that which is far the best and the most desirable for all who are sound and good and prosperous; it is "peace with *dignitas*."[62]

The landmark offered by Utopian leaders is hard to determine, but the dangers of not having a clear one are vividly portrayed in the opening of book 2.

As those opening lines show, the island of Utopia is shaped like a crescent whereby "the whole inner coast is one great harbor": "Being sheltered from the wind by the surrounding land, the bay is not rough, but placid and smooth instead, like a big lake." The narrator then describes

---

Morton's table gives to people of "animi magis excelsi" (*CW* 4, 62/22), but Raphael is quick to condemn this invidious distinction.

[60] *De Officiis* 1.68.

[61] *Pro Sestio*, especially 91–92.

[62] *Pro Sestio* 98. We have no adequate translation of *dignitas*. Cicero identifies it with *honestas*, that is, a human being's distinctive moral excellence; see especially *De Officiis* 1.94–99, 106 and 1.124, which presents the duty of magistrate and citizen as working for "tranquillitas et honestas" and which emphasizes upholding the state's "dignitas," enforcing laws and rights, and living up to "fides."

this bay as an ideal and welcoming port of entry, "across which ships pass in every direction, to the great advantage of the people."[63]

This picture is thoroughly deceptive, however. Hidden shallows and rocks make this harbor not only "very dangerous" but impossible to navigate unless the entering ships use Utopian pilots who "direct their course by some landmarks on the coast" – landmarks that can "be shifted about" to "easily lure to destruction" anyone perceived as an enemy. Ominously, we are also told that the landmarks can be moved so that even Utopian pilots would find it "hardly safe even for themselves."

The tactic of changing landmarks helps to explain the unusual status of Utopian treaties and their conception of *fides*. Morus and his fellow *principes* have come to Bruges to make a new treaty and therefore to strengthen *fides* between their merchants and countries. As Cicero explained, all social transactions require *fides*, as enhanced by the clarity and consensus achieved in good treaties. By contrast, Raphael explains that the Utopians will not make a treaty "at all with any nation."[64] The reason given raises the deepest questions investigated by philosophy:

If nature, they say, doesn't bind man adequately to his fellow man, what good is a treaty? If a man scorns nature herself, is there any reason to think he will care about mere words? They are confirmed in this view by the fact that in that part of the world, treatises and alliances [*foedera pactaque*] between princes are not generally observed with much good faith [*bona fide*].[65]

This provocative formulation poses the issue forcefully: What *is* the relationship between action, "mere words," and *bona fides*? As we have seen, Socrates defined justice in terms of correspondence between thought and action; Regulus died rather than go against his word – both of whom Cicero presents as models of *bona fides*. In addition, More's Epigram 32 presents *fides* and *foedera* as part of good rule. Yet the Utopias go directly contrary to these positions, leading us to ask once again how the *bona fides* of Raphael compares with other characters such as Giles and Morton who are presented as effective leaders well known for their *fides*.[66] So far, we have seen that Raphael puts his strongest faith in a

---

[63] *CW* 4, 110/7–26, but the *CUP Utopia* translation is used in this paragraph and the next.

[64] *CW* 4, 196/14–16: "Foedera quae reliquae inter se gentes toties ineunt, frangunt, ac renovant, ipsi nulla cum gente feriunt."

[65] *CW* 4, 197/20–26, although this translation is taken from *CUP Utopia*, 197–98.

[66] *CW* 4, 48/3, 7; 58/31. Ironically, we are told that Raphael is responsible for the Utopian sailors' reckless "faith" in the new compasses Raphael brought to Utopia (*CW* 4, 52/21).

society that has eliminated private property and money, a society that has been ordered by Utopus. Whom are we to trust: Raphael or Morus?

Raphael tells us that Conqueror Utopus has brought about the ultimate expression of *humanitas*, quickly bringing the "rude and rustic" inhabitants fraught with discord and faction to peace and a "perfection of culture and *humanitas*."[67] How did Utopus achieve this remarkably quick transformation from *vis* to *ius*? By contrast, Cicero warned that decades of study and training would be required for one well-disciplined person to achieve *humanitas*; this demanding education of "self-fashioning" would require mastery of history, philosophy, law, and rhetoric after preliminary training in all the liberal arts. Has this *humanitas* been achieved and maintained in Utopia? And if so, how?

The true landmarks of the Utopians' *humanitas* are difficult to determine, but trustworthiness or *fides* is not one, nor is "peace with dignity." What then is the basis of Utopia's supposed history of idyllic living? And how idyllic is it? Is it like the harbor that is said to be inviting and to be "to the great advantage of the people," but is actually quite the opposite?

How did Utopus transform a country of warring factions, a country like the England dramatized in *Richard III*, into a country of internal peace? Through force, draconian punishments, and constant terror – or so a careful reading of *Utopia* makes clear to "sharp-sighted," "well and wisely trained citizens."[68]

One of the most revealing contradictions in Raphael's account is his boast that fear will disappear once money is eliminated, yet, throughout his story, he points out that Utopia is governed by constant fear, and even terror.[69] As Raphael reports, reason is "insufficient" to guide a life to virtue, peace, and happiness;[70] the state must therefore impose religious beliefs that ensure torturous fear of eternal punishment as the primary motive of action.[71] Without such religious fear, Raphael reports, the Utopians would not hesitate "to seek pleasure by fair means or foul" and would have no incentive to "pursue hard and painful virtue."[72] The

---

[67] CW 4, 112/5.

[68] CW 4, 248/27 and 52/33.

[69] CW 4, 242/5–8; for the role of terror, see 112/15, 202/26, 234/28.

[70] That fear is the primary motive, see CW 4, 220/28- 222/3, 228/2–8, and 234/5–7, even though Utopia's obligatory beliefs also include faith in great eternal pleasure as a reward for good behavior (160/20–162/5, 220/25).

[71] Note the many Utopian citizens who become slaves for their "criminal" actions, despite their having received Utopia's "ideal" education.

[72] CW 4, 162/5–15.

essential role of fear is stated explicitly[73] when Raphael explains Utopus's "tolerant" approach to religion, an approach so tolerant that those who do not acknowledge Utopus's required beliefs are no longer regarded "even as a member of mankind" and can hold no position in the state. We learn that elders with authority are responsible for instilling in Utopian children "a religious fear towards the gods" because such fear is "the greatest and almost the only stimulus to the practice of virtue."[74] Hence, the Utopian priests, who are charged with educating the children in "opinions . . . useful for the preservation of the commonwealth,"[75] elicit terror at the monthly worship services[76] and are the source of the greatest fear.[77]

Fear of the most severe punishment for themselves and of "great disgrace" for their parents is one of the strongest motives, as Raphael reports, for entering marriage, an institution that comes under the heading of "Slavery."[78] Because love is supposedly not strong enough to motivate people to undertake "all the troubles" of marriage, Utopians have exceptionally harsh laws regulating any promiscuous behavior before marriage.[79] This view of love and marriage is in sharp contrast to Cicero's and More's accounts of the tender love that naturally develops between spouses and between spouses and their children.[80] Just this attachment, however, Utopia seeks to prevent.

What Utopia does to normal family life, and the level of terror needed to enforce it, can be glimpsed in what would generally be considered the symbol of family conviviality: the family meal. Instead of conviviality, however, children from the ages of five to seventeen stand along the walls of a large hall in absolute silence waiting for their parents to hand them food – as one would a family pet.[81] Meanwhile the young parents are at

---

[73] CW 4, 220/28–29, 222/1–3, and 234/5–7.

[74] CW 4, 234/2–7.

[75] CW 4, 228/10–11.

[76] CW 4, 234/28–29: "terrorem . . . incutiat"; see also 232/27–31.

[77] CW 4, 228/4–6.

[78] See the heading of this section at CW 4, 184/14; the discussion of marriage begins at 186/22. Raphael and Pico both shun marriage in favor of following their Ulyssean passion for travel. Their indulgence in travel is in sharp contrast to the prohibitions against travel in Utopia. Raphael is explicitly compared to Ulysses (CW 4, 20/27ff., 48/31ff.) because of his wanderings and passion for travel (50/4–5, 10). About Pico, consider again CW 1, 69/21–25: "Liberty above all things he loved, to which both his own natural affection and the study of philosophy inclined him; and for that he was always wandering and flitting and would never take himself to any certain dwelling."

[79] CW 4, 186/24–34.

[80] See notes 69 and 70 of Chapter 8.

[81] Consider the level of terror needed for spirited hungry children to remain absolutely silent and patiently waiting for table scraps.

tables with approved elders on both sides, so that nothing the young say "escapes the notice of the old present on every side."[82] These elders are given the best food, and "at their discretion" they share it with the young. They also introduce "approved" topics of conversation and "provoke" (*provocant*) the young in order "to test" each one as "revealed in the freedom [*libertas*] of mealtime talk." Such behavior does not, of course, elicit any *inuidias* or any disharmony. Everyone, of course, is very happy not to eat in their own homes and not to talk freely among themselves.

In this context, the use of *provocant* and *libertas* gives direction to the obvious irony at play in this passage. In contrast to Utopian citizens, Roman plebs demanded the right of *provocatio* when their *libertas* was threatened.[83] But what appeal is possible for the oppressed Utopians?

As presented by Raphael, the Utopian "citizens" have no protection from the tyranny of life-term senators and *principes*; they have no representatives equivalent to that "bulwark of liberty," the tribunate;[84] they have no courts for appeal; they have no historically developed protections such as England's institution of sanctuary or Rome's institution of *provocatio*. Utopian "citizens" are easily enslaved and are more harshly punished than noncitizens. They are also killed: a practice condemned by Raphael in book 1 but never in book 2, a practice specifically outlawed in Rome without a trial.[85] Because these "citizens" have no right to a trial, no appeal, no legal advocates, and no protections, they have no *libertas*. How this practice compares with the Roman Republic's care for its citizens can be seen in Cicero's rhetorically forceful statement: "No honorable man, even if he is within his rights, wants to put a citizen to death."[86]

But rhetoric has no place in Utopian education or society. Why would it be needed when twenty phylarchs, one *princeps*, and thirteen priests have frightening, unchecked power and where freedom of speech ends in death?[87] The phylarchs, whose name means "fond of power,"[88] and the *princeps*, whose name in Utopian (Ademus) means "without a

---

[82] CW 142/19–34; the syphogrant and his wife also sit at a raised table in the middle "to have the whole company in sight."

[83] Lintott 1972 and 1999.

[84] Livy 3.37.5.

[85] Lintott 1999 33, 37.

[86] *Pro Publio Quinctio* 51.

[87] CW 4, 124/1–2: "To take counsel on matters of common interest outside the senate or the popular assembly is considered a capital offense." And see the telling reason that follows for justifying such a draconian measure.

[88] Commentary at CW 4, 114/7.

people,"[89] do seem to live up to those names. The priests are above the law; they can be "subjected to no tribunal," regardless of "however guilty" they may be (229/24–26).

Utopia claims to have eliminated what *Richard III* revealed as three of the strongest motives behind factions: greed, pride, and ill will.[90] According to Raphael's tale, these were "easily" eliminated once money had been outlawed. But how believable is such a claim? And what motives are absent in Raphael's account? Like Plato, who shows Socrates' eliminating elements such as eros from his tale in the *Republic,* author More leads his careful readers to think through the nature and power of the very motives conspicuously absent.

Utopia's idyllic history of prosperity forged by bland and nameless leaders invites comparison with London's three-hundred-year history of agonies and successes of hard-fought-for self-government, of heroes like Judge John Markham, who loyally served London as recorder and *vice-comites* and then risked his life and office in defending the law against a tyrannous king.

London's three-hundred-year history of self-government was marked by frequent discord between crown and city, and within the city itself. "Sedition," "turmoil," and "war" were constant dangers, as they had been in Rome. Yet these very upheavals became the occasion for new invention of customs, institutions, and laws. In England, these included, to name but a few: the city recorder, special courts, improved trials by jury, the practice of sanctuary, public assemblies in London's magnificent *forum* (i.e., the Guildhall), and improved education for its legal and government professionals. In contrast, Utopia, with its boast of fifty-four peaceful and prosperous Londons and loudly proclaimed hatred for war, is actually a warring state so economically and politically primitive that a prosperous and self-governing London of sixty thousand people could never exist.[91]

Raphael's presentation of easily recognized injustices is laden with pathos and anger, but his solutions are utterly simplistic and mostly unhelpful. His suggestion, for example, to solve the enclosure problem by returning to a more primitive economy overlooks England's unique position as the largest wool producer of the world; it ignores the complexities

---

[89] CW 4, 132/8; Morus calls special attention to this name in his Letter to Giles at 250/14.

[90] CW 4, 240/28–29ff., 242/25/26ff., 244/11. Lust for dominion or power, so obvious and destructive in *Richard III,* is not even mentioned by Raphael as a factor in human and political life.

[91] Raphael claims that Utopia has fifty-four cities, each having 60,000 to 90,000 people.

of national and international supply and demand; it closes future-looking avenues such as those taken by Morus and his fellow ambassadors in developing more sophisticated laws, treatises, and the very arts and sciences excluded from Utopia. Any economic or political scientist would understand immediately why it would be impossible to have fifty-four Londons on one small island as diverse in geography and resources as England.[92] Because of its unique qualities, London became the "first" or leading city of England in financial, cultural, and professional sophistication, allowing a *libertas*, a peace, and a prosperity that Raphael ironically and unknowingly points to.[93]

To appreciate the irony at work, one might consider the passage where Raphael calls the Romans the "greatest experts in administering the commonwealth"[94] and praises their "good arts of peace."[95] Yet the Romans' most famous art is law, which is not highly valued in Utopia. As a result, we are less surprised to discover that the Rome Raphael praises is not the ancient Roman Republic but an imperial Rome with warring Sparta's aspirations. That is the Rome that Utopus and his fellow warlords admire (108/7–8). This clarification makes sense of their justification of wars for expansion (136) and of an economy and society so focused on war that every man, woman, and child practices for war before every religious service (236), that the priests are most famous for their incredibly effective interventions in war,[96] and that every Utopian city not only is walled but protects its water source, ready for any "hostile attack."[97] The Utopians' only children's games are war games (128), and the greatest social pressure is placed upon families to act as a military unit willing to fight to the death (210).

The Rome of Cicero, the London of More, and the *humanitas* that both Cicero and More sought to establish – these are in sharp contrast to Raphael's Utopia. Cicero and More present *amor* and *amicitia* as the best bond in the body politic; Raphael and his Utopians present fear. Cicero and More present trust and treaties as the best policy, even in war; in war, the Utopians boast of deception and craft that destroys trust even

[92] See note 25.
[93] In Utopia, Amaurotum is called the *princeps* of cities at 112/27 despite the insistence that all Utopian cities are the same.
[94] "Romanis administrandae reipublicae peritissimis," 74/15.
[95] "bonis pacis artibus," 56/24.
[96] These truly incredible interventions are examples of More's debt to Lucian. See Wegemer 1996 84–88.
[97] "uis hostium," 118/25.

between brothers or between king and people. And Utopians never make treaties, or so he says. In fact, they do.[98]

Utopus is the antithesis of Cicero's *princeps*, and Utopia is a case study in disguised tyranny beneath a rhetoric of peace and *respublica* – so much so that the frequent repetition of *princeps* and *respublica* by Raphael achieves the same ironic and satiric effect as "Protector" Richard in More's *History of King Richard III*.

If so, why would Morus end by praising Raphael as "most experienced in human things" (*rerum humanarum peritissimo*)? This statement is a classic example of More's most famous form of irony.[99] In appearing to say one thing, he has actually said the opposite. As we saw in Chapter 3, Cicero's "often repeated" principle was that *rerum humanarum* – "passing human things" – are precisely those things that good leaders should scorn. More made the same point in his December 1516 letter to Erasmus. Morus's "praise" of Raphael is similar to the coronation ode's "praise" of the war-hungry adolescent who had just taken the throne. To the "sharp-eyed" reader, these ironic praises reveal the opposite of what appears at first sight.

But a harder question is this: why does *princeps* Morus remain so silent[100] about an issue that he himself characterized as a most important duty?[101] True, there is precedent for silence used as a tactic by the London citizens in *Richard III,* as they watched "kings' games played upon scaffolds." And later, author More would use silence as Speaker of the House, angering Wolsey but defending Parliament's customary liberty.[102] He would also use it at the end of his life as a legal defense in the face of a tyrannous king. In these three cases, silence was a strategy and a clear sign of strong opposition. In the first, the silence of the Londoners

---

[98] Compare CW 4, 196/14–25 (repeated at 198/14–28) with the Utopian treaties at: 148/19 for trade with other countries, 164/19–23 for internal distribution, and 214/7 for truces with enemies.

[99] As seen earlier, Thomas Wilson reports on More's reputation in his 1560 *The Art of Rhetoric*: "Sir Thomas More with us here in England had an excellent gift not only in this kind [of "pleasant dissembling," i.e., of "praising the unworthy"] but also in all other pleasant delights, whose wit even at this hour is a wonder to all the world and shall be undoubtedly even unto the world's end" (175).

[100] In fact, Morus is not silent because he writes up his account and publishes his work despite the supposed reservations he declares in his 1517 Letter to Giles. More draws attention to the importance of publication in his introductory letter to *A Dialogue Concerning Heresies* (CW 6, 21–24).

[101] CW 4, 86/9–10.

[102] Roper 17–19; Hall 1.285–86; Great Britain, *Letters and Papers of Henry VIII* 3, no. 3267 (24 August 1523).

in *Richard III* left Richard and Buckingham disappointed because they "could not see any honorable citizens" in their party.[103] In the second, Wolsey became angry with the opposition represented by the silence of More and the House of Commons and left in frustration. Similarly with the third, Henry VIII and Cromwell became angry and fearful with prisoner More's silence: fearful, because they saw that it was the "occasion of much grudge . . . in the realm."[104]

Yet his silence with Raphael at the end of *Utopia*, we are told by Morus, has a different motive. In book 1, Morus disagreed directly and bluntly with Raphael's position. Raphael claimed that Morus did not have an adequate *imago res publicae* and then spent all of book 2 giving one. When finished, Morus points out that Raphael was tired and had shown his unwillingness to "brook any opposition to his views." Morus then tells us how they ended their afternoon together:

> I therefore praised their way of life [*institutione*] and his speech [*oratione*] and, taking him by the hand, led him in to supper. I first said, nevertheless, that there would be another chance to think about these matters more deeply and to talk them over with him more fully. If only this were some day possible! (244/26–30).

To the readers, however, Morus goes on to say directly that many things were "very absurdly established" – thus giving "sharp-sighted" readers an invitation to look more attentively. But why keep silent with Raphael? Orator Morus is true to the principle he set forth in book 1: "I don't think you should . . . offer advice that you know for certain will not be listened to."[105] Morus also exhibits in deed what More expressed in poetry: that friendship is the best bond in the body politic.[106]

---

[103] *CW* 15, 472/15–16.
[104] *SL* 249–50 and also *SL* 247; these concerns were the reason King Henry gave Cromwell for increasing the pressure for More's compliance or his death.
[105] *CW* 4, 98 but the translation here is from *CUP Utopia* 95.
[106] See especially Epigrams 32, 111, 112.

The Un-Utopian Thomas More Family Portrait

An Icon of Morean Humanitas?

[T]he lad, while *mad*, sought the stars, trusting in new arts, and strove to vanquish true birds in flight, demanding too much of his false wings. . . .[1]

Were it mine to fashion [*fingere*] fate at my will, I would trim my sails to gentle winds, lest my yards tremble, bent 'neath a heavy blast a gentle, moderate breeze that does not heel the side would guide my untroubled boat.[2]

Texts from Seneca that appear in the Thomas More family portrait

The elegant dress of this wealthy family depicted in the portrait *Sir Thomas More and His Family* stands in sharp contrast to the simple unfinished clothes mandated in Utopia. Most striking are old Judge More's bright scarlet robes of office, which remind us that Utopia has no judiciary separate from its senate and *princeps*.[3] Sir Thomas's gold

---

[1] Seneca's *Oedipus*, 893–97, emphasis added in the translation and also in the Latin here. In the family portrait, Margaret is pointing to *demens* (mad). The "lad" refers to Icarus. The words covered by Margaret's hand on this page are in brackets: "astra dum *demens* petit / artibus fi[sus] novis, / certat et ve[ras a]ves / vince[re ac falsis ni]mis / impe[rat pinnis puer] / no. . . . / c. . . ."

[2] These are lines 882–89, with emphasis added: "Fata si liceat mihi / *fingere* arbitrio meo, / temperem zephyro levi / vela, ne pressae gravi / spiritu antennae tremant. / lenis et modice fluens / faura nec ver[gens latus] / ducat in[trepidam ratem]." The concluding couplet of this sentence (lines 890–91) not shown in the painting is: "tuta me media vehat / vita decurrens via" (Running a middle course, my life would carry me safe).

[3] For the problems that arose in Rome when the senate assumed all judicial duties, see, for example, Cicero's *Verrine Oration* 1.37.

An earlier version of this chapter was presented at the 2007 International Thomas More Conference at the Center for Renaissance Studies at the University of Massachusetts in Amherst, 14 August 2007, and published in *Moreana*, no. 173 (June 2008): 103–16.

chain and red-velvet sleeves put him in the company of those Anemolian ambassadors ridiculed by Utopian children, as would the gold jewelry and beautiful attire accented with gold brocade of More's wife and daughters. The humor represented by the family monkey and the professional "fool" in the painting have no parallels in humorless Utopia.

More's secretary, John Harris, stands in the doorway with an official document in hand, reminding us that Utopia does not have the secretarial trade, but it does have slaves.

The beautiful tapestry on the table and the rich gold and green draperies on the wall represent other trades excluded from Utopia, along with the craftsmen of the newfangled clock or the fine woodcarving seen in this portrait.

The books identified in More's painting are all Latin works, whereas the Utopians, we are specifically told, have only those treasured Greek books that Raphael brought with him,[4] because Raphael decidedly favors Greek.

The high culture depicted in this portrait, with musical instruments on the sideboard, fine furniture, beautiful serving dishes and vases, gold-edged and velvet covered books, all stand out in sharp contrast to life in Utopia. All are accurate and characteristic of More's home and of the education he defended and provided.

This painting (Illustration 5) could well represent the most famous day in the lives of Thomas More's three daughters: the day in 1526 that they "disputed in philosophy" before Henry VIII.[5] Holbein sketched his preparatory drawing (see Illustration 4) for this painting in December 1526 or very early in 1527, shortly after he arrived at the home of More, who hosted this young ambitious painter on his first trip to England. If Holbein intended to represent or allude to Henry's visit,[6] the king may just have left because everything needed for his entertainment is displayed, and Margaret and Elizabeth are still deep in thought. Margaret is pointing to a specific word in her open text of Seneca's *Oedipus*, and Elizabeth has Seneca's *Letters* under her arm while she removes her glove. Cecily has the largest book, which is unidentified, but her classical interests are

---

[4] CW 4, 182/33ff. and 180/25ff.
[5] See John Palsgrave's report of this event, *Corr.* 405/76–77. For the proper dating of the letter, see House 211.
[6] One odd detail of the painting is the fool Henry Patensen's unusual resemblance to King Henry, complete with red and white roses on the top of his cap. His frontal stance, gold coat, and hand-on-sword are all standard features Holbein and other painters used in representing Henry.

FAMILIA THOMÆ. MORI ANGL: CANCELL:

Thomas Morus Æ 50. Alicia Thomæ Mori uxor Æ 57. Iohannes Morus pater Æ 76. Iohannes Morus Thomæ filius Æ 19. Anna Grisacria Iohannis Mori Sponsa Æ 15. Margareta Ropera Thomæ Mori filia Æ 22.
Elisabeta Daunc Thomæ Mori filia Æ 21. Cecilia Heronea Thomæ Mori filia Æ 20. Margareta Giga Clementis uxor Mori filiabus Condiscipula et cognata Æ 22. Henricus Patensonus Thomæ Mori morio Æ 40.

ILLUSTRATION 4. *Study for the Thomas More Family Portrait,* the 1526/27 Holbein drawing of the Thomas More family. In December 1526 or early 1527 Hans Holbein sketched this preparatory drawing of More and his family, who hosted him in their home during his first trip to England. More then introduced the young painter to King Henry and to other English leaders.

shown by the medallion of Venus that she is wearing. The nudity of Venus is quite different from Utopia's premarital inspections, but it is the most radical change from Holbein's initial sketch in which Cecily held a rosary and a prayer book. Why More or his family would insist on this change is of interest.[7]

Whatever might be the occasion of this painting, however, it does clearly represent the household's "civic humanism" as the Mores wished it to be remembered, emphasizing the learning and culture of the women of this family and the important civic positions held by Sir Thomas and

---

[7] Whether these changes were the sole decision of Sir Thomas or the collaborative wishes of the family cannot be determined. For our purposes, however, the importance is that this presentation of the family was "published" and then later copied and modified by More's children and grandchildren.

ILLUSTRATION 5. The 1530 and 1593 portrait *Sir Thomas More and His Family* (Nostell Priory, Wakefield, England) depicting the cultural and civic involvements of the family. From left to right are Margaret Giggs (22 years old, adopted), Elizabeth (21), Judge John More (76), Anne Cresacre (15, ward), Sir Thomas More (50), John (18), Henry Patenson (family "fool"), Cecily (20), Margaret (22), John Clement (More's secretary), Lady Alice (57). An unidentified servant is reading in the back room. The family monkey is chained next to Lady Alice's chair.

his father. More's daughters and wife all have books.[8] Before one looks at such details in the painting, however, study of the preparatory drawing can help to appreciate the major changes – requested by More or the family – in the family's representation.

Art historians and More scholars have often asked why the scene of Holbein's famous preliminary drawing of the More family that so clearly depicts the family's piety would be changed to a scene that appears purely secular.[9] Let us consider the painting's three phases in turn.

---

[8] Anne Cresacre, the youngest daughter, is the only woman not shown to have a book. More had taken her into his home as a ward when her parents died, but she was also a well-read and well-educated person who would eventually marry More's son, John.

[9] The relationship between the Nostell Priory painting, the Basel drawing, and the now-lost original water-based portrait requires further investigation. Careful study of the four

In the first phase, Holbein's famous "Basel drawing" of the More family captures a conventional moment of piety:[10] Lady Alice is kneeling with eyes focused on a book that is the same small size as the ones held by Margaret, Cecily, Margaret Giggs, and young John. As Louis Martz pointed out,[11] these are prayer books, which Eamon Duffy recently suggests to be "the Book of Hours."[12] Cecily holds a rosary[13] and is gazing[14] calmly toward the same distant object as her father. As David Piper suggested,[15] an object outside the painting would provide a focal point that is obviously missing in this sketch; that focal point would likely be a sacred image – thus explaining the presence of a lighted candle in daylight.[16] Another rosary hangs from Elizabeth's sash,[17] and the book she has under her arm seems the same as the others in this drawing.[18] Margaret and Elizabeth are shown in a thoughtful or prayerful or "abstracted" frame of mind,[19] like the depiction of their father. Dinner or entertainment of some kind has just finished or will soon begin.[20] Sir Thomas is shown in a pose strikingly different from the one in the famous Frick portrait. As Louis Martz observed about the Basel sketch: "We see the face of a man unguarded, open, vulnerable, seeking, devotional in mood."[21]

other contemporary family paintings can yield important information, as shown by Frank Mitjans's "*Non sum Oedipus, sed Morus.*"

[10] This drawing was brought by Holbein himself to Erasmus, as a gift from More – the reason for its being in Basel. Holbein made detailed preliminary drawings of most if not all of those who appear in this drawing; see Lewi's overview 13–16.

[11] Martz 8.

[12] E. Duffy 58. Duffy's beautifully designed book gives a helpful historical account of this most popular English prayer book, before it was outlawed along with rosary beads in 1538 and 1571.

[13] Rhodes explains that such books as *The Rosary of Our Lady* (1525) were based on the Carthusian practice of combining "an event from Christ's life with a personal petition" (1984 4–17). Rhodes's earlier publication points out that these widespread practices and publications were outlawed already in 1538 (1983 180–91). The further condemnation of these publications and practices in 1571 (E. Duffy 176) could well explain why the texts of these books would be blank in Lockey's painting of 1594.

[14] See Martz's observations about the direction and implications of More's gaze (8).

[15] Piper 742.

[16] The lighted candle is on the right, and the outlines of hills and greenery can be seen through the back window.

[17] For a similar hanging rosary that Holbein painted in the same year, see his *Mary Wotton, Lady Guildford* (City Art Museum, St. Louis) pictured in E. Duffy 56.

[18] In the Nostell Priory painting, the book is larger and is identified as Seneca's *Epistoles.*

[19] David Smith 487.

[20] Note the dishes for hospitality on the sideboard and windowsill, and the exceptionally rich formal attire that everyone wears.

[21] Martz argues (8–9) that the first Windsor drawing (RL 12225) is the study used for the Basel drawing, while the "stronger" Windsor drawing (RL 12268) is the study used

Although this original drawing stresses the family's piety, it is still, overall, an icon of Christian civic humanism. This humanism is represented not only by the elements of the intellectual life but also by signs of full engagement with the practical world of human affairs. Most striking are Thomas More's famous S chain, the formal dress of his elegant family, Judge More's robe of office, the stately character of the room with its artifacts of high culture, and the official documents that More's secretary bears.

That the More family wanted a less ostentatiously pious depiction of themselves is clear from the revisions indicated in brown ink in what is widely taken as Holbein's hand, especially because all the indicated revisions appear in all the later copies. In the second phase of the painting, the strong directions written in German on the sketch beside Lady Alice ("This one should sit")[22] indicate that Lady Alice may well have had strong opinions about being singled out for the greatest public display of her piety.

That the revisions aim at a more secular focus is clear from the many other revisions indicated in brown ink: the monkey crawling up Lady Alice's dress, crossing out the candle, the larger books (definitely not prayer books) scattered on the floor, the musical instrument hanging on the wall, with another note in German indicating that "clavichord and other string instruments [are to be put] on the buffet."[23]

Another curious revision marked in brown ink is the addition of a more expansive open front to Margaret's dress, a change that allows us to see that Margaret – like her two sisters, Elizabeth and Cecily – is pregnant.[24]

---

for the Frick portrait – an argument that S. Foister made in *Drawings by Holbein from the Royal Library Windsor Castle*. Curiously, the Nostell Priory painting shows a facial expression quite distinct from both: it is not as handsome as the Frick portrait and not as youthful as either the Basel drawing or the Frick portrait. Did More insist on greater realism?

[22] "Dise soll sitze" is written in brown ink, distinct from the black ink of the sketch. In the same brown ink, Holbein has sketched in a viola hanging from the ceiling next to the cabinet on the left. In the same hand, presumably Holbein's, a second indication in German is given just above this musical instrument: "Claficordi und ander / seyte spill uf dem buvet." In the same brown ink, a monkey is drawn, tethered to a stone block and climbing up Lady Alice's dress, and three additional books are drawn on the floor to the left of the small bench and one large book on the floor in front of Cecily.

[23] See the previous footnote for the German.

[24] Compare this portrait with Holbein's preparatory sketch. The revisions on the sketch call for Margaret's dress to be modified to show her pregnant. Susan Foister clearly demonstrates Cecily's pregnancy in *Holbein and England* (249–50).

These changes would be in harmony with More's educational aim, which he expressed in a 1521 letter to his recently married daughter, Margaret. Urging her to study medicine as well as theology and the liberal arts, he explains the importance of being "furnished for the whole scope of human life – which is to have a sound mind in a sound body."[25]

These changes, in other words, aim at a fuller and more true-to-life representation of the More family's distinctive form of humanism.

The painting's third and final phase is Lockey's completion of Holbein's oil painting, copied from the tempora. In the Nostell Priory painting of the family of Sir Thomas More,[26] all of the suggestions made in brown ink on the Basel drawing have been followed in some clear way. For example, Lady Alice is not kneeling or focusing on her book, oblivious to all around her as was depicted in the drawing. Instead, she is now sitting in a richly ornate chair, ready for action and giving a knowing glance in our direction, as would be appropriate for the attentive and experienced manager of that busy household and estate.

Although there are no large books scattered on the floor, there are large books in the hands of his children and on the buffet behind More's head.

All of More's daughters are holding books. Margaret is pointing to a specific word in what is arguably the most important choral scene of Seneca's *Oedipus*, and Elizabeth has Seneca's *Epistoles* under her arm rather than a prayer book; both women appear deeply in thought. Cecily is now holding the largest book in the painting, possibly the 1515 collection of Seneca edited by Erasmus while in England and while visiting Thomas More and his family.[27] Instead of the rosary that was so noticeable in the Basel drawing, she is now wearing a striking ivory medallion with a naked Venus leaning on a pillar.[28] This Greek or Roman medallion shows that

[25] *SL* 149. The Latin is "quo nusquam tibi desint ad humanae vitae scopum adminicula (nempe vt sit mens sana in corpora sano)," quoting Juvenal X.356 (*Corr.* 255).

[26] For recent studies of this painting, see David R. Smith, Lesley Lewis, Ruth Norrington, Angela Lewi. That Lockey's skill did not match Holbein's is seen especially in details such as More's and Elizabeth's hands.

[27] The size appears the same as the 1515 edition (see Illustration 1), and it would make sense that she would also have a book by Seneca since her two sisters do – *if* this were indeed a sisterly disputation, as suggested.

[28] A naked Venus is surprising to some, given the known piety of this family. In all subsequent copies of the painting, the figure is obscured so that one cannot tell if the medallion is a Madonna with Child or some other standing figure. This important difference would suggest that the Nostell Priory painting may indeed be a faithful copy of the original.

Cecily has an interest in classical art as do her sisters, even though her book is unlabeled. It may also suggest that she strongly objected to the proposed display of her piety by having her hold a rosary and a prayer book in the Basel drawing.

Margaret Roper – the eldest child of this London family – is presented as a woman sophisticated in the ways of the world in several ways, including her spectacular dress. She is so richly dressed, in fact, that one must wonder why.[29] Why do her jewels far, far surpass those of her mother, her sisters, and her wealthy future sisters-in-law? Margaret's headpiece and gown display scores of pearls or pearl-shaped stones,[30] while Elizabeth's has fewer than ten and her mother even fewer than that.

Other changes have also been made that strengthen a secular rather than a devotional focus.

Engaged in secular action is John Harris, More's secretary, who has been added in the doorway and who holds an official document in hand, a document complete with seals as he looks attentively toward Chancellor More.

In addition, the secular fruitfulness of this family is stressed in this painting. Margaret and Elizabeth and Cecily are pregnant with the next generation,[31] and we are reminded by the inscribed names that John

[29] The Nostell Priory painting has been in the Roper family since it was completed. If this is the "Roper version" commissioned of the More family portrait, then the Ropers would want Margaret to stand out in some significant way. If the original painting did depict the evening when More's daughters disputed philosophy before Henry VIII, then Margaret as the eldest and as the most brilliant of More's children might also have played the leading role that evening. In any case, the Roper family would want this famous woman to stand out in a painting it paid for; she stands out not only by her dress, but first and foremost by her active engagement with a classical text, shown by her thoughtful gaze and her pointing to a specific Latin word that has special significance in this famous tragedy.

[30] Notice that Lady Guildford's headpiece has similar stones, but her dress does not have as many as Margaret's (see note 17).

[31] Margaret married William Roper on 2 July 1521; Elizabeth married William Dauncey and Cecily married Giles Heron on 29 September 1525 in a double wedding ceremony. The Ropers had five children who lived to adulthood: Margaret, Elizabeth, Mary, Thomas, and Anthony. The first child was born in 1523; Thomas, the eldest surviving son, was born in 1534. Margaret died at Christmas 1544. On 4 August 1540 Giles had been hung, drawn, and quartered after being attainted of treason by Parliament but never given a trial. In 1543 William Roper was suspected of treason and imprisoned, but later released. William Dauncey and John More were also accused of "treasonable words"; they were imprisoned, and their goods were confiscated but then restored in April 1544. These events undoubtedly contributed to Margaret's early death. We do not know when Elizabeth's and Cecily's children were born.

would soon marry Anne Cresacre,[32] because she is identified as the "betrothed of John More" in the Basel drawing and the Nostell Priory Painting; that his cousin Margaret Giggs has – in 1527 – already married More's "promising young" Dr. John Clement;[33] and that John Harris[34] would marry Meg's maid, Dorothy Colley.[35] This fruitfulness is emphasized by the presence of the fruit dish and ripe apple on the windowsill on the right and by the abundance of flowers in the room.

The flowers,[36] along with the musical instruments and crowded intimacy of elegant "family-togetherness," connote a sense of worldly beauty, harmony, and happiness. The room is marked by warmth of color, including the carpet of green rushes. It is significant that the setting is not the cold, formal Great Hall of the house.

The classical books identified in the painting suggest a common theme, the theme of happiness: its nature and its possibility in this troubled and stormy world. Margaret, shown deeply in thought, is pointing to the word *demens* (mad) in the famously controversial chorus[37] of the fourth act of Seneca's *Oedipus*.[38] (See Illustration 6.) Oedipus is the best-known tragic character of classical antiquity. He begins being blind in terms of

---

[32] Anne Cresacre is identified in the 1527 Basel drawing and in the 1593 Nostell Priory painting as John More's betrothed ("Anna Crisacria Joannes/ Mori Sponsa anno 15"); Margaret Giggs is identified as John Clement's wife ("Uxor Johannes/ Clement"); John Harris is identified as belonging to Thomas More's family ("Johanes Haresius Thomae / Mori famul: Anno 27"). It is interesting to note that all three of More's daughters are identified with their husbands' names: "Elizabeta Dancea / Thomae Mori Filia anno 21"; "Cecilia.Herond.Thomae.Mori / filia anno.20"; "Margareta Ropera Thomae Mori/ filia anno.22."

[33] Margaret Giggs married John Clement in 1526, and their daughter Winifred was born in 1527. Then Clement went into exile with Rastell, who wrote a biography of More (now lost) and published More's *English Workes*. In *Utopia*, John Clement accompanied More on his mission and is present while Raphael speaks.

[34] "Heresius" is written above John's portrait; this is a Latinized version of his last name, "Harris." John was More's secretary, whom More called "my friend" (*SL* 224). He was also a tutor to More's "school" and was responsible for saving many of More's letters by bringing them into exile with him to Louvain. John More married Anne Cresacre in 1529.

[35] Dorothy Colly was Margaret Roper's maid. More mentions her in his last letter; she cared for him while imprisoned; after his execution, she was among the three women who tended to his burial. John and Dorothy Harris were the major source of documents used by Stapleton for his biography of More.

[36] The flowers in the left vase are Madonna Lilies and red and pink carnations. The other vases contain borages, columbines, purple irises, and peonies. See Lewi 6, 22.

[37] For recent commentary of this particular passage, see Jessica Winston, Bruce R. Smith, and Frederick Kiefer.

[38] See the second note of this chapter. On the left-hand side of the book, "fate" is given first place.

ILLUSTRATION 6. Detail of Margaret and text of her book. Margaret points to the word *demens* (mad) in this choral passage from act 4 of Seneca's *Oedipus*.

self-knowledge and then proceeds "madly"[39] to take out his own eyes once he comes to know himself and his actions for what they are.

The opposite page gives another approach to the troubles that "fate" seems to bring. Using terms from sailing, the Chorus of the play advises: "Were it mine to fashion [*fingere*] fate at my will, I would trim my sails to gentle winds, lest my yards tremble, bent 'neath a heavy blast."

This formulation by the Chorus raises difficult questions: Is it ours to shape fate at our will? If not, then how can one deal with a "heavy blast"

[39] Notice on line 103 that Oedipus refers to his own action as "demens."

ILLUSTRATION 7. Detail of Elizabeth and titles of her books. Elizabeth carries Seneca's *Epistoles* under her arm; on the sideboard is Boethius's *Consolationis Philosophiae.*

such as the one that bends Oedipus? Boethius's *Consolation of Philosophy* (on the cupboard behind Judge More's head; see Illustration 7) deals with just this issue, both dramatically and philosophically: Boethius,[40] imprisoned and awaiting execution by the king he has loyally served, weeps and wails in misery until Lady Philosophy in torn dress enters and

---

[40] Thomas More refers to Boethius as "that great wise and well learned man" (*CW* 8, 939/1), and he commends to his children "that beautiful and holy poem of Boethius" (*SL* 146; *Corr.* 250/21; *TMSB* 202). That More knew Boethius's *Consolation of Philosophy* very well is shown in these other passages: *Corr.* 519; *CW* 11, 84/33n; *CW* 12, 258/13n. The parallels between Boethius and More are striking: both were philosophers, poets, and political leaders; both wrote works of consolation while in prison; both lost favor with their rulers and were subsequently executed, leaving behind wives and children.

commands him to stop. She then leads Boethius to remember what he had earlier seen about the nature of happiness; eventually, Boethius – unlike Oedipus – is able to face the cruelties of life with calm and resignation, and perhaps even happiness. Seneca deals with these same issues in his letters,[41] a copy of which Elizabeth has under her arm; he too ended his life in service to a ruler he faithfully served, with Stoic resignation,[42] for which he became famous – unlike mad Oedipus.

The Consolation of Philosophy also uses the same sailing metaphor as in the choral text of *Oedipus*. In correcting Boethius, Lady Philosophy warns: "If you set up your sails to the wind, you will be carried not where your will desires, but where the gale drives."[43]

Both Boethius and Seneca deal with the possibility of happiness in the midst of fate's powerful workings, a topic that More treated throughout his life,[44] a topic so central and so difficult and yet so practical and so fitting – even for a king – that it may well have been the issue he chose for the disputation that his three daughters held at Chelsea for King Henry VIII shortly before the Basel drawing was done.[45]

But with this emphasis on worldly wisdom and engagement, what has happened to the famed devotional life of the More family?

Close inspection of the Nostell Priory painting shows the family's piety to be still present, but in more subtle ways. Although Cecily and

---

[41] See, for example, Letters 23 ("On the True Joy Which Comes from Philosophy"), 37 ("On Allegiance to Virtue"), 61 ("On Meeting Death Cheerfully"), 67 ("On Ill-Health and Endurance of Suffering"), 78 ("On the Healing Power of the Mind"), 92 ("On the Happy Life"), 96 ("On Facing Hardships"), 105 ("On Facing the World with Confidence"), 110 ("On True and False Riches"), 124 ("On the True Good as Attained by Reason").

[42] Boethius's Lady Philosophy complains that the "inept schools of Epicureans, Stoics, and others, each seeking its own interests, tried to steal the inheritance of Socrates [i.e., of genuine philosophic consolation in the face of unjust execution] and to possess me (in spite of my protests and struggles), as though I were the spoils of their quarreling. They tore this robe which I had woven with my own hands and, having ripped off some little pieces of it, went away supposing that they possessed me wholly" (1.Prose 3). Thomas More goes farther: he insists that *all* the ancient philosophers' attempts at consolation are inadequate (*Dialogue of Comfort* 1.1).

[43] 2.Prose 1: "Si uentis uela committeres, non quo uoluntas peteret sed quo flatus impellerent, promoueres."

[44] Consider, for example, More's early poem on fortune, the many references to fortune or fate in *Richard III*, his treatment of fortune in *Dialogue of Comfort*, and his two prison poems on fortune.

[45] For the date of this event, Elizabeth F. Rogers suggested 1529 in 1947 (*Corr.* 403, 405), but she and subsequent scholars showed the necessity of 1525 or 1526 (*SL* 83n2; Reed 27; Reynolds 49; House 211n10).

Elizabeth no longer have rosaries, and although no family member's piety is ostentatiously on display, we discover that piety is an integral part of this icon of Christian civic humanism. One must look closely to see that the beads hanging from the purse on Margaret Giggs's belt are a rosary; that Henry Pattenson has one around his left hand; and that two rosary cases are in the cupboard behind Margaret Giggs and that, out of one of these, white beads are hanging.

In the Nostell Priory painting, there is not one cross, but four. In addition to Lady Alice's ornate crucifix,[46] which is in the Basel drawing, Henry Pattenson is wearing a simple one around his neck, and he has the red cross of London on his cap. Elizabeth also has a beautiful cross surrounded by pearls hanging from her neck.

Although Lady Alice is no longer kneeling, she holds a prayer book with a beautifully bejeweled, deep-green velvet casing. This small gold-edged book matches the small gold-edged books held by young John and by Margaret Giggs, indicating that the moment captured is indeed the same as in the revised Basel sketch, but without drawing obvious attention to the piety of any one family member. That these books all have blank pages is most easily explained by the fact that the prayer books depicted with print in Holbein's original painting would have been outlawed when this copy was made, thus posing a serious danger for its recusant owner. Significantly, the seventeenth-century unprofessional copy now at Chelsea Old Town Hall has lines in at least one of these prayer books, as does the Basel drawing.

These details indicate that the moment captured in the Nostell Priory painting remains essentially the same as the one represented in the revised Basel drawing, but in a fuller and more true-to-life manner. Including these devotional elements suggests a response to fate and to the question of happiness markedly different from the responses given by Seneca and Boethius, or by the Utopians or the nobles in *Richard III*. Taken as a whole, this portrait – like the revised Basel drawing – presents a Christian family well "furnished for the whole scope of human life."

To appreciate most fully what is distinctive of More's humanism, however, one must account for the dozen or so lines of dramatic verse from Seneca's *Oedipus* that this life-size painting invites us to read.

The painting also asks us to consider the importance of Seneca's *Epistulae*,[47] which Elizabeth carries under her arm. (See Illustration 7.)

---

[46] This cross in now in the British Museum, on loan from Stonyhurst College.
[47] They were the most popular of Seneca's writings throughout medieval times and into More's.

This collection of 124 letters was designed to lead the young not only to Seneca's dialectical understanding of wisdom and virtue,[48] but also to the arduous training needed to form the character it reveals. Hence, the rhetorical, or what one might call the motivational, aspects of the work are an integral part of its humanistic intent.

Seneca scholar Anna Motto explains that these 124 letters are addressed to young Lucilius and focus upon "ardent concern for the journey to wisdom." *Epistulae* 1–50 are "concerned with increasing one's devotion to studies and eliminating many a passion and vice"; *Epistulae* 51–90 concern a "middle period [which] displays one as master of his passions, but subject . . . to relapses," while *Epistulae* 91–123 represent "the last period [which] urges putting wisdom into practice, testing it," thus preparing for *Epistulae* 124 that deals "with the very doorstep of wisdom, discussing . . . the good as it is to be fully attained by reason."[49] As a whole, therefore, these letters represent the *humanitas* that constitutes Seneca's standard and goal of human and political action.

In this context, the passages in Margaret's open book pose a personal and rather daunting challenge.

Margaret is pointing to the word *demens* (mad) in the following passage of act four in Seneca's *Oedipus*. (See portrait detail, Illustration 6.)

[T]he lad, while mad, sought the stars, trusting in new arts, and strove to vanquish true birds in flight, demanding too much of his false wings.[50] (893–898, emphasis added)

This "lad" is Icarus, who, in escaping unjust imprisonment by King Minos, disobeyed his father Daedalus and flew too close to the sun, thus misusing the "false wings" Daedalus had devised. "[W]hile mad" refers to Icarus's intoxication with the exhilaration of flight.

If one cannot and should not be "trusting in new arts" (*artibus novis*) of Icarus's "false wings," what arts are worthy of trust? For Seneca, philosophy alone is the most trustworthy art, and the liberal arts constitute the necessary preparation for that highest of arts.[51] Only the art of philosophy reveals those basic truths that have been tested by time and that are needed for a happy, free, and prosperous life. It alone can

---

[48] These letters, when read as a sequence and as a whole, can be seen in dialectical relationship one to the other. In fact, many sources refer to them as "dialogues" because they continue ongoing philosophic conversations.

[49] Motto 1973 54–55.

[50] The first note of this chapter gives the Latin text.

[51] See in particular Letter 88 on the liberal arts.

adequately respond to everyone's need to "know thyself" and one's place in a complex and often frightening world.[52]

If one should not "trust" in new arts,[53] in what should one trust? Raising the issue of trust or *fides* has a significance we have already seen. Seneca calls *fides* – trustworthiness – the "holiest good" of human beings (*Epistulae* 88.29), one that the "wise alone" achieve (*Epistulae* 81.12), because only the wise have harmony between their words and actions (*Epistulae* 20.2–5, 31.8), the mark of true *humanitas*.[54]

Seneca taught that "all men but the wise are mad,"[55] because the wise alone have learned to govern their passions.[56] Seneca explains that "false conceptions of things render them mad,"[57] conceptions that can lead whole nations to insane action such as unnecessary war. "Mad" is also a word and a theme that occurs frequently in More's writings.

Turning next to the left-hand page of Margaret's open book, we find a naive contrast to Oedipus's mad action. The Chorus wistfully expresses a desire for another approach to the troubles that "fate" brings to people like Oedipus and Icarus. Using terms from sailing, the Chorus of citizens says:

"Were it mine to fashion [*fingere*] fate at my will, I would trim my sails to gentle winds, lest my yards tremble, bent 'neath a heavy blast a gentle, moderate breeze that does not heel the side would guide my untroubled boat."[58]

The Latin gives first place to "fate," and the Chorus assumes it has no power over that force. Yet Seneca and the tradition he represents would strongly reject that assumption, convinced by the power of philosophy in guiding one to a life free from fate's power by forming one's character upon truths that are not prey to the false promises of fate. In Seneca's

---

[52] Seneca, *Epistulae* 30.3, 53.12, 82.5–6, 88.28, 90.1–7, 95.32, 111.2–4.

[53] See the epigraph opening this chapter; Seneca uses the word *fisus*, the participial form of *fidere*.

[54] See Chapters 1, 2, and 11.

[55] See Motto 1970 xvi and 67–68, for references in Seneca to this common disease of madness.

[56] Seneca is not a typical Stoic. Stoics also developed the theme of mad versus wise, but Stoics believed that passion should be eliminated rather than governed. Here, Cicero and Seneca disagree. For Seneca's playful admission of the perennial presence of passion, see his Letter 56. See also Seneca's distinction between the "Stoic strain" and his own "milder style" in *Epistulae* 13.4.

[57] *De Tranquilitate Animi* 12.5; *Epistulae* 94. 17, 32–50.

[58] The second note of this chapter gives the Latin text.

famous words, "fate has no right [*ius*] over character."[59] And so Humanitas can triumph over Time and Nemesis because the wise can learn to trim their sails, to "govern" themselves despite the storms that arise.[60] As More would put it in the last year of his life: one must "set a cross upon the ship of his heart, and bear a low sail thereon, that the boisterous blast of pride blow him not under the water."[61] And his last two poems, written in prison, both mocked the pretensions of fortune[62] – as he did early in life.[63]

[59] *Epistulae* 36.6.
[60] This passage calls to mind again that "govern" comes from *gubernare*, to pilot or navigate. For More's lifelong use of this traditional metaphor, see CW 1, 45; CW 2, 78/12–21 and CW 15, 476/12; CW 4, 52/18 and, most famously, 98/27; CW 3.2, Epigram 19/184; CW 12, 6/13, 29/6, 57/30–58/1; SL 233; CW 14, 265.
[61] CW 12, 29/5–7. See also Seneca's moral essay *De Ira* 2.31.6: "No pilot [*gubernator*] is ever so reckless as to unfurl all his canvas without having his tackle in order for quickly shortening sail."
[62] CW 1, 45–46: "Lewis the Lost Lover" and "Davy the Dicer."
[63] See Chapter 4.

I I

The Arts of Liberty

Can Peace and Prosperity Be Fashioned
by "Sound Deliberation"?

WHAT IS THE BEST FORM OF THE RESPUBLICA?

A senator is elected by the people to rule; a king attains this end by being born. In the one case blind chance rules; in the other, sound deliberation.

Thomas More, Epigram 198/1, 12–13[1]

If perchance wrath were to bring powerful chieftains to war, your *nod* will promptly put an end to that wrath, such reverence for your sacred majesty have your virtues merited.

Thomas More, Coronation Ode for Henry VIII (1509), 19/146–49

We are taught... by the authoritative *nod* of the laws to subdue our passions, to bridle every lust, to protect our own property, and to keep our thoughts, eyes, and hands off what belongs to others.

Cicero, *De Oratore* 1.194

In every human being, "reason ought to reign like a king," and in every *respublica*, "sound deliberation" is the best way to rule. So we saw in Chapter 7. If that were true, a nation could be ruled "by the authoritative *nod* of the laws"[2] – wisely, freely, without violence. Yet, is that not

---

[1] "QVIS OPTIMVS REIPVB. STATVS./ ... Alter ut eligitur populo, sic nascitur alter. / Sors hic caeca regit, *certum* ibi *consilium*" (CW 3.2; emphasis added).
[2] Apart from the ironic reference to eighteen-year-old Henry VIII, the other persons said by Thomas More to govern "with a nod" are the cardinal in *Richardi Tertii* who directs "with a nod" the conversation of his faction so as to persuade the queen to give her son to Richard (CW 15, 384/17); Richard, who is said to be able to "kill [the young princes] *with a nod*, and would certainly dare to do so" (CW 15, 398/13–15); and Cardinal Morton, who when he "saw there would be no end [to the angry quarrel at his table], he sent away the hanger-on *with a nod* and tactfully turned the conversation to another subject"

utopian? Is that not utterly impossible? Certainly it is, without a nation's education in the arts of liberty, which are the work of deliberative reason. At their best, those arts have given rise to good customs and good fashionings of law that protect self-governing and free citizens: fashionings such as private property, money, and contracts; fashionings that are grounded in a careful and extensive study of the human soul and the universe. So Cicero and More argued.[3]

An example of such careful study is Plato's exploration of private property, a complex topic that some consider "the most pressing problem of political theory."[4] In his *Laws*, Plato poses the foundational question: is one's soul private or public? Such is the context Plato sets up when the Athenian Stranger argues that the soul of each person is the "most precious possession" that is "most truly" one's own.[5] The issue regarding the soul's relation to the state is posed with great force by Plato but also by More, not only in his fictional *Utopia* but also in later life when the issue would arise in a dramatically personal way because he found that neither laws nor rhetorical speech could save him from execution for a silence that he insisted was required by his soul.[6]

How private are one's emotions, or one's own body? Should a citizen be able to take what another freely creates? Violent and flagrantly unjust takeovers have always existed, in every type of society. So what is to be done when faced by the violent, or by the tyrannical, who often use craft and deception to appear otherwise?

(CW 4, 84/17–19). As seen at the end of Chapter 4, More used this phrase to refer to Londoners' willingness to follow wise and trusted John Colet (*Corr.* 6/11).This phrase also occurs in the original text of Pico's *Life* in reference to God's use of thunderbolts and man's terrified obedience to God's "nod"; as seen in Chapter 5, More eliminates this description and adds a phrase describing God as "a very tender loving father" (cf. CW 1, 379 and 120, 123). For other examples from Cicero, see *Tusculanae Disputationes* 5.61, *De Oratore* 138, *Epistulae ad Familiares* 11.22.2, *Epistulae ad Quintum fratrem* 94, *Philippics* 10.19, *De Re Rublica* 1.43; but consider especially *Tusculanae Disputationes.* 2.51: "The wise person . . . will govern [*imperabit*] that lower part of his nature as a just parent governs sons of good character: he will secure the carrying out of his wishes *with a nod. . . .*" See also Virgil, *Aeneid* 7.592 and 10.115; Homer, *Iliad* 1.524–28, 8.246, and 15.75; and Homer, *Odyssey* 13.133, 16.164, 16.283, and 21.130, 431.

[3] For More's defense of private property and law, see CW 5, 274–281; for his defense of wealth and private property, see CW 12, 174–84. Cicero's most famous defenses of private property and contracts are in *De Officiis*; his most famous defenses of law include *Pro Cluentio* 146, *De Legibus* 1.18–23, 2.8, 12–13, and *Pro Sestio* 92.

[4] See Kathy Eden's treatment at 86ff.

[5] Plato's *Laws* 731c and 726.

[6] More argued that his life was protected by the oldest and most authoritative laws of England, such as Magna Carta and the king's own coronation oath.

Because human beings are free, tyranny with its savage horrors is always possible – in a household, or in a country. Such horrors, Cicero notes, are present not among animals but only among humans because only we human beings guide ourselves by chosen ideas of the good, mistaken or incomplete as those ideas often are.[7] Given this reality, study of the liberal arts has for thousands of years been recognized as a necessary component of a free, happy, and just society. By careful study of the range of ideas about a flourishing life, citizens can be informed before each must choose.[8]

Plato dramatized that all-important choice at the end of his *Republic*. In the Myth of Er in book 10, all souls have the freedom to choose another life for their reincarnation. The first soul who selects, viewing superficially the complete span of possibilities, decides on the life of tyranny. The last soul to select is famous Odysseus, who "from memory of its former toils having flung away ambition," searches carefully for "the life of an ordinary citizen who minded his own business."[9] As Socrates points out, the first soul chose without "adequate examination" or the help of philosophy and therefore did not "notice that eating his own children and other evils were fated to be a part of that life" (619b–c). The last soul, however, "with difficulty found [its choice] lying in some corner disregarded by the others, and upon seeing it said that it would have done the same had it drawn the first lot, and chose it gladly" (619c–d).

Unguided by "sound deliberation," the first soul – like King Edward IV[10] – shows that the appetite for glamour, wealth, pleasure, and power grows to monstrous, tyrannical proportions. For that reason, Cicero advised and warned in his last major work: "Work out your own ideas and sift your thoughts so as to see what conception and idea of a good person they contain"; otherwise you can end up as a "Caesar [who] overturned all the laws, human and divine, to achieve for himself a *principate* fashioned [*finxerat*] according to his own erroneous opinion."[11] More suggests a similar assessment when he compares Henry VIII's "lust

[7] Consider *De Officiis* 2.12, 1.26, and 3.81.
[8] In his last major work, written as a letter of advice to his talented son, Cicero points out that choosing one's path in life is "the most difficult problem in the world" because the choice is made when one is young and inexperienced (*De Officiis* 1.117).
[9] Plato's *Republic* 620c, Paul Shorey's translation. For the importance given this quote by Thomas More, see Chapter 4, especially note 68.
[10] See the beginning of Chapter 8.
[11] Cicero, *De Officiis* 3.81: "Explica atque excute intellegentiam tuam, ut videas, quae sit in ea [species] forma et notio viri boni"; 1.26: "Caesaris... omnia iura divina et humana pervertit propter eum, quem sibi ipse opinionis errore finxerat, principatum."

for dominion" with that of Caesar's,[12] but then expresses the hope that Henry will allow his study of the liberal arts[13] to act as a corrective.[14]

The study of tyranny has, for thousands of years, been a necessary component of a liberal arts education, that type of education designed for those whom *Utopia's* Morus calls "well and wisely trained citizens."[15] More's own liberal education is instructive. Although he had the comprehensive education Cicero advised, including mathematics and science,[16] More's writings show his emphasis on those areas of learning that dealt most directly with "well and wisely trained citizens."

By twenty-four, More had read so widely in the Latin classics that he gave public lectures on the most comprehensive critique ever written of those classics: Augustine's thousand-page *City of God*. From age twenty-four to twenty-seven, More mastered Greek, joined Erasmus in translating Lucian's dialogues,[17] and challenged Erasmus to write a competing declamation on tyrannicide.[18]

For the next fourteen years, More immersed himself in the Latin and Greek classics. This he did especially from two o'clock to seven every morning – a rare feat made possible because More was a person who needed little sleep and therefore was able to carry on two professions: scholar and poet by night and London *princeps* by day. In the quiet of early morning, he composed his own history of England on the basis of classical models, his own version of Plato's *Republic*, and a body of 281 Latin poems often based on Greek sources.[19] In the business of the day, he practiced law for seventeen years by working on commercial transactions for the London trade guilds, on public projects such as the construction of sewers to control the ever-flooding Thames River, and on international agreements as seen in book 1 of *Utopia*; for eight of those years, he served as undersheriff of London.

---

[12] See Chapter 7.
[13] "ingenuis artibus," CW 3.2, no. 19/117. Cicero uses the same phrase in *De Oratore* 1.73 and *Epistulae ad Familiares* 4.3.4.
[14] See the analyses of Epigrams 243–44 in Chapter 7 and of Epigram 19 in Chapter 6.
[15] CW 4, 52/33.
[16] Stapleton 14; EE 2750; Roper 11 or TMSB 22/20.
[17] Erasmus became a friend of such depth that he would write at More's death that "there was but one soul between us" (EE 3049/163–64). Through Erasmus, More had access to the leading minds of Europe.
[18] Later Erasmus could speak with firsthand knowledge about Londoner More's special hatred for tyranny and his love for liberty (EE 999/88–94 or TMSB 6).
[19] There are "281 extant Latin poems" of More (CW 3.2, 11); 102 are translations from the *Greek Anthology* (Willow 7).

As undersheriff, More was the professional legal adviser to the elected citizen-sheriff in a way similar to the recorder, who served as professional legal adviser to the elected citizen-mayor. More described the recorder's work in his *Richard III*, indicating its importance to Londoners: "The Londoners use the title 'recorder' for a mayoral assistant well trained in the laws of his country who prevents any erroneous judgments from being given through ignorance of the law."[20] In *Richard III*, the recorder's role in London was so important and so well recognized that the mayor reminds the powerful and perturbed Duke of Buckingham that "it was not the custom for any proposal to be put to the citizens in any other voice besides the recorder's."[21] When the narrator of *Richard III* refers to the recorder as "the mouth of the city,"[22] he could have said the same about Undersheriff More because his work as legal adviser for the sheriff was much the same.

By the time More accepted a position at King Henry's court, at age forty-one, he was recognized as one of the leading humanist scholars and lawyers of his day, but he was also one of the most experienced and recognized "first citizens" of England, having been selected to serve as a member of Parliament twice, undersheriff of London for eight years, member of Doctors' Common, public orator on various occasions, an ambassador on two foreign embassies, twice a lecturer of law, and continuously an officer at the inns of court.

When More was twenty-four, he also decided to learn from the London Carthusians the arts of self-rule needed for such qualities as *fides* and *constantia* that Cicero considered necessary for the clear-sighted and courageous ruler capable of doing what *princeps* Scipio or Crassus or Regulus had done. During this time, More began reading Pico della Mirandola, a reading that eventually led him to develop in verse his distinctively Christian articulation of *humanitas,* as seen especially in his "Rules" and "Weapons" of spiritual battle and his own unique account of "The Twelve Properties of a Lover."[23]

Years later, More explained the importance of an education that would strengthen reason, character, and law – an education that develops "the one special thing without which all learning is half-lame . . . a good mother

[20] CW 15, 470/7–9.
[21] CW 15, 470/4–5.
[22] CW 2, 75/21.
[23] See Chapter 5. It is notable that More's poetic additions are the longest single portion – over one-third – of the book.

wit."[24] Yet More realized that to expect reason, character, and law to exercise such power was indeed daunting, almost utopian, given the fact that history seems to present more war than peace, more discord than harmony, and more laws broken than kept. Nonetheless, he saw this daunting task to be possible only to the extent that the arts of liberty – education, law, and rhetoric – fashioned the works of reason to counter prejudice, misguided passion, and thoughtless self-interest. This task was and is so difficult that most political philosophers after More abandoned the cultural project that he and his classical and biblical predecessors saw as the irreplaceable support for just government. Yet conscious of all the difficulties involved, More was convinced that "sound deliberation" by wise and experienced citizens was an irreplaceable dimension of free self-government.[25]

In these matters, More would later strongly oppose Luther's positions on the corruption of reason and on the denial of free will, arguing that these dogmas of Luther were untrue to human nature and thus served to undermine the political and educational mainstays that he and his fellow followers of Ciceronian *humanitas* judged to be the only means to peace, to a mature and prosperous political community, and to ongoing reform in society.

If More had such confidence in the power of education in "good letters," why did he not publish his own *Richard III*? The apparent mystery of More's laboring upon *Richard III* for many years without publishing it becomes understandable when we consider the lessons of civic liberty that are proposed, lessons similar to those set forth by Cicero and Sallust, who sought to educate civic leaders to that level of virtue, shrewdness, and citizenship needed to accomplish the most difficult work of justice and peace. Such an education aims at a type of judgment and character lacking in *Richard III*'s Hastings and Queen, but found in the narrator, in Chief Justice Markum, in Thomas Morus's fellow *principes* as *Utopia* opens, and perhaps in Bishop Morton.[26]

---

[24] CW 6, 132/13–16; see the many earlier references, especially those in Chapter 1 regarding the necessity of becoming "prudent as the serpent."

[25] More gives a detailed account of Livy's portrayal of the problems of a free and self-governing city in dealing with factions (CW 9, 79–80, recounting Livy 23.2–3). Although More clearly presents the senate's crucial role, he discreetly omits the judgment given in Livy that "a senate [is] the only deliberative body in a free state" (Habenicht 149).

[26] Consider the ambiguity of More's judgment that Morton's last days were so godly that they "well changed his life" (CW 2, 91/17). Undoubtedly, however, Morton played a leading role in bringing the English civil wars of his time to an end with the skills seen in diffusing the escalating war at his own dinner table in *Utopia*.

To the reader exercising sharp-sighted prudence, *Richard III* reveals dramatically and with penetrating irony how a nation fails in self-government. In doing so, *Richard III* points to clear principles and highly valuable prudential advice about good self-government; it points to the importance of institutions such as London's often-annually elected "senate" of aldermen,[27] annually elected mayors and sheriffs, professionally trained civil magistrates such as the recorder, and the availability of courts governed by established law.[28] It also points to the odd and imperfect but effective custom of sanctuary, an institution that receives what appears to be disproportionately long attention in his short history. Yet *Richard III* shows how leaders of a people can and must invent such novel and even peculiar protections, cleverly responding to grave threats to the lives of citizens.

In *Richard III,* even Buckingham, who strongly argues against the queen's right to use sanctuary, acknowledges that the institution of sanctuary still has great force.[29] He also "concede[s] it was virtuous and merciful to have some haven" for specific cases such as the following one, the one that matches perfectly the queen and her sons' situation then and fourteen years earlier:

And if (as has happened a number of times) someone's title to the throne is disputed, when the title is determined by warfare and each side treats the other as traitors, it makes sense to have some place where each side can be safe in uncertain or threatening circumstances as victory swings from one side to the other.[30]

Buckingham acknowledges this situation as the "true and original function of sanctuaries," but he disingenuously denies that this situation exists in the queen's case. Nonetheless, he goes on to give an arresting explanation of why the "privilege" of sanctuary arose: "[I]t is when the source of danger is the law itself that one has to resort to a privilege for protection; and I believe it is from this necessity that the custom of sanctuaries arose and grew up."[31]

What is the "law itself" that is the source of the danger of *Richard III*? Is it the law of hereditary monarchy, that form of government that

---

[27] The long struggles between hereditary and elected and then annual and life terms are clearly presented in Barron 136ff.

[28] See especially the importance given to Westminster as the seat of judgment according to law (CW 15, 482/26–27), to the court of a Chief Justice Markham who resigns his office rather than violate the law (CW 15, 458/7), and to city courts such as the Court of Hustings (CW 2, [English] 69/15). See Barron 128 on London's "many courts."

[29] CW 15, 368/26–29.

[30] CW 15, 371.

[31] CW 15, 373–75.

Aristotle and Erasmus both identified as "primitive," an institution that necessarily evolves out of existence because of the demands of human nature and political development? Reflection guided by *Richard III* requires that this question be asked if the Ciceronian and Roman arguments are weighed, especially the problems of pride and faction they show as consequences of placing power over merit, thus encouraging arrogance and *inuidia* (i.e., envy or ill will).

But if More spent years writing both an English and a Latin version of *Richard III*, why did he then decide to publish *Utopia* in Latin and *Richard III* not at all in his own lifetime? Simply put: because *Richard III* would have been too dangerous because it is too direct, in either version. Not only does it name and show powerful political families in egregious corruption; it also names and shows the major weaknesses of a primitive and defective government doomed to produce bitter factions, as seen in Chapter 8.[32] The solutions artfully alluded to in *Richard III* for England's strife-ridden government are not the ones Conqueror Utopus would use – that is, military force and tyrannical rule. The solutions suggested are (and eventually became) something closer to the best that the wise *principes* of Rome and of London had developed over generations of painful trial and error, of long and careful deliberation: stronger laws and more effective institutions and customs allowing for such goods as the following – the allotment of power based on merit, effective protections of citizen safety and rights, honors bestowed according to *humanitas*, good advice privileged on the basis of reason rather than appetite and self-interest, and "apt"[33] education of "well and wisely trained citizens" who are capable of devising adequate customs, laws, institutions, and literary arts for governing themselves in freedom, in *libertas*.

One such custom that More sought to advance as a first-time speaker of the House of Commons was freedom of political speech. More argued to a young King Henry VIII: Parliament is "a very substantial assembly of right wise and politic persons"; its members are "the most discreet persons out of every quarter" of England. They will, however, be unable to "giv[e] of their advice and counsel" regarding "matter of weight and importance"

---

[32] That the cycle seen in *Richard III* would (and did) continue is seen in the narrator's references to the pretender Perkin Warbeck (CW 2, 82/22, 83/2). As Ann Wroe shows, Warbeck posed a serious political problem for eight years; he led three invasions and was promoted by Henry VII's rivals as a legitimate claimant to the English throne.

[33] For the distinctively Roman character of this virtue, see *De Oratore* 2.17 and 18. As Crassus points out there, "[O]f all the words in the Latin language, none has so wide a signification as this word"; regarding its opposite, "the Greeks have not even bestowed a name upon the fault in question."

unless they are granted freedom of speech and thus "utterly discharged of all doubt and fear" caused by the "dread" that their "timorous hearts" have before the king. Unless each is given the freedom "to discharge his conscience," More went on to argue, the "profit of England will suffer."[34] For that Parliament of 1523, Henry VIII granted More's request.

Seven years earlier, More had explored the issue of free speech in *Utopia*. How to rule free citizens? – that is the broader context of free speech presented in *Utopia*; that is the major question artfully raised and profoundly explored; that is the major interest expressed by Morus before inviting Raphael to tell his story;[35] that is the major appeal that Raphael himself makes in rejecting the monarch's willful "life of pleasure and self-indulgence" and in speaking on behalf of free citizens. Raphael makes his powerful plea against tyrannous monarchs in the name of citizens with *libertas*:

> To have a single person enjoy a life of pleasure and self-indulgence amid the groans and lamentations of all around him is to be the keeper, not of a kingdom, but of a jail. In fine, as he is an incompetent physician who cannot cure one disease except by creating another, so he who cannot reform the lives of citizens in any other way than by depriving them of the good things of life must admit that he does not know *how to rule free citizens*.[36]

When this appeal is compared to the actual place he praises, however, Utopia can be seen as the opposite of what Raphael promises; rather than a paradise, it is more a jail in which "citizens" are regularly deprived of the very goods valued most by the free. Nevertheless, Raphael's appeal to the "rule of free citizens" prepares us for his insistence on *respublica*[37] and for the apparent similarities between *Utopia* and Aristotle's and Cicero's mixed forms of government designed specifically to remedy the divisions and animosities between classes of rich and poor. Yet the constant refrain of calling freedomless Utopia a "republic" acquires the same powerful ironic effect as the constant refrain of calling murderous Richard the "protector." Without directly saying so, the author cleverly and effectively invites the careful reader to participate in discovering the true nature of things: Utopia is the opposite of the "property of the people," just as Richard is the opposite of a protector. In Utopia, all ownership is

---

34 Roper 12–16 or *TMSB* 24–25.
35 *CW* 4, 52/30–54/1.
36 *CW* 4, 94/37–96/3, emphasis added.
37 More uses *respublica* more than sixty times in *Utopia*; *princeps* is used even more frequently.

supposedly outlawed, but the sharp-sighted reader will discover the sub-terfuge of Conqueror Utopus and his military heirs, that is, those war lords, officials, and quaestors who direct Utopia's aggressive and impe-rialistic war plans and who are rewarded by living abroad "in opulence and a grand manner."[38]

When Raphael speaks of the Roman arts of rule[39] and "arts of peace,"[40] most would at first think of Rome's famous rule by law, love for *libertas,* and protection of citizens' rights – rights that included legal and institutional protections from slavery and from execution without a trial. Yet, unlike the Romans, Utopia boasts of having few and simple laws, with the result that the people have no *libertas* because they have no protections from being enslaved and executed – the opposite of a good government that, as Raphael boasted of Utopia, "know[s] how to rule the free."[41]

Repeatedly, Raphael tells us one thing but shows us another. He tells us that the harbor of Utopia allows travel to and fro for the good of the people, but then we learn that is dangerously not true. He tells us that it is easy to do what he himself most enjoys, which is travel, but then we learn that is dangerously untrue as well. He tells us that all live a simple, trusting, and virtuous life, but we discover Machiavellian tactics, especially in imperialist wars designed to destroy trust and augment fear, that are anything but simple and virtuous. He tells us that Utopia hates slavery, yet the entire economy of this small island is based on tens of thousands of slaves, many of whom are its own citizens enslaved for having thought or acted freely.

Repeatedly, Raphael insists that his ideal social order has eliminated three factors identified by the Greek and Roman historians and by the Bible and church fathers as the causes of disharmony and war: pride, greed, ill will. This claim by Raphael, like the many claims seen in Chapter 9, is wholly implausible. So why would an author like Thomas More "record" for us the sailor-tales of such an unreliable person as Raphael,[42] Speaker-of-Nonsense?[43]

---

[38] CW 4, 214/25–26.
[39] CW 4, 108/7–8.
[40] CW 4, 56/24.
[41] CW 4, 96/3.
[42] Consider the role of the Recorder, "mouth of the city" (CW 2, 75/21), seen in *Richard III,* and Morus's insistence at CW 4, 250/20ff. that he is simply reporting what Raphael said.
[43] See note 39 of Chapter 9.

One reason Morus makes explicit: to exercise our sharp-sightedness in prudent assessment.[44] If Raphael is wrong about human nature, readers must ask why. If Raphael's proposals are not viable solutions to the pressing issues of obvious injustice, readers must ask why not and then decide what might be better.

Any experienced leader knows that pointing out injustices and inadequacies is easy, while finding genuine solutions to these is often extraordinarily difficult and personally demanding. The starvation, unemployment, and unrest that Raphael points out in England, for example, are obvious injustices. But his simplistic solutions lack the inventive resourcefulness and personal industry that arise from a deep and sharp-eyed understanding of causes. Reverting to medieval England's system of open fields and primitive farming will not solve England's social and economic problems. Mere reversion to primitive custom does not acknowledge, for example, England's unique role as the greatest wool producer of that time.[45] Nor is idle Raphael willing to become personally involved. In contrast, Morus has freely answered at great personal cost the request of his fellow Londoners and the king to serve as their "orator"[46] on an embassy to address the international complexities involved in a world that requires international cooperation and harmony, rather than the imperial dominion that a primitive Utopia claims to deserve – thus raising an even larger and more complex issue posed earlier by Cicero: how does one free people rule itself in a world with countries composed of other people who wish to be free?[47]

Through *Utopia*, More ironically reveals that money, private property, law, and effective institutions of self-government are not only helpful but necessary inventions of good reason; they are fashionings of art refined over time in adapting to new economic, political, cultural, and historical developments. As *Utopia* suggests, London was an evolving embodiment of these inventive fashionings, but unlike Utopia, London was marked by unusual freedom; it allowed no slavery and offered genuine social and

---

[44] See the letter of 1517 that More appended to the second edition of *Utopia*, *CW* 4, 248–52.

[45] To remind English legislators and judges of this fact, judges and members of the House of Lords sat on woolsacks. See the Parliament Roll paintings of the king in Parliament from that time.

[46] *CW* 4, 46/12.

[47] By raising such an issue, one can see some basis for the surprising claim that More's *Utopia* "rivals" and "surpasses" Plato's *Republic* (*CW* 4, 20/5 and 18–19, also 18/23–26).

economic mobility in its customs of apprenticeship and self-regulating trades.[48]

After much trial and error, the city of London decided "in 1389 to allow no one to serve as mayor for more than one year at a time, and no one to be reelected to the office until five years had passed" – despite the obvious practical difficulties of such frequent elections. Why? So factions did not form around individuals holding the city's power.[49]

Thomas More, as "Citizen & Vicecomes of London,"[50] artfully makes a similar recommendation in Epigram 198, which shows the advantages of an elected "consul" who is accountable to the people.[51] Epigram 121 expresses the position of popular sovereignty, as does the Latin version of *Richard III*.[52] As we have also seen, the narrator of *Richard III* shows in many ways that "long-confirmed power turns many *principes* to pride." Most dramatically, King Edward admits on his deathbed that he "as a private citizen" had not exercised his liberty "to foresee and anticipate" the "ill effects" of his unchecked ambitions. The dying king goes on to confess: if I had foreseen the "ill effects as distinctly in thought as I later experienced them in deed, with less pleasure than pain, on my life, I would never have sacrificed so many men's heads to see men on their knees doing me honor."[53] More's own literary art has just that objective, as did Plato's and Homer's: to show "distinctly in thought" the effects of free choice.

Utopia is an art of this same kind. Its dialectical design invites the attentive reader to similar depth and comprehensiveness of thought about the human condition and the free choices each must make. Ultimately, *Utopia's* irony reveals not only the importance but the absolute necessity of the very realities that Raphael belittles and even rejects,[54] such as mandatory limitations of power along with strong and enforceable protections so that reason can reign over prejudice, passion, and thoughtless indulgence. Attentive readers of *Utopia* are invited to discover reasons

---

[48] See especially Barron and Nightingale.

[49] Barron 148 and n. 27.

[50] The first editions of the 1518 Epigrams identify More as "civis et vicecomitis Londinensis" (CW3.2, 272/3v–4v). See also notes 11 and 12 of Chapter 9.

[51] See Chapter 6 and consider the title of this epigram, "Quis Optimus Rei Publicae Status?" in relationship to *Utopia's* actual title, which begins *De Optimo Reipublicae Statu. . . .* As indicated in the beginning of Chapter 7, More planned to have the epigrams printed with *Utopia*.

[52] See Chapters 7 and 8.

[53] CW 15, 22–26.

[54] As did Pico.

for protections such as sophisticated laws, private property, and money; they are invited to discover why Cicero would argue that trustworthiness or *fides* should be lived with everyone including enemies, and why virtue can never be based on pleasure; they are invited to see why agents and "embodiments" of the law such as lawyers and magistrates are practical necessities if peace and prosperity are to reign in the midst of constant change. In other words, the dialectical character of *Utopia* is designed for a self-education that genuinely equips citizens to value their liberty and to learn what is needed for its existence. By inviting friendly deliberation about such issues,[55] this work fosters a self-education that not only leads future *principes* to an understanding of both the causes of violence and the character of those arts necessary for liberty, peace, and mere survival but also motivates them to work hard enough to acquire those arts they have discovered to be necessary for that liberty, peace, and survival.

If reason is to be king, genuine deliberation must be fostered, trained, tricked, and corrected, and then trained again with deepened determination and more ardent desire. Toward this end, liberal education has traditionally been seen since the time of the Greeks as the necessary education for those entrusted with piloting (*gubernans*) the ship of state. Just as expert captains must know the character and qualities of different kinds of ships and sailing conditions, and just as the doctor must know the character and qualities that make up health and sickness, so expert "first citizens" must know the character and qualities of our human condition, but they must also have labored to acquire the historian's appreciation of their country, the poet's sympathy for the human heart, the orator's and legislator's skills in moving that heart, and the Stoic's endurance come what may – all in a spirit of trustworthy friendship and dedicated industry.

For thousands of years, the *studia humanitatis* or a liberal education – devised by "sound deliberation" – has served to advance just these purposes so that well-trained first citizens could be agents for the difficult work of achieving some measure of justice, prosperity, liberty, and peace. Young More not only studied these arts, these "good letters";[56] he also

---

55 Consider the generous action and friendly speech that persona Morus exhibits toward Raphael. Despite his ambassadorial position, Morus does not take offense at Raphael's harsh and even insulting manner. Morus brings Raphael to his home, feeds him lunch and dinner (unlike Socrates in the *Republic*), and takes pains not to cause old Raphael offense despite their major differences.

56 See the opening of Chapter 1 for a listing of the various English and Latin phrases for liberal education.

contributed to them, most clearly with *Richard III* and *Utopia* – masterful puzzles that exercise the subtle and kingly prudence they artfully advocate.[57]

As this book has tried to demonstrate, More presented his solutions to England's civil wars with the same subtlety that he admired in those classical authors who were master artisans of *humanitas*. More's solutions were not simplistic reorganization or precise forms of institution. His solutions were eminently Ciceronian in calling for the comprehensive education of leading citizens as master artists so they could fashion a more just and peaceful order from the particulars of their people's history, geography, economics, laws, customs, and institutions, always in light of the broadest possible understanding of human nature and the universe as they exist. Only this comprehensive education could provide the perspective that free and careful judgment needs to fashion wise decisions about pressing particulars. Only leaders educated in this way could fashion the strategy needed to guide their ships of state in the midst of constantly changing conditions, of storms and calms, of dangerous waters, and of riotous crews.

Yet for the captain, the doctor, and the citizen, knowledge and judgment are not enough. Absolutely necessary are highly motivated,[58] finely fashioned[59] characters possessing the self-mastery and courage needed to exercise those arts in a trustworthy manner despite the most difficult of conditions. As seen in More's letter of 1516, the ideal citizen generals are clothed in the peace-loving Franciscan's simple garb and are so trained for endurance that not even the temptations of glory and unsurpassed wealth can distract them from their arts.[60]

[57] Consider again humanist Froben's book device of the crowned serpents fashioned in the shape symbolizing health as they protect the innocent dove.
[58] See *De Oratore* 1.134 for the need to have *studium*, "something like the passion of love" to achieve such difficult goods.
[59] See notes 1 of Chapter 1 and note 61 of Chapter 2 and Cicero's metaphor of "forging and fashioning" one's character as fine sculptors fashion their art: *De Officiis* 1.13–14, *De Finibus* 4.35, *De Oratore* 3.58. See also Seneca, *Epistulae* 65.7.
[60] An effective leader cannot be, as More put it in his last work, "a cowardly ship's captain who is so disheartened by the furious din of a storm that he deserts the helm, hides away cowering in some cranny, and abandons the ship to the waves"(CW 14, 265). Or, as the text chosen for the portrait *Sir Thomas More and His Family* reads: each must be a master able to "trim my sails...lest my yards tremble, bent beneath a heavy blast" (Chapter 10). More's own use of this same metaphor of trimming sails appears a few years after this painting was completed: in *A Dialogue of Comfort*, old Anthony reminds Vincent that "[w]hen God send the tempest, he wills that the sailors shall get themselves to their tackling and do the best they can for themselves that the sea not eat them up"

To "fashion" a character and a nation "in *humanitas* and virtue" was Cicero's and Seneca's challenge to their fellow Romans. It was Homer's and Plato's challenge to their fellow Greeks. It is the challenge recorded in the portrait *Sir Thomas More and His Family*. It was the challenge young More posed to England, and to himself, even in his earliest poetry. But would he live up to that challenge in the tempestuous years to follow? And would England?

(*CW* 12, 57/30ff.). Earlier, Vincent began by recounting his urgent need to "govern and stay the ship of our kin, and keep it afloat" (6/13). But More used these metaphors, as did Cicero, throughout his writings.

Works Cited

Ackroyd, Peter. *The Life of Thomas More*. London: Chatto & Windus, 1998.

Adams, Robert P. *The Better Part of Valor: More, Erasmus, Colet, and Vives, on Humanism, War, and Peace, 1496–1535*. Seattle: University of Washington Press, 1962.

Aesop. *Aesop's Fables*. Trans. Laura Gibbs. Oxford: Oxford University Press, 2002.

Allen, Ward. "Speculations on Thomas More's Use of Hesychius." *Philological Quarterly* 46.2 (April 1967): 156–66.

Aquinas, Thomas. *Expositio S. Thomae in decem libros* Ethicorum ad Nicomachum, Aristotelis. Turin: Marietti, 1934.

Aristotle. *Basic Works*. Ed. Richard McKeon. New York: Random House, 1941.
  Nicomachean Ethics. Trans. H. Rackham. Loeb Classical Library. Cambridge, MA: Harvard University Press, 1934.
  Politics. Trans. H. Rackham. Loeb Classical Library. Cambridge, MA: Harvard University Press, 1944.

Astin, A. E. *Scipio Aemilianus*. Oxford: Oxford University Press, 1967.

Austin, R. G., ed. *Aeneidos, Liber Primus with a Commentary*. Oxford: Clarendon Press, 1971.

Baker, David. "First among Equals: The Utopian *Princeps*." *Moreana*, nos. 115–16 (December 1993): 33–45.

Baker-Smith, Dominic. *More's Utopia*. Toronto: University of Toronto Press, 2000.

Barron, Caroline M. *London in the Later Middle Ages: Government and People, 1200–1500*. Oxford: Oxford University Press, 2004.

Basil the Great. *How to Profit from Pagan Literature*. In *The Letters*, 4:378–35. Trans. Roy Deferrari and Martin McGuire. Loeb Classical Library. Cambridge, MA: Harvard University Press, 1939.

Batstone, William W. "The Antithesis of Virtue: Sallust's *Synkrisis* and the Crisis of the Late Republic." *Classical Antiquity* 7.1 (April 1988): 1–29.

Beier, Benjamin V. "The Subordination of Humanism: Young More's 'Profitable' Work, *The Life of John Picus*." *Moreana*, nos. 179–80 (June 2010): 23–44.

Black, Crofton. *Pico's Heptaplus and Biblical Hermeneutics*. Boston: Brill, 2006.

Blum, Paul R. "Pico, Theology, and the Church." In *Pico della Mirandola: New Essays*, ed. M. V. Dougherty, 37–60. Cambridge: Cambridge University Press, 2008.

Boethius. *Consolation of Philosophy*. Trans. Richard Green. New York: Macmillan, 1962.

Borghesi, Francesco. "A Life in Works." In *Pico della Mirandola: New Essays*, ed. M. V. Dougherty, 202–19. Cambridge: Cambridge University Press, 2008.

Bostaph, Samuel. "Deepening the Irony of *Utopia*: An Economic Perspective." *History of Political Economy* 42.2 (Summer 2010): 361–82.

Brooke, Christopher. *London, 800–1216: The Shaping of a City*. Berkeley: University of California Press, 1975.

Brunt, P. A. *The Fall of the Roman Republic and Related Essays*. Oxford: Oxford University Press, 1988.

Chambers, Richard W. *Thomas More*. London: Jonathan Cape, 1935.

Cicero. *Academica*. Trans. H. Rackham. Loeb Classical Library. Cambridge, MA: Harvard University Press, 1933.

Brutus. Trans. G. L. Hendrickson. Loeb Classical Library. Cambridge, MA: Harvard University Press, 1952.

De Amicitia. Trans. W. Falconer. Loeb Classical Library. Cambridge, MA: Harvard University Press, 1923.

De Fato. In *De Oratore*, vol. 2. Loeb Classical Library. Cambridge, MA: Harvard University Press, 1942.

De Finibus. Trans. H. Rackham. Loeb Classical Library. Cambridge, MA: Harvard University Press, 1931.

De Inventione. Trans. H. M. Hubbell. Loeb Classical Library. Cambridge, MA: Harvard University Press, 1949.

De Lege Agraria. Trans. J. H. Freese. Loeb Classical Library. Cambridge, MA: Harvard University Press, 1967.

De Legibus. Trans. C. W. Keyes. Loeb Classical Library. Cambridge, MA: Harvard University Press, 1928.

De Natura Deorum. Trans. H. Rackham. Loeb Classical Library. Cambridge, MA: Harvard University Press, 1933.

De Officiis. Trans. Walter Miller. Loeb Classical Library. Cambridge, MA: Harvard University Press, 1913.

De Oratore. Trans. E. W. Sutton and H. Rackham. 2 vols. Loeb Classical Library. Cambridge, MA: Harvard University Press, 1942.

De Re Publica. Trans. C. W. Keyes. Loeb Classical Library. Cambridge, MA: Harvard University Press, 1928.

Epistulae ad Atticum. Trans. E. O. Winstedt. Loeb Classical Library. Cambridge, MA: Harvard University Press, 1970.

Epistulae ad Familiares. Trans. W. G. Williams. Loeb Classical Library. Cambridge, MA: Harvard University Press, 1958.

Epistulae ad Quintum fratrem. Trans. D. R. Bailey. Loeb Classical Library. Cambridge, MA: Harvard University Press, 1972.

In Pisonem. Trans. N. H. Watts. Loeb Classical Library. Cambridge, MA: Harvard University Press, 1953.

Orator. Trans. H. M. Hubbell. Loeb Classical Library. Cambridge, MA: Harvard University Press, 1952.

Pro Archia. Trans. N. H. Watts. Loeb Classical Library. Cambridge, MA: Harvard University Press, 1935.

Pro Balbo. Trans. R. Gardner. Loeb Classical Library. Cambridge, MA: Harvard University Press, 1958.

Pro Caelio. Trans. R. Gardner. Loeb Classical Library. Cambridge, MA: Harvard University Press, 1958.

Pro Cluentio. Trans. H. Grose Hodge. Loeb Classical Library. Cambridge, MA: Harvard University Press, 1927.

Pro Murena. Trans. Louis E. Lord. Loeb Classical Library. Cambridge, MA: Harvard University Press, 1937.

Pro Publio Quinctio. Trans. John H. Freese. Loeb Classical Library. Cambridge, MA: Harvard University Press, 1930.

Pro Sestio. Trans. R. Gardner. Loeb Classical Library. Cambridge, MA: Harvard University Press, 1958.

Pro Sexto Roscio Amerino. Trans. J. H. Freese. Loeb Classical Library. Cambridge, MA: Harvard University Press, 1930.

Pro T. Annio Milone. Trans. N. H. Watts. Loeb Classical Library. Cambridge, MA: Harvard University Press, 1953.

Tusculan Disputations. Trans. J. E. King. Loeb Classical Library. Cambridge, MA: Harvard University Press, 1945.

Verrine Orations. Trans. L. H. G. Greenwood. 2 vols. Loeb Classical Library. Cambridge, MA: Harvard University Press, 1948.

Cousins, A. D. "More's 'Pageant Verses,' the History of Human Life and the Pursuit of the Common Weal." In *Renaissance Historicisms: Essays in Honor of Arthur F. Kinney,* ed. James M. Dutcher and Anne Lake Prescott, 36–53. Newark: University of Delaware Press, 2008.

"St. Thomas More as English Poet." In *Thomas More: Essays on the Icon,* ed. Damian Grace and Brian Byron, 43–52. Melbourne, Australia: Dover Communications, 1980.

DiLorenzo, Raymond. "The Critique of Socrates in Cicero's *De Oratore*: *Ornatus* and the Nature of Wisdom." *Philosophy and Rhetoric* 11.4 (Fall 1978): 247–61.

Dougherty, M. V., ed. *Pico della Mirandola: New Essays.* Cambridge: Cambridge University Press, 2008.

Duffy, Eamon. *Marking the Hours: English People and Their Prayers, 1240–1570.* New Haven, CT: Yale University Press, 2006.

Dyck, Andrew R. *A Commentary on Cicero, De Officiis.* Ann Arbor: University of Michigan Press, 1996.

Eden, Kathy. *Friends Hold All Things in Common: Tradition, Intellectual Property, and the* Adages *of Erasmus.* New Haven, CT: Yale University Press, 2001.

Erasmus, Desiderius. *The Collected Works of Erasmus*. Ed. Craig R. Thompson
  et al. Toronto: University of Toronto Press, 1974–.
  The Education of a Christian Prince. Trans. and ed. Lisa Jardin. Cambridge:
  Cambridge University Press, 1997.
  Erasmi Epistolae. Ed. P. S. Allen et al. 12 vols. Oxford: Oxford University
  Press, 1906–55.
  Institutio Principis Christiani. *Opera Omnia*, 4.1. Amsterdam: North-Holland,
  1974.
Fantham, Elaine. *The Roman World of Cicero's* De Oratore. Oxford: Oxford
  University Press, 2004.
Ferrary, Jean-Louis. "The Statesman and the Law in the Political Philosophy of
  Cicero." In *Justice and Generosity: Studies in Hellenistic Social and Political
  Philosophy Proceedings of the Sixth Symposium Hellenisticum*, ed. Andre
  Laks and Malcolm Scholfield, 48–73. Cambridge: Cambridge University
  Press: 1995.
Foister, Susan. *Drawings by Holbein from the Royal Library Windsor Castle*.
  New York: Harcourt Brace Jovanovich, 1983.
  Holbein and England. New Haven, CT: Yale University Press, 2004.
Fox, Alistair. *Thomas More: History and Providence*. New Haven, CT: Yale
  University Press, 1983.
Frank, William. "Cicero's Civic Metaphysics as a Basis for Responsibility." In
  *Verantwortung in einer komplexen Gesellschaft – Responsibility: Recogni-
  tion and Limits*, ed. Anton Rauscher, 175–92. Berlin: Duncker & Humblot,
  2010.
Garrison, James D. *Dryden and the Tradition of Panegyric*. Berkeley: University
  of California Press, 1975.
Georgiadou, Agathi. "Political Terminology and Ideology in Thucydides." Ph.D.
  thesis, King's College, London, 1988.
Gleason, John B. *John Colet*. Berkeley: University of California Press, 1989.
Gordon, Walter M. "*Maiestas* in Thomas More's Political Thought." *Moreana*,
  no. 129 (March 1997): 5–20.
Grace, Damian. "Subjects or Citizens? *Populi* and *Cives* in More's *Epigrammata*."
  Moreana, no. 97 (March 1988): 133–36.
  "Thomas More's *Epigrammata*: Political Theory in a Poetic Idiom." *Parergon*,
  n.s., 3 (1985): 115–29.
Graves, Michael A. R. *Henry VIII: A Study in Kingship*. London: Pearson, 2003.
Great Britain. Public Records Office. *Calendar of State Papers, Spanish*. London:
  Longmans, 1866.
  Letters and Papers of Henry VIII. Ed. J. S. Brewer and James Gairdner. London:
  Longmans, 1882.
The Greek Anthology. Ed. and trans. W. R. Paton, Loeb Classical Library.
  Cambridge, MA: Harvard University Press, 1958.
Greenblatt, Stephen. *Renaissance Self-Fashioning: From More to Shakespeare*.
  Chicago: University of Chicago Press, 1984.
Gunn, Steven. "The French Wars of Henry VIII." In *The Origins of War in
  Early Modern Europe*, ed. Jeremy Black., 28–51. Edinburgh: John Donald
  Publishers, 1987.

Guy, John. *A Daughter's Love: Thomas and Margaret More.* London: Fourth Estate, 2008.

———. *Thomas More.* New York: Oxford University Press, 2000.

———. *Tudor England.* New York: Oxford University Press, 1988.

Habenicht, Rudolph E. *A Thomas More Reader.* Naalehu, HI: Chelsea Press, 1998.

Hall, Edward. *Lives of the Kings: Henry VIII.* 2 vols. London: T. C. and E. C. Jack, 1904.

Harpsfield, Nicholas. *The Life and Death of Sir Thomas Moore, Knight, Sometymes Lord High Chancellor of England.* London: Oxford University Press for Early English Text Society, 1932.

Heath, T. G. "Another Look at Thomas More's *Richard.*" *Moreana,* nos. 19–20 (November 1968): 11–19.

Heiserman, A. R. "Satire in the *Utopia.*" *PMLA* 78 (1963): 163–74.

Heraclitus. *Fragments: The Collected Wisdom of Heraclitus.* Trans. Brooks Haxton. New York: Viking, 2001.

Herman, Peter C. "Henrician Historiography and the Voice of the People: The Cases of More and Hall." *Texas Studies in Literature and Language* 39.3 (Fall 1997): 259–83.

———. "'O, tis a gallant king': Shakespeare's *Henry V* and the Crisis of the 1590s." *Tudor Political Culture,* ed. Dale Hoak, 204–25. Cambridge: Cambridge University Press, 1995.

Hobbes, Thomas, trans. *The Peloponnesian War/Thucydides.* Notes and introduction by David Grene. Chicago: University of Chicago Press, 1989.

Holmes, T. Rice. *The Architect of the Roman Empire, 44 B.C. – 27 B.C.* Oxford: Oxford University Press, 1928.

Homer. *The Iliad.* Trans. Richmond Lattimore. Chicago: University of Chicago Press, 1951.

———. *The Odyssey.* Trans. Richmond Lattimore. New York: Harper & Row, 1965.

Horace. *The Odes and Epodes.* Trans. C. E. Bennett. Loeb Classical Library. Cambridge, MA: Harvard University Press, 1927.

———. *Satires, Epistles and Ars Poetica.* Trans. H. Rushton Fairclough. Loeb Classical Library. Cambridge, MA: Harvard University Press, 1926.

Hosington, Brenda M. "More's Use of English Proverbs in *The History of King Richard III.*" *Moreana,* no. 134 (June 1998): 5–24.

Hoskins, W. G. *The Age of Plunder: King Henry's England, 1500–1547.* New York: Longman, 1976.

House, Seymour Baker. "Sir Thomas More as Church Patron." *Journal of Ecclesiastical History* 40.2 (April 1989): 208–18.

Jerome. *On Illustrious Men.* Trans. Thomas Halton. Washington, DC: Catholic University of America Press, 1999.

Juvenal. *Juvenal and Persius.* Trans. G. G. Ramsay. Loeb Classical Library. Cambridge, MA: Harvard University Press, 1961.

Kiefer, Frederick. *Fortune and Elizabethan Tragedy.* San Marino, CA: Huntington Library, 1983.

Kinney, Arthur F. *Humanist Poetics: Thought, Rhetoric and Fiction in Sixteenth-Century England.* Amherst: University of Massachusetts, 1986.

Koterski, Joseph W. "Circe's Beasts and the Image of God: More's Creative Appropriation of Pico's Humanist Spirituality." *Moreana,* nos. 179–80 (June 2010): 45–62.

Lewi, Angela. *The Thomas More Family Group.* London: Her Majesty's Stationery Office, 1974.

Lewis, Lesley. *The Thomas More Family Group Portraits after Holbein.* Herefordshire: Gracewing, 1998.

Lintott, Andrew. *The Constitution of the Roman Republic.* Oxford: Oxford University Press, 1999.

"Provocatio: From the Struggle of the Orders to the Principate." *Aufstieg und Niedergang der römischen Welt* 1.2 (1972): 226–67.

Violence in Republican Rome. Oxford: Oxford University Press, 1968.

Livy. *History of Rome.* Trans. Frank G. Moore. Loeb Classical Library. Cambridge, MA: Harvard University Press, 1919–59.

Logan, George M. *The Meaning of More's "Utopia."* Princeton, NJ: Princeton University Press, 1983.

Lucian. *The Works of Lucian of Samosata.* Trans. H. W. Fowler and F. G. Fowler. Oxford: Clarendon Press, 1905.

Machiavelli, Niccolò. *The Prince.* Ed. Quentin Skinner and Russell Price. Cambridge: Cambridge University Press, 1988.

MacKendrick, Paul. *The Philosophical Books of Cicero.* London: Duckworth, 1989.

Maitland, Frederic William. *Domesday Book and Beyond.* New York: Norton, 1966.

Martial. *Epigrams.* 2 vols. Trans. Walter Ker. Loeb Classical Library. Cambridge, MA: Harvard University Press, 1961.

Martz, Louis. *Thomas More: The Search for the Inner Man.* New Haven, CT: Yale University Press, 1990.

McConica, James K. "The Patrimony of Thomas More." In *History and Imagination: Essays in Honor of H. R. Trevor-Roper,* ed. Hugh Lloyd-Jones, Valerie Pearl, and Blair Worden, 56–71. New York: Holmes & Meier Publishers, 1981.

Mitchell, Thomas N. *Cicero: The Ascending Years.* New Haven, CT: Yale University Press, 1979.

Cicero: The Senior Statesman. New Haven, CT: Yale University Press, 1991.

"Cicero on the Moral Crisis of the Late Republic." *Hermathena* 136 (1984): 21–41.

Mitjans, Frank. "Non sum Oedipus, sed Morus." Moreana, nos. 168–70 (March–June 2007): 12–67.

More, Thomas. *Correspondence of Sir Thomas More.* Ed. Elizabeth F. Rogers. Princeton, NJ: Princeton University Press, 1947.

The English Works of Sir Thomas More. 2 vols. Ed. W. E. Campbell. London: Eyre and Spottiswoode, 1931.

Selected Letters. Trans. Elizabeth F. Rogers. Princeton, NJ: Princeton University Press, 1947.

A Thomas More Source Book. Ed. Gerard B. Wegemer and Stephen W. Smith. Washington, DC: Catholic University of America Press, 2004.

Utopia: Latin Text and English Translation. Ed. George M. Logan, Robert M. Adams, Clarence H. Miller. Cambridge: Cambridge University Press: 1995.

The Yale Edition of the Complete Works of St. Thomas More. New Haven, CT: Yale University Press, 1963–97. Hereafter, *CW*.

CW 1, *English Poems, Life of Pico, The Last Things*. Ed. Anthony S. Edwards, Katherine G. Rodgers, and Clarence H. Miller. 1997.

CW 2, *The History of King Richard III*. Ed. Richard S. Sylvester. 1963.

CW 3.1, *Translations of Lucian*. Ed. Craig R. Thompson. 1974.

CW 3.2, *The Latin Poems*. Ed. Clarence H. Miller, Leicester Bradner, Charles A. Lynch, and Revilo P. Oliver. 1984.

CW 4, *Utopia*. Ed. Edward Surtz and J. H. Hexter. 1965.

CW 5, *Responsio ad Lutherum*. Ed. J. M. Headley. 1969.

CW 6, *A Dialogue Concerning Heresies*. Ed. Thomas Lawler, Germain Marc'hadour, and Richard Marius. 1981.

CW 7, *Letter to Bugenhagen, Supplication of Souls, Letter against Frith*. Ed. Frank Manley, Germain Marc'hadour, Richard Marius, and Clarence H. Miller. 1990.

CW 8, *Confutation of Tyndale's Answer*. Ed. Louis Schuster, Richard Marius, James Lusardi, and Richard Schoeck. 1973.

CW 9, *The Apology*. Ed. J. B. Trapp. 1979.

CW 10, *The Debellation of Salem and Bizance*. Ed. John Guy, Ralph Keen, Clarence H. Miller, and Ruth McGugan. 1987.

CW 11, *The Answer to a Poisoned Book*. Ed. Stephen M. Foley and Clarence H. Miller. 1985.

CW 12, *A Dialogue of Comfort against Tribulation*. Ed. L. L. Martz and Frank Manley. 1976.

CW 13, *A Treatise on the Passion*. Ed. Garry E. Haupt. 1976.

CW 14, *De Tristitia Christi*. Ed. Clarence M. Miller. 1976.

CW 15, *In Defense of Humanism*. Ed. Daniel Kinney. 1986.

Motto, Anna Lydia. *Seneca*. New York: Twayne Publishers, 1973.

Seneca Source Book: Guide to the Thought of Lucius Annaeus Seneca. Amsterdam: Adolf M. Hakkert Publisher, 1970.

Muller, Bearbeitet von Christian. *Die Druckgraphik im Kupferstichkabinett Basel*. Basel: Schwabe, 1997.

Munday, Anthony, et al. *Sir Thomas More: A Play by Anthony Munday and Others*. Ed. Vittorio Gabrieli and Giorgio Melchiori. Manchester: Manchester University Press, 1990.

Nelson, William. "Thomas More, Grammarian and Orator." In *Essential Article: Thomas More*, ed. Richard Sylvester and Germain Marc'hadour, 150–60. Hamden, CT: Archon Books, 1977.

Nicgorski, Walter. "Cicero and the Rebirth of Political Philosophy." *Political Science Reviewer* 8 (1978): 63–101.

"Cicero, Citizenship, and the Epicurean Temptation." In *Cultivating Citizens: Soulcraft and Citizenship in Contemporary America*, ed. Dwight D. Allman and Michael D. Beaty, 3–28. New York: Lexington Books, 2002.

"Cicero's Distinctive Voice on Friendship: *De Amicitia* and *De Republica*." In *Friendship and Politics: Essays in Political Thought*, ed. John von Heyking and Richard Avramenko, 84–111. Notre Dame, IN: University of Notre Dame Press, 2008.

"Cicero's Focus: From the Best Regime to the Model Statesman." *Political Theory* 19 (1991): 230–51.

"Cicero's Paradoxes and His Idea of Utility." *Political Theory* 12 (1984): 557–78.

"Cicero's Socrates: Assessment of 'The Socratic Turn.'" In *Law and Philosophy: The Practice of Theory*, vol. 1, ed. John A. Murley, Robert L. Stone, William T. Braithwaite, 213–33. Athens: Ohio University Press, 1992.

"Nationalism and Transnationalism in Cicero." *History of European Ideas* 16.4–6 (1993): 785–91.

Nightingale, Pamela. *A Medieval Mercantile Community: The Grocers' Company and the Politics and Trade of London, 1000–1485*. New Haven, CT: Yale University Press, 1995.

Norrington, Ruth. *The Household of Sir Thomas More*. Charlbury, Oxon: Kylin Press, 1985.

Ogilvie, R. M. *A Commentary on Livy, Books 1–5*. London: Oxford University Press, 1965.

Osmond, Patricia J. "*Princeps Historiae Romanae*: Sallust in Renaissance Political Thought." *Memoirs of the American Academy in Rome* 40 (1995): 101–43.

"Sallust and Machiavelli: From Civic Humanism to Political Prudence." *Journal of Medieval and Renaissance Studies* 23.3 (1993): 407–38.

Oxford Latin Dictionary. Ed. P. G. W. Glare. Oxford: Clarendon Press, 2005.

Parks, George B. "Pico della Mirandola in Tudor Translation." In *Philosophy and Humanism: Renaissance Essay in Honor of Paul Oskar Kristeller*, ed. Edward Mahoney, 352-69. Leiden: Brill, 1976.

Pawlowski, Mary. "Thomas More's Mis-translations of Lucian's *Cynic, Menippus,* and *Tyrannicide*." *Moreana*, nos. 179–80 (June 2010): 85–101.

Piper, David. "Holbein the Younger in England." *Journal of the Royal Society of Art* 111 (1963): 736–55.

Plato. *Collected Dialogues*. Ed. Edith Hamilton and Huntington Cairns. Princeton, NJ: Princeton University Press, 1961.

The Republic. Trans. Paul Shorey. 2 vols. Loeb Classical Library. Cambridge, MA: Harvard University Press, 1935.

Pliny the Elder. *Natural History*. Trans. H. Rackham. Loeb Classical Library. Cambridge, MA: Harvard University Press, 1938–63.

Plutarch. *Plutarch's Lives*. Trans. John Dryden. 2 vols. New York: Modern Library, 2001.

Moralia. Trans. Frank C. Babbitt. 15 vols. Loeb Classical Library. Cambridge, MA: Harvard University Press, 1929–69.

Pohl, F. J. *Amerigo Vespucci: Pilot Major*. New York: Columbia University Press, 1944.

Quintilian. *Institutio Oratoria*. Trans. and ed. H. E. Butler. 4 vols. Loeb Classical Library. Cambridge, MA: Harvard University Press, 1921.

Raaflaub, Kurt A., and Mark Toher, eds. *Between Republic and Empire: Interpretations of Augustus and His Principate*. Berkeley: University of California Press, 1990.

Rawson, Elizabeth. *Cicero: A Portrait.* Ithaca, NY: Cornell University Press, 1983.

Reed, A. *Under God and Law.* Oxford: Oxford University Press, 1949.

Reynolds, E. E. *Margaret Roper.* New York: P. J. Kenedy & Sons, 1960.

Rhodes, Jan. "The Rosary in Sixteenth-Century England I." *Mount Carmel* 31.4 (Winter 1983): 180–91.

"The Rosary in Sixteenth-Century England II." *Mount Carmel* 32.1 (Spring 1984): 4–17.

Roper, William. *The Lyfe of Sir Thomas Moore.* Ed. E. V. Hitchcock. London: Oxford University Press for Early English Text Society, 1935.

Rundle, David. "Erasmus, Panegyric, and the Art of Teaching Princes." In *Pedagogy and Power: Rhetorics of Classical Learning,* ed. Yun Lee Too and Niall Livingstone, 148–69. Cambridge: Cambridge University Press, 1998.

"A New Golden Age? More, Skelton and the Accession Verses of 1509." *Renaissance Studies* 9.1 (1995): 58–76.

Sallust. *Works.* Trans. J. C. Rolfe. Loeb Classical Library. Cambridge, MA: Harvard University Press, 1931.

Scarisbrick, J. J. *Henry VIII.* New Haven, CT: Yale University Press, 1997.

Seneca. *Epistulae Morales.* Trans. R. M. Gummere. 3 vols. Loeb Classical Library. Cambridge, MA: Harvard University Press, 1917.

Moral Essays. Trans. J. W. Basore. 3 vols. Loeb Classical Library. Cambridge, MA: Harvard University Press, 1928.

Tragedies. Trans. Frank J. Miller. Loeb Classical Library. Cambridge, MA: Harvard University Press, 1917.

Shakespeare, William. *The Riverside Shakespeare.* 2nd ed. Boston: Houghton Mifflin, 1997.

Skinner, Quentin. "Thomas More's *Utopia* and the Virtue of True Nobility." In *Visions of Politics, vol. 2, Renaissance Virtues,* 213–44. Cambridge: Cambridge University Press, 2002.

Smith, Bruce R. *Ancient Scripts and Modern Experience on the English Stage, 1500–1700.* Princeton, NJ: Princeton University Press, 1988.

Smith, David. "Portrait and Counter-Portrait in Holbein's *The Family of Sir Thomas More.*" *Art Bulletin* 87.3 (September 2005): 484–506.

Smith, William. *A Dictionary of Greek and Roman Antiquities.* London: Longman, Green, 1870.

Sparshott, Francis Edward. *Taking Life Seriously: A Study of the Argument of the Nicomachean Ethics.* Toronto: University of Toronto Press, 1994.

Starkey, David. *Henry: Virtuous Prince.* London: Harper Press, 2008.

Stapleton, Thomas. *The Life and Illustrious Martyrdom of Sir Thomas More.* Trans. Philip E. Hallet, ed. E. E. Reynolds. New York: Fordham University Press, 1966.

Summers, Walter C. *Selected Letters of Seneca.* Bristol: Bristol Classical Press, 1983.

Sylvester, R. S. "'Si Hythlodaeo Credimus': Vision and Revision in Thomas More's *Utopia.*" *Soundings* 51 (1968): 272–89.

Tacitus. *Annals*. Trans. John Jackson. Loeb Classical Library. Cambridge, MA: Harvard University Press, 1956.
  The Histories. Trans. Clifford H. Moore. Loeb Classical Library. Cambridge, MA: Harvard University Press, 1962.
Terence. *Plays*. 2 vols. Trans. John Barsby. Loeb Classical Library. Cambridge, MA: Harvard University Press, 2001.
Thucydides. *The Peloponnesian War*. Trans. Thomas Hobbes. Notes and introduction by David Grene. Chicago: Chicago University Press, 1989.
Wegemer, Gerard. *Thomas More on Statesmanship*. Washington, DC: Catholic University of America Press, 1996.
Williams, Gwyn A. *Medieval London: From Commune to Capital*. London: Athlone Press, 1963.
Willow, Mary Edith. *An Analysis of the English Poems of St. Thomas More*. Nieuwkoop: B. De Graaf, 1974.
Wilson, S. J. *The Thought of Cicero*. Bristol: Bristol Classical Press, 1993.
Wilson, Thomas. *The Art of Rhetoric*. Ed. Peter Medine. University Park: Pennsylvania State University Press, 1994.
Winston, Jessica. "Seneca in Early Elizabethan England." *Renaissance Quarterly* 59 (2006): 29–58.
Wirszubski, Chaim. "Cicero's *cum dignitate otium*: A Reconsideration." *Journal of Roman Studies* 44 (1954): 1–13.
  Libertas as a Political Idea at Rome during the Late Republic and Early Principate. Cambridge: Cambridge University Press, 1968.
Wood, Neal. *Cicero's Social and Political Thought*. Berkeley: University of California Press, 1988.
Wroe, Ann. *The Perfect Prince: The Mystery of Perkin Warbeck and His Quest for the Throne of England*. New York: Random House, 2003.
Xenophon. *Memorabilia and Oeconomicus*. Trans. E. C. Marchant. Loeb Classical Library. Cambridge, MA: Harvard University Press, 1923.

Index

Ackroyd, Peter, 51, 148
Adams, Robert P., 12, 110
Aesop, 46
Allen, Ward, 155
American Founders, 44, 47
amore, 7, 46, 97, 105, 114
apt, 33, 35, 69, 183
Aquinas, Thomas, 9, 17, 26, 28, 48
Aristotle, 17, 18, 22, 23–29, 32, 45, 49, 50, 74, 113, 114, 140, 144, 146, 183, 184
  Metaphysics, 25, 26
  Nicomachean Ethics, 18, 25, 26, 27, 28, 32
  Parts of Animals, 25, 26, 27
  Physics, 25
  Politics, 25, 50, 144
  Protrepticus, 25
art(s)
  of good living, 75, 86
  law as Rome's most famous, 157, 185
  of peace
    in Rome, 157, 185
    in *Sir Thomas More*, 33
    in *Utopia*, 185
  philosophy as most fruitful, 29, 30
  of rule, 23, 94
  of virtue, 18, 26, 29, 32

virtue as primary and wisdom as great of all, 8, 25
arts of liberty. *See* education; law; and rhetoric
Astin, A. E., 42
Augustine, 30, 38, 46, 49, 50, 61, 137, 179
  City of God, 30, 38, 46, 49, 50, 61, 137, 179
Austin, R. G., 37

Baker, David, 37
Baker-Smith, Dominic, 38, 39, 84
Barron, Caroline M., 132, 141, 187
Basil the Great, St., 8, 17, 20
Batstone, William W., 18, 126
beast fable, 102, 107
Beier, Ben, 78
Bible, 21
Black, Crofton, 73, 75, 77
body politic, 40, 45, 114
Boethius, 3, 114, 170, 171, 172
Borghesi, Francesco, 72, 73, 77
Bostaph, Samuel, 144
Brixius, 99, 133, 143, 148
Brooke, Christopher, 141

Chambers, Richard W., 100, 143
charity, 120